Carmen Concilio (ed.)
Imagining Ageing

Aging Studies | Volume 18

The series is edited by Heike Hartung, Ulla Kriebernegg and Roberta Maierhofer.

CARMEN CONCILIO (ED.)
Imagining Ageing
Representations of Age and Ageing in Anglophone Literatures

[transcript]

This book was published with the financial support of the Department of Foreign Languages, Literatures and Modern Cultures, University of Turin, Italy: Dipartimento di Lingue e Letterature Straniere e Culture Moderne.

This volume saw the light under the aegis of the International Research Project launched by the University of Turin, Italy: #hackunito4ageing.

Bibliographic information published by the Deutsche Nationalbibliothek
The Deutsche Nationalbibliothek lists this publication in the Deutsche Nationalbibliografie; detailed bibliographic data are available in the Internet at http://dnb.d-nb.de

© 2018 transcript Verlag, Bielefeld

Cover concept: Kordula Röckenhaus, Bielefeld
Cover illustration: Old Tree Silhouette, Public Domain (www.goodfreephotos.com)
Printed and bound in Great Britain by Marston Book Services Ltd, Oxfordshire
Print-ISBN 978-3-8376-4426-5
PDF-ISBN 978-3-8394-4426-9
https://doi.org/10.14361/9783839444269

Contents

Editor's Introduction
Carmen Concilio | 7

Preface
Ageing in a Faraway Land
Licia Canton | 13

Shakespeare's Grandiose Old Men
Paolo Bertinetti | 19

Ageing and the Attainment of Form in *Robinson Crusoe*
Lucia Folena | 27

The Ageing Confessor and the Young Villain:
Shadowy Encounters of a Mirrored Self
in Julian Barnes's *The Sense of an Ending*
Pier Paolo Piciucco | 41

"Making Sense or No Sense of Existence":
The 'Plot' of Thomas Kinsella's *Late Poems*
in the Light of Norberto Bobbio's *De senectute*
Donatella Badin | 61

A Voice Fit for Winter: Seamus Heaney's Poetry
on Ageing in *Human Chain*
Irene De Angelis | 85

"The Mark on the Floor": Alice Munro on Ageing and
Alzheimer's Disease in *The Bear Came Over the Mountain*
and Sarah Polley's *Away From Her*
Carmen Concilio | 103

Coming to Terms: Ageing and Moral Regeneration
in J.M. Coetzee's *Age of Iron* and *Elizabeth Costello*
Blossom Fondo | 127

Imagi(ni)ng Ageing: Old Women in J.M. Coetzee and
Virginia Woolf. Mrs Curren and Mrs Dalloway.
Carmen Concilio | 141

"Representing Age and Ageing in New Zealand Literature":
The Māori Case
Paola Della Valle | 165

Ageing and Neurologic Disease
Enrica Favaro | 183

Contributors | 203

Editor's Introduction

CARMEN CONCILIO, UNIVERSITY OF TURIN

The present volume explores some literary representations of ageing in British and Anglophone literature. The authors and the texts studied are *exempla* for various reasons. Licia Canton, one of the Italian creative voices in Montreal, provides in her *Preface: Ageing in a Faraway Land* a moving portrait of first and second generation Italian migrants to Canada. Their getting older means to observe – from a window, from a park bench – how their own children have grown up, how someone else is taking care of his/her own grandchildren, how life suddenly might turn into waiting for a visit, when the children and grandchildren move on in their lives. Sometimes, loneliness makes two souls closer, talking about culinary affinities, some Italian specialties to possibly taste together and share.

One tragically emblematic relationship between a father and his children is certainly Shakespere's *King Lear*. Paolo Bertinetti, having dedicated his life-scholarly work to English drama, presents Lear as a model of an un-wise old man, who stumbles upon one mistake after another. His fondness to his favourite daughter, Cordelia, is also his doom, his 'dotage'. After the capital sin of renouncing his sovereignty, and the fracturing of his reign in favour of his two undeserving daughters, his body weakens and his mind vacillates to the point of being suspected of what we now would call 'dementia', as defined by Enrica Favaro in this volume. According to Shakespeare's parallel plots, misplaced trust also tragically drags Gloucester, another father, to his ruin. Bertinetti stresses how Lear is an old man whose views on politics and life are untenable and therefore wiped out by his profiteering daughters. Yet, Lear is contextualised in Shakespeare's wider production, from his *Sonnets*, where ageing is often (but not always) connoted in negative terms, to history plays and comedies, where Falstaff provides a more complex portrait of an old man.

Lucia Folena, a scholar in early modern English literature, starts by illustrating how the Old Man is a recurrent figure in medieval narratives. He is generally a secondary character who assists the protagonist by advising him and explaining the 'actual' meaning of events and encounters. She further examines how, in the novel, as defined by the first full-fledged example of the genre, *Robinson Crusoe*, the Old Man's counselling is turned into a necessary starting point of the narrative, in terms of something that needs to be rejected in order for the story to exist. Neither the protagonist nor the reader may now accept that kind of guidance. To both of them the novel opens up territories which they must needs discover for themselves, no matter how often those regions have already been explored by their elders. Finally, Folena demonstrates how 'Form' and the power of interpretation are no longer legacies to be handed down from one generation to the following: they have turned into the very goals of their protagonists' quests.

With a time-leap from early modern English Literature to 2011 Booker Prize winner, Pier Paolo Piciucco introduces *The Sense of an Ending* by Julian Barnes. Piciucco frames within postmodern parameters an anti-hero, who seems to finally understand – retrospectively – what really happened in his whole life only later in his life age. The tragic death of his best friend, his relationship with his best friend's fiancé, and his former fiancé, all these are facts lived through almost without consequences. Those same facts slowly clear up when the older self makes an assessment and comes to terms with his younger self. Getting older implies here a splitting of the subject, for the older judge puts the younger culprit under trial. Ageing is modelled as a retrospective looking back to a life that has not necessarily been exemplary, and to avoid a traditional and consolatory happy ending, this looking back involves neither remorse nor repentance. The villain, after all, remains ambiguously and ironically indifferent to revelations and redemption.

Assessment of one's life, "sense of one's life" is also the object of Thomas Kinsella's *Late Poems*. The Irish studies scholar, Donatella Badin, reads Kinsella in light of the Italian philosopher Norberto Bobbio's essay *De senectute*. Both men, the Irish poet and the Italian intellectual, in their old age, resort to memory as an hermeneutic and philosophical tool to comprehend their past lives, writings, activities, and ideals. Ageing in their case does not so much imply a retrospective look, but rather an inner look in order to reach knowledge of the self. Beneath the scrutiny of Kinsella's everyday and past life and relationships, including love for his wife, surfaces the memory of the mythical past of Ireland. The mood of these poems, self-published as a sort of journal before being turned on to major publishing houses, is not one of grievance but of appreciation for the gift of understanding. One may detect a certain circular pattern in his life-series of poems, that seem to reconfirm already well-established and recurrent themes to the point of revisiting titles and poems of the past. Finally, in taking stock of their lives, both Bobbio and Kinsella exorcise through their writings weakness, physical impairments, thoughts of illness and death. Yet, their literary exploration of ageing shapes a robust, agnostic and articulate corpus bridging to the future.

In Ireland the voice of another bard pays tribute to the physical impairments that characterize old age: 1995 Nobel Prize winner Seamus Heaney. Irene De Angelis, a scholar in Irish studies too, analyses a late collection of the bard's poems, *Human Chain*, where Heaney comes to terms with a stroke that hit him while visiting friend poets and participating in a party. This experience is however lyrically translated into imagery of re-awakening for the renewal of life coincides with a revived creative impetus. Thus the poet resorts to a more intimate tone, dedicating his lyrics to the loved ones, particularly to his own old father, now almost identifying with him. Also artists and friends, already passed away, find space in his verses, portraits of elderly people, partly disabled by ageing, but all firmly determined in their life. The poet then dedicates a final thought to his grandchildren teaching them to flying kites over a hill, as his father did with him, in a poem reminiscent of a similar poetic composition by the Italian poet Giovanni Pascoli. Heaney's subtle irony, capacity of renewal and flights of joy are exemplary of a process of ageing that goes hand in hand with a poetic creativity that sees death as a possibility.

As a postcolonial studies scholar, I based my contribution on a reading of 2013 Nobel Prize winner Alice Munro's best-known short story *The Bear Came Over the Mountain* and of its transposition into a film, by the Canadian director Sarah Polley, *Away from Her* (2006). In this case ageing is emblematically represented by a woman who chooses a retiring home where to spend her last days for she is affected by Alzheimer's Disease. Both the short story and the film pivot around two elderly couples, their different choices, their different social status and material conditions, their encounters inside and outside the clinic. These two mononuclear families demonstrate how ageing affects lonely people in contemporary societies, where there is no longer a sense of a community. While the short story attributes a strong agency to Fiona, the main protagonist, the film seems to pick on that to stress how all the four characters involved, disabled or not, manage to articulate their agency till the very end. Dealing with the ineluctability of Alzheimer's, Munro could but create for her character an exit "with a little grace".

A similar exit with grace is imagined by J.M. Coetzee for his older women-protagonists: Elizabeth Costello and Mrs Curren. Blossom Fondo, working with the theoretical tools of ageing studies within a postcolonial framework, and writing from Cameroon, establishes a relationship between gerontology and literary postcolonial works, an area still to be explored and to be emancipated from marginality. Analysing the works of 2003 Nobel Prize winner J.M. Coetzee, Fondo articulates her relevant thesis. Coetzee's elderly women protagonists produce an increasing firm ethical stance, a sort of shield to the current corruption that might be inversely proportional to their weakening bodies. To Coetzee, old age, both in apartheid-torn South Africa and in contemporary scientific and academic enclaves, seems to be an armour of solid moral and humanist principles. Both Elizabeth Costello in *Elizabeth Costello* and Mrs Curren in *Age of Iron* acknowledge the rights of respectively non-humans and despondent others with lucid inflexibility, holding ethical agency against their own various physical invalidity.

Mrs Curren and *Age of Iron* are further object of study in my second essay, whose interest in South African literature goes back to my majoring with a dissertation on J.M. Coetzee. This time, Coetzee's 'portrait of an old woman' is referred back to Virginia Woolf's Modernist masterpiece, *Mrs Dalloway*, where surprisingly, metaphors, iconic images and discourses on ageing women reverberate with striking and even unexpected affinities. Acknowledging Coetzee's indebtedness to Modernism also means here to compare ageing processes across time, cultures and urban geographies, opening up ageing studies to postcolonial countries.

Paola Della Valle, a scholar in New Zealand and Oceania studies shows how Aotearoa New Zealand appears as a particularly meaningful example of how ageing can become an issue of an on-going negotiation of cultural concepts, social practices, ideals and behaviours between social and ethnic groups: the Pākehā and the Māori communities, whose philosophies, healing practice and experience, but also ageing processes differ enormously. This process is evident in the rise of distinct Māori-defined frameworks for health, well-being and positive ageing that appeared in response to the 'Positive Ageing Strategy' (PAS) – an official government Decalogue of best practices to empower older people in Aotearoa New Zealand – in order to comply with Māori needs and views on ageing. From Māori culture and literature, particularly from the works by Māori writers Witi Ihimaera and Patricia Grace, we learn that old age is endowed with a moral stance, a political vision and is treasured as a repository of ancient knowledge, philosophy, beliefs. Old age is neither isolated nor marginalized, for intergenerational transmission and contact are encouraged and are normal best practices among the Māori people. Both the community and single individuals benefit from the well-being of all its members including ageing and aged people.

Enrica Favaro, a scholar in Medical science and responsible for a programme of well-being for seniors at the University of Turin, called "Terzo Tempo / Third Time" – including multidisciplinary laboratories with activities aiming at increasing awareness about ageing processes and encouraging good practices to achieve well-being – offers an informative contribution listing and illustrating major impairments, disabilities, illnesses and pathologies affecting elderly people. Moreover, this scientific contribution has the merit of highlighting certain features – both physical and psychological – of the literary figures met in the first part of the present volume, from Lear's senility to Heaney's light stroke, to Fiona's Alzheimer's, to Mrs Curren's terminal cancer.

Thus, this volume creates a fruitful cross-fertilization and an interdisciplinary connection among literary studies, ageing studies, postcolonial studies, and medical studies. Touching countries such as Canada, England, Ireland, South Africa, New Zealand and Italy, it might be an effective instrument in the didactics of English and Postcolonial literature, particularly in academic courses that take into account gender and ageing studies. A culturally aware critical and theoretical approach allows this volume a certain versatility and multidisciplinarity in terms of its use, while offering a wide perspective on outstanding writers of both the past and present literary canon, it might give doctors (literary) descriptions of symptoms, illnesses, healing processes to work on.

Apart from keeping oneself healthy and fit, eating sensibly, resorting to medical care and becoming more aware of what expects us all when ageing and what is expected from us in our contemporary societies, some best practices have been mentioned. For instance, Licia Canton hints at projects that involve seniors on University Campuses, so that they can enjoy the company and presence of youths. A similar project was launched in Italy, too, encouraging elderly people to rent their spare room to students, who in exchange should accompany them in their daily errands such as shopping or buying medicines. While the experiments in Canada and in the Netherlands seem to work well and provide benefits in terms of well-being, in Italy the results of such a project have not been assessed yet.

Another prize-worthy initiative are the so-called healing gardens for Alzheimer's patients, based on gardening activities that have a double effect, that of keeping fit and that of providing a pleasant aesthetic experience. Many more examples could be mentioned, but ageing processes vary according to innumerable variables, depending on genetics, geography, social status, income, gender and education.

While talking about experimental clinics that offer various forms of both medically-based and/or socially-oriented types of therapies, there are countries where all this is still a dream, if the internationally renowned South African artist William Kentridge could still write, in 2010: "Pensioners still get taken over the hills of Kwa-Zulu Natal in wheelbarrows to the pension office to get their pensions every month and are wheeled back home over the hills by their nephews or grandsons or whoever they are." (2017: 46)[1] He stressed how this image, which strikes as surprising, is also 'authentic', that is to say its specificity is stronger than what an artist could invent. This last iconic example clearly shows how ageing, even in the present era promoting medical, sports and cultural campaigns of awareness and information, is a right we might aspire to, particularly now that life-expectancy has increased enormously. Ageing is and should primarily be a matter of 'social justice'.

Carmen Concilio,
Turin – June 1, 2018

---

1 Cp. *Footnotes for the Panther. Conversations between William Kentridge and Denis Hirson*, Johannesburg: Fourthwall Books, 2017.

Preface

Ageing in a Faraway Land

LICIA CANTON, MONTREAL

Ageing is something that concerns me daily. I ponder the brown spots on my hands and the tinsel growing in my hair. I am attuned to the increasing aches and pains as I approach sixty. On a recent trip to Turin, the jet lag lasted much longer than usual upon my return home to Montreal. I wonder how much of this is due to the fact that I am getting older.

In April, I had the pleasure of leading a writing workshop with students at the University of Turin. When I asked them to share the name of a person that they look up to, I was particularly struck by a quiet blond girl in the last row. "My 94-year-old grandfather," she said proudly. "He is the man I admire and respect the most." She went on to list the characteristics that make her grandfather an impressive role model.

Like that student, I am very aware of the contribution that the elderly have made to my generation and to my children's. I was born in Italy and raised in Canada, and I am particularly sensitive to the condition of retired immigrants. They left their homeland to pursue opportunities in a foreign country, whose hosts were not always welcoming. Those who left post-World War II Italy were mostly uneducated labourers. They emigrated from small rural towns where everyone knew each other and settled in big urban centres, where they were practically invisible. They made a comfortable living as simple construction workers or piece workers in clothing factories. They saved their pennies to buy that first house and to send their children to university. Now in their seventies, eighties or nineties, they wait for their (grand)children to visit. Old age is a time of rest for them, but it is also a very lonely period. When the grandchildren were small, the grandparents played a vital role: they accompanied their grandchildren to and from school, helped them to do homework, and often made them dinner before the parents arrived to take them home. Many of the elderly who gave their time to the young ones are not getting the same in return.

Years ago I wrote the poem "Chi non viene" (2006), self-translated into French as "Ceux qui ne viennent pas," to honour my 90-year-old grandmother who spent her day waiting for visitors. And in my most recent collection, *The Pink House and Other Stories* (2018), the first and last of the fifteen stories act as bookends, an acknowledgement to the first generation immigrants who are now seniors in their adopted land. The first story, "Watching Them Laugh," is about the special relationship between a grandmother and her granddaughter and the laughter they share when they are together. In the last story, "The Motorcycle," an eighty-year-old man renews his motorcycle license. The man is hard of hearing, he walks very slowly, and he falls asleep in the waiting area. He may never ride the motorcycle again, but he is adamant about renewing his license just in case his granddaughter (who is in university) needs his help to learn to ride a motorcycle. He cannot let go of his need to be useful.

Elizabeth Cinello's short story "Food Companion Wanted" (2011) is an ode to the elderly: those who mistakenly think that they have no purpose in society. Two lonely seniors, Alberto and Nina, come together because of their love of food – the genuine staples of their Italian heritage. During a conversation on a park bench, their sense of uselessness is replaced by a mutual culinary communion. Away from Toronto's urban traffic, Nina and Alberto meet in a green space which recalls their country of origin. The meeting in the park is about negotiating an arrangement that would improve their present reality on both counts: Alberto "wants to eat again" for he has not had a good meal since his wife's passing. Nina wants to escape her daughter's ultra-urban household, where no one speaks to her, where she feels isolated and useless.

Twenty-five years ago, as a soon-to-be mother, I moved to a new home in St. Leonard (on the island of Montreal) – a well-to-do neighbourhood with many retired first-generation Italian immigrants. Back then, the bocce courts were always full. Summer evenings I pushed the stroller around the park and stopped to listen to the bocce players, men and women, who spoke

Italian or dialect as they excitedly discussed their performance or argued about the distance between the bocce. The last time I walked by the bocce court a few nights ago, the lights were on, but there was no one there. And yet, the weather was mild. There should have been players on the court. The truth is that many of them have passed away, and the others may be too old to play. Their decreased mobility is keeping them at home, thus reducing the likelihood of human interaction, and increasing their isolation and loneliness.

When I moved into my corner house in St. Leonard, there were two elderly couples living on either side. Each couple had three adult children, but I noted that they did not visit very often. My neighbours were proud to introduce their children whenever they did visit. They explained that their children had very busy lives, demanding jobs or they lived too far away.

Summers, these elderly neighbours watched my children play in our backyard. They came out to chat about how tall the children had grown or how well behaved they were. When my daughter played the flute on the balcony, the neighbours took their chairs to their own balconies to listen. Her practice sessions became mini-concerts. Then, about ten years ago, one couple sold their house and moved to a retirement home. And, from my kitchen window, I could see that the other neighbour kept the light on, day and night. She had been a widow for two years. She felt more comfortable with the lights on. She confessed that she had no reason for living after her husband died. She, too, sold the house and went to a seniors' residence.

Now, there is a young family living next door. I have watched the young couple have one, two and three children. Summers they play on the swings and the seesaw; they run around the yard under the watchful eye of a parent. Winters they build snowmen and high mountains of snow, then come sliding down.

When I am alone, I let go of the tears as I watch the little children play from my kitchen window. I miss those days with my own children. Watching the neighbours' children playing takes me back to my thirties. And yes, it is a reminder that I am ageing. That is what the tears are for: the passing of time, the inability to stop the speedy process, the inevitability of the life cycle. I am now the one watching the neighbours' children playing, and soon I will yearn for my own adult kids to come visit.

There is a special relationship between the young and the elderly. I see it in my own family: there is nothing that the grandchildren can do wrong in the eyes of their grandparents ... and vice versa. And yet they are at polar opposites. My grown children are open-minded and inclusive. Their immigrant grandparents are products of their generation with the customs, traditions and codes of behaviour that they took to Canada when they left Italy in the 1950s and 1960s. But hugs are universal.

They say that the last phase of life is similar to the first: as one reaches the end of life, there is a regression towards childhood. Some communities have seen the benefits of bringing seniors and children together. They have put preschools in nursing homes so that the elderly benefit from the presence of youth and the children learn to interact with the aged and the disabled. In an article titled "The Preschool Inside a Nursing Home," Tiffany R. Jansen writes that "Numerous studies have linked social interaction with decreased loneliness, delayed mental decline, lower blood pressure, and reduced risk of disease and death in elders. Socializing across generations has also been shown to increase the amount of smiling and conversation among older adults...".[1]

Jansen goes on to say that "kids who have early contact with older people are less likely to view them as incompetent – and simply exposing children to positive depictions of elders makes them less likely to exhibit ageism. These intergenerational interactions also enhance children's social and personal development." In Deventer, The Netherlands, university students are offered free lodging in a retirement home in exchange for keeping the elderly company for 30 hours per month. It is part of a project "aimed at warding off the negative effects of ageing."[2] And at the Université de Moncton, New Brunswick, a retirement complex with 65 residents was opened on the university campus.[3]

Through the Canadian Mental Health Association of Toronto, I have visited groups of seniors to speak about healing through writing and to engage them in literary activities. They are lonely. They need to talk. They

---

[1] Cp. (https://www.theatlantic.com/education/archive/2016/01/the-preschool-inside-a-nursing-home/424827/). Last Accessed May 28, 2018.

[2] Cp. *PBS News Hour*, April 5, 2015, (https://www.pbs.org/newshour/world/dutch-retirement-home-offers-rent-free-housing-students-one-condition). Last accessed May 28, 2018. Web.

[3] Cp. *Maclean's*, Feb. 10, 2018, (https://www.macleans.ca/education/seniors-universite-moncton/). Last accessed May 28, 2018. Web.

need to share their stories. Although I listen patiently for as long as I can, it is not enough. And when I am obliged to excuse myself in order to move on with the rest of my day, I always feel guilty about leaving them.

I would like to think that most of our senior citizens are leading a serene existence and that they smile as they reflect on their experiences, accomplishments and relationships. I would like to think that they have a strong sense of pride in the last phase of life, even though the decades have whizzed by, loved ones have passed away, and they've had to slow down due to physical deterioration. When I think of the elderly, I think of their vulnerability. But I also think of their wisdom and experience, and how much we could learn from them if we took the time to do so.

Licia Canton
Montreal, May 2018

BIBLIOGRAPHY

Canton, Licia (2018): *The Pink House and Other Stories*, Montreal (QC): Longbridge Books.

Cinello, Elizabeth (2011): "Food Companion Wanted". In: *Accenti Magazine*, Summer, (http://www.accenti.ca/news-archives-issue-22/feature-food-companion-wanted-elizabeth-cinello).

SITOGRAPHY

Cadoff, Emily Baron (2018): "Université de Moncton: The new seniors on campus." In: *Maclean's*, February 10, 2018 last accessed May 28, 2018 (https://www.macleans.ca/education/seniors-universite-moncton/). Web.

Jansen, Tiffany R. (2016): "The Preschool Inside a Nursing Home." In: *The Atlantic*, January 20, last accessed May 28, 2018 (https://www.theatlantic.com/education/archive/2016/01/the-preschool-inside-a-nursing-home/424827/). Web.

Reed, Carey (2015): "Dutch nursing home offers rent-free housing to students." In: *PBSONEWSHOUR*, April 5, last accessed May 28, 2018 (https://www.pbs.org/newshour/world/dutch-retirement-home-offers-rent-free-housing-students-one-condition).Web.

Shakespeare's Grandiose Old Men

PAOLO BERTINETTI, UNIVERSITY OF TURIN

This essay intends to be a consideration on the different and sundry ways in which the topic of ageing and deteriorating occurs in Shakespeare's works. Shakespeare divides human existence into seven phases (seven was a sort of magic number in the culture of his time): Jacques, in *As You Like It*, after illustrating the first six ages of man, ends his monologue describing the seventh age:

> Last scene of all,
> That ends this strange, eventful history,
> Is second childishness and mere oblivion,
> Sans teeth, sans eyes, sans taste, sans everything. (Act II, Scene vii, 64-66, p. 266)[1]

In the same scene, the melancholic Jacques had just reported the profound declaration of Touchstone, one of Shakespeare's wise fools: "And so from hour to hour we ripe and ripe, / And then from hour to hour we rot and rot." (Act II, Scene vii, 63-64, p. 264) Undoubtedly, there are several equally gloomy and disconsolate quotes about old age in other Shakespeare's plays; and in his sonnets he dedicates numerous verses to the anguish of the passing of time, the impassive time that carves deep marks of ruination on man's body and face. Frequently, time is described as the never resting

---

1 All references to Shakespearean texts are from William Shakespeare (1964), *The Complete Works*, ed. by Peter Alexander, London: Collins.

agent that brings about annihilation and destruction, as Guiderius states in *Cymbeline*: "Golden girls and lads all must / As chimney sweepers come to dust." (Act IV, Scene ii, 262-263) And in describing old age in Sonnet 2, Shakespeare underlines the signs that time engraves on man's face, ploughed through by wrinkles compared to trenches:

> When forty winters shall besiege thy brow,
> And dig deep trenches in thy beauty's field,
> Thy youth's proud livery, so gazed on now,
> Will be tattered weed, of small worth held. (p. 1308)

Shakespeare here employs two brilliant and impressive metaphors. The first one is linked to the image of war, and the verb to besiege expresses the idea of an unremitting battle between man and time. The second one relates to clothing: appearance becomes substance, as the proud livery will become tattered weed.

The fact that ageing is such a significant theme in Shakespeare could be proof of his own anxieties about growing old, as the first stanza of Sonnet 73 suggests:

> That time of year thou mayst in me behold
> When yellow leaves, or none, or few, do hang
> Upon those boughs which shake against the cold,
> Bare ruined choirs, where late the sweet birds sang. (p. 1320)

The final couplet of the same sonnet, though, could suggest, on the contrary, that Shakespeare's interest in the subject of growing old demonstrates the serenity (as we find in Latin poets such as Catullus) with which he faced the prospect. "This", that is to say the twilight of his life, tells the poet to the young man is addressing, you perceive, and "makes thy love more strong / To love that well which thou must leave ere long" (Sonnet 73, p. 1320).

It is obvious that at the time ageing and death were omnipresent and, so to speak, part of daily life. Shakespeare died when he was 52, but we must bear in mind that in his time life expectancy was of approximately 35 years: it is a fact that Shakespeare outlived many of his friends and relatives, even one of his own children, and experienced death as a familiar and prominent aspect of everyday life. The twilight of one's existence was something to be serenely accepted as a precious aspect of life, not necessarily as a harbinger of death. Some Shakespearean philologists claim that in the last verse the poet is saying that the young man should now understand that he will lose his own youth and passion and that therefore Sonnet 73 ends on a deeply melancholic and not on a serene note; at least in this particular case sensibility should prevail over philology.

The topic of ageing undoubtedly crops up throughout Shakespeare's texts in various and even contradictory ways, but *King Lear* is the most significant play for a reflection of ageing in his work. *Lear* is a tragedy in which all the principles that we think of as protecting our recognition of humanity are attacked: children turn on their parents, and the elderly are tortured. As the social, ethical and familial bonds between people are severed, individuals lose their sense of self and go mad. The play centers on an old man, an old king, who loses his kingdom, his daughters and his mind after having handed over authority to his children. Having done this, as he is old and has no power, he is doomed to be mistreated and discarded.

At the beginning of the tragedy, Lear announces his decision to abdicate. According to the map he has reflected on, he intends to divide his kingdom into three parts in order "to shake all cares and business" from his age. He seems to accept the fact that he is no longer capable of ruling his kingdom and that therefore he should confer his power to his young daughters ("younger strengths") while he will crawl towards death.

Lear describes his abdication as an act of divestiture of rule and "cares of state": he is yearning to be a free man, to become a private citizen, but he is not aware of the consequences of his decision.

Unlike Shakespeare's other tragic protagonists, Lear has no soliloquies, no moments to reflect privately on his state of mind and on the action of the play. The Fool, who is the only character allowed to speak the truth to the old king (Kent is banished in the first scene for attempting to counsel him) provides a means for Lear to use a more intimate and unguarded voice: he vividly figures Lear as putting down his "breeches" so that his mother-daughters may use 'the rod' on him. The Fool's image suggests that Lear himself is responsible for creating disorder by promoting his daughters above their king and father. But his greater mistake has been not to take into account the weakness of old age.

At the beginning of the play we learn that he intends to abdicate but without parting with "all addition to a king". Lear is clearly vain and whiny as he declares that he has decided to divide his kingdom among his three daughters after having imposed on them a ludicrous and nonsensical love test (in itself a sign of inept senility). Before the test begins, we are enabled to understand that he has reserved the best part to Cordelia, his youngest daughter and his favourite one. Yet the question on which his final decision depends is absurd and foolish in the extreme: he wants to be told who loves him "most". Goneril and Regan speak first, using the vain and pompous rhetoric all expect of them. When it is Cordelia's turn, at first she declares that she has nothing to say and then she adds that she loves him according "to her bond". Her honest words incense him and in his anger he disinherits and repudiates her:

> Here I disclaim all my paternal care,
> Propinquity and property of blood,
> And as a stranger to my heart and me
> Hold thee, from this, for ever. (Act I, Scene i, 112-115, p. 1074)

Everyone is aware of the fact that, as his two daughters' speeches are nothing else than empty rhetoric, Lear's reaction is a sign of folly. And also, according to Goneril's consideration during the conversation with her sister Regan that takes place at the end of the same scene, a sign of unchecked senility.

> You see how full of changes his age is. The observation we have made of it hath not been little. He always loved our sister most; and with what poor judgment he hath now cast her off appears too grossly. (Act I, Scene i, 287-291, p. 1076)

And Regan adds: "Tis the infirmity of his age." (Act I, Scene i, 294, p. 1076) The two sisters talk about their father in terms that we would now associate with dementia. They are concerned with his old age and his mental impairment: he is "rash", is given to "unconstant starts", is impetuous and irrational. And therefore they set about conceiving a plan in order to deal with a man who is at the threshold of senility and second childhood. The two things go together. As we have seen, also Jacques speaks of second childishness; but in point of fact it is Lear himself that hints at such an identification when he says that he "crawls" toward death, an image that will often occur later in the tragedy.

The two sisters' plan is a conspiracy; but a conspiracy promptly triggered against a king who, in the very first verses of the play seems to admit that he is no longer capable of ruling his kingdom. In the third scene Goneril, describing her father to her servant Oswald as an "idle old man", prepares the ground for the first step of the conspiracy. "Idle" not only means "lazy", but, above all in this instance, also means "foolish": he is so foolish that he "still would manage those authorities / That he hath given away!" (Act I, Scene iii, 18-19, p. 1079). Lear is idle and infantile. Goneril underlines with lofty contempt the fact that her father has reverted to second childhood: he is a senile old man who must be dealt with exactly as one would with babies, scolding, rebuking and flattering him.

Another crucial word used by Goneril in the same scene is "dotage", a term that not only indicates the state of one who dotes, who is characterized (through old age) by an excessive fondness and a foolish affection for the woman he loves – or is just infatuated with. Dotage is a word also used in reference to the loss of cognitive powers. Being almost a synonym of senility and second childhood. Eventually, in the fourth act, Lear, after his return to sanity, recognizes his disgraceful mistake and the feebleness of his mind due to his age: "I am a very foolish, fond old man" (Act IV, Scene vii, 60, p. 1107), he says to Cordelia ("fond" is a synonym of foolish) and meekly begs her pardon.

The theme of Lear as an old man reverberates in the figure of Gloucester, whose age is not stated but who is referred to as white-haired (Regan picks white hairs from his beard). Edmund, his illegitimate son, whose plan to deceive him corresponds to the defiance of Goneril and Regan to their father, uses the same terms, "idle" and "fond", to express his revolt against the "aged tyranny" of his father.

The deeds of Lear and Gloucester and the corresponding ones of the two sisters and of Edmund strengthen the role of ageing in the tragedy. In the last scene, the concluding words pronounced by Edgard, Edmund's younger brother:

The oldest hath borne most; we that are young
Shall never see so much, nor live so long. (Act V, Scene iii, 325-326, p. 1113)

could suggest that the theme of the play is the clash between youth and age. But they could also be interpreted as the acknowledgment that Lear and Gloucester have achieved through suffering that kind of wisdom that only the old can achieve. In Shakespeare's plays we meet several old men who carry positive connotations, who are the epitome of wisdom, understanding and judgment, such as Duke Senior and Old Adam in *As You Like It*, or Gonzalo in *The Tempest*. Also the Earl of Warwick, counselor to the king, could be seen as a valid specimen of wise old man. His part in *Henry IV Part 2* is not a large one; but he is definitely the wisest of the king's counselors and the character who gives Henry IV an explanation of the "logic" of the events that occurred during his reign. Warwick is not always played by an old actor, but by Elizabethan standards he *was* an old man.

The main reason to mention him here, though, is that *Henry IV*, *Part 1* and *Part 2* (along with *The Merry Wives of Windsor*) are the plays of the triumph – and the fall – of Falstaff, one of the greatest characters created by Shakespeare, that we can rate as an almost mythical figure, as Hamlet, Othello, Macbeth, and Romeo and Juliet are. Falstaff is an anomalous old man, not wise, not reliable, but utterly likeable as a stage character.

When the Lord Chief Justice, whom Falstaff, pretending to be young, addresses as an old man ("You that are old consider not the capacities of us that are young", Act I, Scene ii, 166, p. 519), on his turn addresses angrily Falstaff attributing to him the various conventional infirmities of old age, the fat "irregular humorist" replies that he is old only in "judgment and understanding" (Act I, Scene ii, 178, p. 519) and that although he limps because of his gout, he is still a vigorous man, capable of turning diseases to advantage. Falstaff is verbally imaginative, quick-witted, inexhaustibly witty. When he first appears in the play, in the second scene of the first act, he asks Page what the doctor has said about the analysis of his urine and Page tells that the urine is healthier than the patient (who *is* an old man), Falstaff pronounces one of his most brilliant and famous lines "I am not only witty in myself, but the cause that wit is in other men" (Act I, Scene ii, 10-12, p. 517).

Falstaff, being the English version of Plautus' *miles gloriosus*, informs the Lord of Justice of his military valour and of his deeds on the battlefield, where his name was "so terrible" to the enemy: which is why he is needed in the King's army. It is obvious (to us) that he is lying, but he is doing it with extraordinary self-assurance and acting ability. The fact is that Falstaff is a shrewd actor, who lives in a "world of play" and who knows that old men are subject "to this vice of lying". But in spite of his "vices" he is an admirable character and the quintessence of vitality and joy of life.

Nicolas Rowe maintained that Queen Elizabeth was so pleased with his personage that she "commanded" Shakespeare to write a comedy based on Falstaff. The result was *The Merry Wives of Windsor*, a play that W.H. Auden considered a failure, stating that its only merit resided in having enabled Giuseppe Verdi to compose his brilliant "commedia lirica" *Falstaff*. Shakespeare's comedy presents a different Falstaff from the one that appears in *Henry IV*. In *The Merry Wives*, Falstaff, in order to mend his fortunes, plans to court two wealthy married women; but as the two merry wives are obviously not interested in him, they decide to have fun at his expense pretending to be engrossed by his advances. The audience is supposed to have fun as well, and a compulsory happy ending concludes the play.

The protagonist of *The Merry Wives* is just a comic character who has little to do with the grand characters of the two history plays, whose reckless vitality, whose *joie de vivre*, whose brazenness, are accompanied by the awareness of the limits of age. In the second act of *Henry IV Part 2* Falstaff has a telling conversation with Doll Tearsheet, a sort of sentimental harlot in Mistress Quickly's tavern. Falstaff seems older and less vigorous than before, and acutely aware of his declining years: "I am old, I am old" he repeats. But Doll replies that she loves him better than "ever a scurvy young boy of them all" (Act II, Scene iv, 262-263, p. 528). The scene ends on a sentimental note, with Doll in tears and Mistress Quickly praising Falstaff for his honesty and true-heartedness. This explains why the spurning of Falstaff by Prince Hal, just become King Henry V, is such an emotional and dramatic event:

> I know thee not, old man. Fall to thy prayers.
> How ill white hairs becomes a fool and jester.
> I have long dreamt of such a kind of man,
> So surfeit-swelled, so old and so profane,
> But being awaked I do despise my dream. (Act V, Scene v, 48-52, p. 549)

The stress is on "old man", as if age could be Falstaff's main fault. Henry V cannot accuse the fat knight of doing what he himself has done. He accuses him of being an old man who does not know how to behave as an old man. Fun is for the young, the elderly have to be happy to say: "We have heard the chimes at midnight." (Act III, Scene ii, 210, p. 533) Now that they are old, they must not hear them any longer. Such a belief was common sense in Shakespeare's time – and it is today.

But why not following instead Dylan Thomas's advice to his aged dying father?

> Do not go gentle into that good night.
> Old age should burn and rave at close of day;
> Rage, rage against the dying of the light. (2014: 193)

BIBLIOGRAPHY

Bertinetti, Paolo (2016): "*400 anni fa, William Shakespeare.*" In: *Lo Straniero*, Roma: Contrasto Editore, anno XX, n. 188, febbraio, pp. 5-18.

Bloom, Harold (1999): *The Invention of the Human*, London: Fourth Estate.

Dylan, Thomas (2014): *The Collected Poems*, John Goodby (ed.), London: Centenary Edition, p. 193.

Greenblatt, Stephen (2004): *Will in the World*, New York/London: W.W. Norton & Company.

Pogue Harrison, Robert (2014): *Juvenescence, A cultural History of Our Age*, Chicago/London: The University of Chicago Press, pp. 67-71.

Shakespeare, William (2004): *King Lear*, Paolo Bertinetti (ed.), Torino: Einaudi.

_____ (1964): *The Complete Works*, Peter Alexander (ed.), London/Glasgow: Collins.

Ageing and the Attainment of Form in *Robinson Crusoe*

LUCIA FOLENA, UNIVERSITY OF TURIN

In the initial lines of "Sailing to Byzantium" (Ll. 1-10) William Butler Yeats opposes youth – as a time of existential plenitude and full immersion in the joys of carnality and sense – to the irresistible physical decay brought about by the process of growing old. An awareness of this spoliation, however, does not necessarily entail only loss and despair. For the gradual ebbing away of corporal faculties leaves increasing ground for the intellectual and spiritual progresses of the "soul" (L. 11), to the point where it becomes possible to imagine a final metamorphosis of the passionate and transient living body into a detached and eternal artistic masterpiece graced with an absolute perfection of form.[1] Thus, paradoxically, ageing may turn into an aesthetic experience. And there are cases in which, instead of positing the antithetical nature of the two terms involved – 'life' and 'art' – in its definitively lifting the individual him/herself out of the pathway of the former up to the sanctuary of the latter, such an experience results in reducing or denying the opposition by directly transfiguring one of the terms into the other: converting the whole existential itinerary that has produced the now-aged individual into an aesthetically and intellectually gratifying object.

Any creative product invested with an aesthetic function – as well as art in general, including literature – may be regarded as an attempt to impose

---

1 Frank Kermode stresses that Yeats's "'artifice of eternity' is a striking periphrasis for 'form'" (2000: 3).

form and legibility – i.e., 'meaning' – upon the chaotic, irrational, ultimately unreadable, fluidity of life. But 'art' is not always the outcome of a deliberate intervention on the raw materials of existence; it is also the natural point of arrival of life itself, since it is precisely the latter's fluidity that generates, in the course of time, the possibility of its being transcended, 'dynamic' confusion eventually freezing into 'static' order, harmony, and peace.

On one level, a narrative, regardless of its specific characteristics, is always and invariably an account of the process through which its protagonist gets hold of form, finally acquiring the hindsight that enables him/her – and/or the reader – to pronounce a conclusive statement on his/her experiential itinerary, which at that point has lost the inevitable fragmentariness of its former day-to-day development to display itself as a continuous line, no matter how circuitous, conducting from beginning to end.[2] This characteristic, however, becomes decidedly more prominent in the early novel, which is structurally dependent on it, partly at least on account of the usually greater length of the time span covered – years, decades, occasionally a whole lifetime, whereas previous narratives (with the notable exception of the picaresque) often limit themselves to the recounting of one or few momentous adventures or episodes in the protagonist's existence.

The 18th-century English novel constructs a new kind of subjectivity based on a linear notion of time. Like the early novel, late-medieval and early-modern romances also often foreground discovery, and self-discovery, as a central object of the character's action, but in that case what comes to light eventually, rather than appearing as the creation of time, trial, error, and commitment, manifests itself as having already been there, though hidden – as having been constantly present in a state of latency. It is in the novel that the final discovery gets equated with the awareness of 'new' components having added themselves to one's individuality.

---

2   In the words of Georg Lukács (1971: 80), the "inner form of the novel" is "the process of the problematic individual's journeying towards himself, the road from dull captivity within a merely present reality – a reality that is heterogeneous in itself and meaningless to the individual – towards clear self-recognition. After such self-recognition has been attained, the ideal thus formed irradiates the individual's life as its immanent meaning."

The Old Man (far more rarely the Old Woman) is a recurrent figure in medieval narratives, especially in chivalric romances. He does not usually appear as a protagonist, nor does he get directly involved in the action – whose military and athletic character obviously calls for physical exuberance, ardent vigor and the kind of naïve assurance that is ascribed to the prime of youth – but he still plays a fundamental, twofold role vis-à-vis the central character, acting simultaneously as counselor and interpreter. In this second function he also integrates a metatextual component designed to instruct the reader. For not only does he (intratextually) palliate with his sage advice the inexperience and lack of foresight which are seen as typifying the earlier phases of human life; he provides (both intra- and extratextually) indispensable contributions to the unfolding of the true 'sense' or 'meaning' of events and adventures. Without him the story he gets involved in would remain at least partly obscure or ambiguous in its implications.[3]

The first English novel – for, all in all, *Robinson Crusoe* undoubtedly deserves that label – attributes to the Old(er) Man an analogous form of wisdom: the ability to see beyond appearances and predict the negative consequences of younger people's inappropriate conduct or unrestrained desires. The father's interdiction – an extreme, authoritarian rather than merely authoritative variant of the Old Man's counsel despite the affection for the son he displays and the tears he sheds – takes up the opening of the narrative and works as the initial catalyst of its action (Defoe 2007: 5-8).[4] There the eighteen-year old is quite significantly entreated "not to play the young Man" (7), as if it were possible for him to divest himself of an age which endows him with the very traits that make him a credible potential adventurer and, in effect, a far more coherent up-and-coming capitalist than his overly prudent interlocutor.[5] No "young Man" governed by restlessness

---

3   Cp. Todorov 1977: 120-42.
4   That this is no mere advice but an actual veto is stressed immediately afterwards by the father himself, in his dialogue with the mother: "That Boy might be happy if he would stay at home, but if he goes abroad he will be the miserablest Wretch that was ever born: *I can give no Consent to it.*" (Defoe 2007: 8; emphasis added)
5   Ian Watt observes that "the argument between his parents and himself is a debate, not about filial duty or religion, but about whether going or staying is

and desire, no story. *Felix culpa*: as in the biblical account of the Fall, an "original sin" of disobedience (Defoe 2007: 164) must needs inaugurate events and prefigure their development in terms of a gradual bridging of the gap between son and father through the agency of time and experience.

Just a few pages later another Old Man intervenes with his judicious warnings in an equally unsuccessful attempt to change the course of the protagonist's insubordinate existence:

Young Man, says he, you ought never to go to Sea any more, you ought to take this for a plain and visible Token that you are not to be a Seafaring Man [. . .]. And young Man, said he, depend upon it, if you do not go back, where-ever you go, you will meet with nothing but Disasters and Disappointments till your Father's Words are fulfilled upon you. (Defoe 2007: 14-15; original emphasis)

Robinson's unwillingness to take such advice – the impossibility, in fact, for him at that early stage of being to do so – marks one primary difference between the novel and its predecessor, the romance. The Young Man can no longer adopt his older counterpart's view sic et simpliciter: he must literally convert himself into the Old Man in order to be able to see things that way. He must ripen from Son into Father, as Robinson symbolically does not only by growing in years and judgment but by 'educating' Friday.[6] Such a metamorphosis evidently entails an extensive and painful itinerary through life and experience. It requires, first and foremost, a large amount of time, the chronicle of which is precisely the main theme of the tale. The new 'Grail' of the novel coincides with the second function assigned to the

---

likely to be the most advantageous course materially: both sides accept the economic argument as primary. And, of course, Crusoe actually gains by his 'original sin', and becomes richer than his father was". Watt adds that such an "original sin" is actually "the dynamic tendency of capitalism itself, whose aim is never merely to maintain the status quo, but to transform it incessantly" (1957: 64).

6 "[N]ever Man had a more faithful, loving, sincere Servant, than *Friday* was to me; without Passions, Sullenness or Designs, perfectly oblig'd and engag'd; *his very Affections were ty'd to me, like those of a Child to a Father*; and I dare say, he would have sacrific'd his Life for the saving mine, upon any occasion whatsoever" (Defoe 2007: 176; emphasis added).

elderly mentor in the romance – that of revealing hidden meanings. This has become the object of a lifelong quest whereby it is no longer a secondary character but the hero who gains the power of interpretation and explains to the reader the consequences and significations of his younger self's errors and misfortunes.

This kind of evolution might be regarded as not entirely new, considering that a very ancient narrative such as *Beowulf* already, and rather uncharacteristically, features a protagonist who is fifty years older at the end than in his inaugural confrontations with Grendel and his mother, and on whom time has bestowed wisdom as well as renown – the aristocratic counterpart of the bourgeois respectability that Robinson eventually conquers. There is, however, an enormous difference between the Anglo-Saxon epic and the 18th-century novel. First and foremost, the time separating Beowulf's initial and final adventures is far from being treated as worthy of more than a cursory mention, which takes up just three out of the poem's 3182 lines. When Hygelac, the previous king of the Geats, dies,

> the wide kingdom
> reverted to Beowulf. He ruled it well
> for fifty winters, grew old and wise
> as warden of the land.[7]

The narrator then hastens on to the final battle with the dragon. Furthermore, Beowulf's growing "old and wise" does not seem to have really changed him much. His prowess has remained unaltered, and so has his pride, which is what prevents him – against the prudence he is supposed to have gained – from seeking the help of his warriors in facing the phenomenally dreadful enemy (Ll. 2345-47), and thus leads him to his heroic death. The only difference between the young hero and his elderly upshot therefore resides in the inevitable physical deterioration that has taken place in the half-century interval.

When the protagonist of *Robinson Crusoe* starts his autobiographical account, he is about seventy-two years old, having been born in 1632, as he informs the reader at the very beginning of the novel, while his final words

---

7 Ll. 2207-10 (*Beowulf* 2000: 151).

state that he has been carrying on an existence rich in "surprizing Incidents" and "new Adventures" for "ten Years more" after his 1694 voyage "as a private Trader to the *East Indies*" (Defoe 2007: 257-58; original emphasis). It is evidently only in that advanced phase of his life that he feels he has acquired the detachment and perspective necessary to reconstruct all that preceded it as a continuous and teleological progression in time, arranging meaningful splinters of past events into a coherent, causal sequence. Only now has he at last become a master of form, a creator/discloser – one who can produce legible shapes out of the primal chaos of human reality as well as reveal the pattern hidden in that chaos and explain its implications. Reaching such a stage is like attaining a summit whence one may survey the whole of the itinerary which has led to it, and 'refigure' it as a historically-determined progression.[8]

First-person narratives, especially when fashioned as fictional autobiographies like those of Daniel Defoe, are particularly dependent on this motif. When the account, rather than coming directly from the subject of the experiences reported, is delivered by an external voice, the imposition of 'meaning' on existential disorder is partly – often largely – allocated to it, while the lack of another figure of mediation between text and reader in stories told by their supposed protagonists turns the latter into their own exegetists and moralizers. Hence their lives become not only quests for happiness and a place in the world, but routes through an anarchic, incomprehensible proliferation of unrelatable phenomena towards a final attainment of form and unity – an attainment which coincides with the end of the story and the coming of old age. The early novel, at least in Defoe's hands, is thus the story of how, in the progression of time, a common, undistinguished human being immersed in a flux of events ultimately achieves narratorial authority and the power of endowing the tale told with emblematic significance.

---

8   For refiguration, or "mimesis 3", cp. Ricoeur 1984: 52-87. Refiguration is the outcome of an act of reading, so that it is generally presupposed by a text as its potential and necessary destination, but not contained in it – not actualized until that text enters the domain of reception. Now autobiography – no matter how fictional – incorporates, to a far larger extent than any other narrative form, an enactment of that very process by the protagonist, who presents him/herself as the first reader of his/her past experiences.

The novel as such presupposes not only the centrality of time as an agent of change, but a way of relating to time that differs profoundly from that which characterized previous narrative forms. It is, as a matter of fact, a wholly new concept of temporality that comes into play here. Ian Watt opposes the Platonic view permeating ancient philosophy and literature to the modern one surfacing in the Renaissance but manifesting itself fully only with the rise of the novel. For in Shakespeare as well as in Spenser, and still in Bunyan, "the sequence of events is set in a very abstract continuum of time and space, and allows very little importance to time as a factor in human relationships" (Watt 1957: 22).[9]

The Platonic outlook, in its positing Ideas, which were "timeless and unchanging", as "the ultimate realities behind the concrete objects of the temporal world", gave time a very limited role in determining worldly events and affairs (Watt 1957: 20-21). Even more widely influential, the traditional Christian viewpoint characteristic of the Middle Ages, despite its differing from the classical one in its setting up a "quantitative rather than a qualitative difference between time and eternity" (Le Goff 1980: 31), concurred with it in denying the crucial function of time in shaping the itinerary towards salvation: "for the Christian in the Middle Ages [...] to feel his existence was to feel his being, and to feel his being was to feel himself not changing, not succeeding himself in time, but subsisting" (Poulet 1956: 3-4). Moreover, Christian time belonged to God only and humans had no right to sell and buy it.[10]

---

9   Analogously, Jacques Le Goff points out that the late-medieval "epic and gest were [...] negations of history by feudal society, which used historical items only to strip them of historicity in the context of an atemporal ideal" (1980: 32). In the courtly romance, whose "fundamental purpose" is a "self-portrayal of feudal knighthood with its mores and ideals", as Erich Auerbach emphasizes, "the indications of time are as reminiscent of fairy tale as the indications of place" (2013: 130-31). On the simultaneity of past and present in Arthurian romance, cp. also Todorov 1977: 134.

10 Le Goff cites the way in which a 14th-century Franciscan lector-general settled a dispute on this issue: "Question: is a merchant entitled, in a given type of business transaction, to demand a greater payment from one who cannot settle his account immediately than from one who can? The answer argued for is no,

Around the 12th century the increasing social weight of the mercantile middle class and the needs of the rising commercial capitalism, the very existence of which depended on the appropriation and marketability of time, began opening up a drastically new perspective in which time itself was gradually transformed into a measurable and monetarily evaluable commodity. Rather than mutually exclusive, Church time and commercial time then became complementary, as belonging to two distinct spheres of reality – the spiritual and the pragmatic. The Christian merchant started dividing his life into two separate segments, making Church time into "a second horizon of his existence": the "time in which he worked professionally was not the time in which he lived religiously. Where salvation was concerned, he was content to accept the Church's teaching and directives" (Le Goff 1980: 37). It was only, however, between the late 17th and the early 18th century, when the middle class started supplanting the aristocracy in terms of ideological hegemony over the rest of society, offering it its own values and beliefs as universal principles to be espoused by all, that this major change became apparent in literature, turning into one of the decisive components of the new, bourgeois fiction identified as the novel.

In *Robinson Crusoe* the presence of time is constantly perceptible and often explicitly drawn attention to. The very first line of the narrative outlines the protagonist's identity in terms of when – and where – his existence began, and only after that inaugural characterization are his social and national origins specified: "I Was born in the Year 1632, in the City of York, of a good Family, tho' not of that Country [...]." (Defoe 2007: 5) The reader is later recurrently, scrupulously informed about the years, and even the months and presumed days, that have elapsed since the outset of Crusoe's "strange surprizing adventures", and eventually assured that the measurement effected by the protagonist was largely if not entirely accurate: "as for an exact Reckoning of Days, after I had once lost it, I could never recover it again; nor had I kept even the Number of Years so punctually, as to be sure that I was right, tho' as it prov'd, when I afterwards examin'd my Account, I found I had kept a true Reckoning of Years." (Defoe 2007: 209) He had in fact, at the very beginning of his stay

---

because *in doing so he would be selling time* and would be committing usury *by selling what does not belong to him*" (1980: 29; original emphasis).

on the island, erected a kind of monument to the succession of temporal splinters he expected to live through:

> I cut it with my Knife upon a large Post, in Capital Letters, and making it into a great Cross I set it up on the Shore where I first landed, viz. *I came on Shore here on the 30th of* Sept. 1659. Upon the Sides of this square Post I cut every Day a Notch with my Knife, and every seventh Notch was as long again as the rest, and every first Day of the Month as long again as that long one, and thus I kept my Kalander, or weekly, monthly, and yearly reckoning of Time. (Defoe 2007: 55-56; original emphasis)

Furthermore, Robinson's constant, uninterrupted preoccupation with time may be symbolized in the name he imposes on the young native he saves from the anthropophagic designs the members of another tribal group have on him – the name of a fraction in his personal history, a day of the week:

> I made him know his Name should be *Friday*, which was the Day I sav'd his Life; I call'd him so for the Memory of the Time; I likewise taught him to say *Master*, and then let him know, that was to be my Name. (Defoe 2007: 174; original emphasis)

Through this double baptism he of course also defines his future rapport with the newcomer, establishing once and for all his own superiority over him.[11] But the symbolism involved in enclosing a person's identity in the name of a day perhaps extends to the choice of "Master" as a self-appellation. When measured and segmented into a sequence of units – which are differentiated and rendered unique by the specific positions they occupy vis-à-vis other units – time turns from a mysterious, impersonal and overpowering entity controlling people's lives into something manageable, capable of being mastered and governed, and 'makes sense' to humans thanks to the 'syntactic' reorganization the self-same separating gesture produces on the newly-identified components.

The Journal incorporated in the retrospective narration (Defoe 2007: 60-113) offers a further tangible attestation of the constant need Robinson experiences to measure time and to establish a precise correspondence between days and events – "to minute down the Days of the Month on

---

11 Cp. Novak 1997: 117; Keane 1997: 115.

which any remarkable Thing happen'd to me" (113) – thus simulating and thematizing that "reinscription of phenomenological time onto cosmological time", to use Ricoeur's formula (1988: 180-182), which is one salient feature of novel-writing and of the historiographical modality that it imitates. The intelligibility of life and the world, then, depends on a double gesture: demolition – the dissection of time entrusted to the Young Man in his progress through the events – must precede that activity of (re)construction which is only accessible to the Old Man.

Division and differentiation occur on all levels, from the macroscopic one of years and seasons (Defoe 2007: 90-91) to the microscopic one of daily activities assigned to precise hours (97-98). This temporal fragmentation matches the spatial one that gradually turns the originally indistinct, unknown body of the Island of Despair (Defoe 2007: 60) into the anthropized, syntactically organized territory of a colony – however scantly peopled – as in an ideal step-by-step transformation of the land into its own map. Essentially, the stretch of time involved in this process gets subjected to a remarkably similar mapping process. Such a twofold charting may be taken to suggest, metatextually, the pioneering work of the bourgeois writer colonizing narrative space and time for his own class. It also functions as a general metaphor of human life, in a Lockean psychological ontogenesis of sorts where the "white paper"[12] in the new-born human's mind mirrors and duplicates the temporal and spatial *tabula rasa* outside him/her: for 'falling' into life is like finding oneself in an unfamiliar region – in time and space – that one, little by little, has to take possession of and to make meaningful to oneself. Old age is the phase when the exploration is more or less complete and a map may be drawn on the basis of a process of refiguration. It is as if, when he reaches his island after the shipwreck, Robinson is 'born again', in both literal and religious senses; and the account of the initial phases of his new existence shows that the steady acquisition of knowledge and manual and intellectual skills he experiences is absolutely inseparable from the spiritual and moral growth that leads him to recognize and honor God's presence in himself and in the physical world around him. Analogously, within the basic pattern of linearity which underlies the representation of time as an agent of change in this novel – and in the large majority of its descendants – the temporal syntax the narrator sets up reintroduces a form

---

12 Locke 2017: 18.

of circularity that in all likelihood, rather than looking back to the romance, secularizes the biblical prototype and the practice of the typological interpretation of scriptural history, where past, present and future are intrinsically connected, to the point of being essentially homogeneous if not identical, by the recurrence of events or figures whose entire meanings are only elucidated in juxtaposition.[13] The narrator makes the curvature explicit through declaring, "I remember that there was a strange Concurrence of Days, in the various Providences which befel"; examples of those temporal coincidences are provided immediately afterwards (Defoe 2007: 113).[14] As happens very visibly in *Moll Flanders* (Watt 1957: 97-98), and indeed in many other passages of *Robinson Crusoe*, here two voices are anachronistically merged: that of the Young Protagonist who is gradually discovering the 'figure in the carpet' of his earthly adventure, and that of the Aged Narrator – the wise, discerning old person who sees the whole picture retrospectively and is in a position to explain the implications and connections of events in light of what came to pass afterwards.[15]

---

13 For this kind of interpretation, which originated in the early centuries of Christianity and was still in use in Protestant contexts at the beginning of the 18th century, cp. Auerbach 1994. This connection with typology is part of *Robinson Crusoe*'s more general dependence, in structure as well as content, on the model of the Puritan narrative and the spiritual autobiography. The novel "is structured on the basis of a familiar Christian pattern of disobedience punishment-repentance-deliverance, a pattern set up in the first few pages of the book" (Hunter 1966: 19).

14 "First I had observed, that the same Day that I broke away from my Father and my Friends, and run away to *Hull*, in order to go to Sea; the same Day afterwards I was taken by the *Sallee* Man of War, and made a Slave. The same Day of the Year that I escaped out of the Wreck of that Ship in *Yarmouth* Rodes, that same Day-Year afterwards I made my escape from *Sallee* in the Boat. The same Day of the Year I was born on (*viz.*) the 30*th* of *September*, that same Day, I had my Life so miraculously saved 26 Year after, when I was cast on Shore in this Island, so that my wicked Life, and my solitary Life begun both on a Day." (Defoe 2007: 113; original emphasis)

15 This juxtaposition of points of view is also suggested by the wavering recourse to present and past tenses in the passage: "I [now, while writing this story]

The combination of those two distant points of view is particularly frequent in the Journal, despite its being initially presented as an accurate reproduction of the actual logbook Young Crusoe produces before running out of ink. At the same time at which this section enters the text as a body of documental evidence aimed at confirming the veridical nature of its account, it introduces a significant fissure, if not an outright contradiction, into the otherwise solid autobiographical makeup of the story. In general, diaristic and epistolary novels tend to appear as 'configurations', or 'emplotments', rather than refigurations, of experience:[16] the first-person narrator is not in a position to see beyond the episode he/she is relating, or its immediate reverberations, so as to foretell the direction his/her existential itinerary is actually taking and to disclose the 'meaning' and 'shape' it bears; and in the absence of the Interpreter embodied by the Old(er) Protagonist in an autobiographic tale, or by a third-person narrator in other novelistic forms, the same uncertainty is shared by the reader. Contrariwise, in *Robinson Crusoe* the day-by-day record often gives way to reflections and moral judgments that are clearly only possible a long while *ex post facto*. One of the most manifest examples of Old Robinson's sermonizing intrusions is provided by his severe comments on Young Robinson's past obstinacy in repeatedly rejecting both his father's good

---

remember [. . . the] strange Concurrence of Days" versus "I had observed [then, while experiencing each second episode which recalled a previous one]." (ibid)

16 Ricoeur derives the notion of emplotment from Aristotle and explains it thus: "Plot is mediating in at least three ways. First, it is a mediation between the individual events or incidents and a story taken as a whole. In this respect, we may say equivalently that it draws a meaningful story from a diversity of events or incidents (Aristotle's *pragmata)* or that it transforms the events or incidents into a story. The two reciprocal relations expressed by *from* and *into* characterize the plot as mediating between events and a narrated story. As a consequence, an event must be more than just a singular occurrence. It gets its definition from its contribution to the development of the plot. A story, too, must be more than just an enumeration of events in serial order; it must organize them into an intelligible whole, of a sort such that we can always ask what is the 'thought' of this story. In short, emplotment is the operation that draws a configuration out of a simple succession" (Ricoeur 1984: 65).

advice and God's help before the "terrible Dream" of the man with the spear (Defoe 2007: 75-78).

Such relentless counseling is of course perfectly useless, for neither the protagonist nor the reader may accept that kind of guidance. To both of them the genre of the novel, as 'invented' by Defoe, opens up territories which they must needs discover for themselves, no matter how often those regions have already been explored by their elders. 'Form' and the power of interpretation are no longer legacies to be handed down from one generation to the following: they have turned into the very goals of their protagonists' quests.

BIBLIOGRAPHY

Auerbach, Erich (1994 [1938]): "Figura". In: Erich Auerbach, *Scenes from the Drama of European Literature*, trans. Ralph Manheim, Minneapolis: Univ. of Minnesota Press, pp. 11-76.

Auerbach, Erich (2013 [1946]): *Mimesis: The Representation of Reality in Western Literature*. Trans. Willard R. Trask, Princeton: Princeton UP.

Beowulf (2000). Trans. Seamus Heaney, New York–London: Norton.

Defoe, Daniel (2007 [1719]): *Robinson Crusoe*. Ed. Thomas Keymer, Oxford-New York: Oxford UP.

Hunter, J. Paul (1966): *The Reluctant Pilgrim: Defoe's Emblematic Method and Quest for Form in* Robinson Crusoe, Baltimore: Johns Hopkins UP.

Keane, Patrick (1997): "Slavery and the Slave Trade: Crusoe as Defoe's Representative". In: Roger D. Lund (ed.), *Critical Essays on Daniel Defoe*, New York: G. K. Hall, pp. 97-120.

Kermode, Frank (2000 [1966]): *The Sense of an Ending: Studies in the Theory of Fiction*, Oxford-New York: Oxford UP.

Le Goff, Jacques (1980 [1977]): "Merchant's Time and Church's Time in the Middle Ages". In: Jacques Le Goff, *Time, Work, and Culture in the Middle Ages*. Trans. A. Goldhammer, Chicago-London: The University of Chicago Press, pp. 29-42.

Locke, John (2017 [1689-90]): *An Essay Concerning Human Understanding*, Book 2. Ed. J. Bennett. Last accessed March 6, 2018 (http://www.earlymoderntexts.com/assets/pdfs/locke1690book2.pdf).

Lukács, Georg (1971 [1920]): *The Theory of the Novel*. Trans. Anna Bostock, Cambridge, Mass.: MIT Press.

Novak, Maximilian (1997): "Friday: Or, The Power of Naming". In: Albert J. Rivero (ed.), *Augustan Subjects: Essays in Honor of Martin C. Battestin*, Newark: University of Delaware Press, pp. 110-122.

Poulet, Georges (1956): *Studies in Human Time*. Trans. Elliott Coleman, Baltimore: Johns Hopkins UP.

Ricoeur, Paul (1984, 1985, 1988 [1983, 1984, 1985]): *Time and Narrative*, 3 vols. Trans. K. McLaughlin and D. Pellauer, Chicago: The University of Chicago Press.

Todorov, Tzvetan (1977 [1971]): *The Poetics of Prose*. Trans. Richard Howard, Ithaca - London: Cornell University Press.

Watt, Ian (1957): *The Rise of the Novel*, Berkeley-Los Angeles: University of California Press.

Yeats, William Butler (1989): "Sailing to Byzantium". In: A. Norman Jeffares (ed.), *Yeat's Poems*, London: Gill and Macmillan, pp. 301-302.

The Ageing Confessor and the Young Villain

Shadowy Encounters of a Mirrored Self in Julian Barnes's
The Sense of An Ending

PIER PAOLO PICIUCCO, UNIVERSITY OF TURIN

In his discussion of Julian Barnes's *The Sense of an Ending* (2011), Ivan Callus claims that the British novelist reveals connections with the postmodern aesthetics that remain "a little less evident than in, say, *Flaubert's Parrot* (1984) or *A History of the World in 10½ Chapters* (1989)" (2012: 55). While in fact his first two literary works display a flamboyant inventiveness that has also contributed to widening the boundaries of postmodern fiction, *The Sense of an Ending*, both because of its brevity and because of the apparently unpretentious ways of its narrator, does not appear as a trend-setter. Nevertheless, *The Sense of an Ending*, reviewed as "a page-turner" (Wallen 2017: 1) or as "a strange and oddly powerful book" (Tóibín 2012: online), is a novel that perceptively plays with the inner constituents of confessional fiction with such a craft as to hide them at times from the reader. The plot of Julian Barnes's literary work, to start with, creates a duality between past and present sequences that interact with, echo, contradict and, ultimately, re-write each other, displaying the quintessential obsession found in such works of fiction "with the question of how we can come to know the past today" (Hutcheon 1989: 47).

The whole story then is told to us by a narrator who defends his unreliability from the very first page. This happens before the reader has even had the chance to understand that this tale relies entirely on a work of memory, the narrator has already marked his own territory: "what you end up remembering isn't always the same as what you have witnessed." (Barnes 2011: 4) Incidentally, in dealing with contemporary literature originated from memory, Shields has made a sharp comment that seems to be in keeping with the narrator, Antony Webster, and his convoluted efforts at remembering his past: "Anything processed by memory is fiction," he writes (2010: 57). A vague and indistinct capriciousness on the part of the narrating voice directly calls into question the centrality of subjectivity that in this story plays the lion's share. Its function in postmodern writing is explained by Bram Nichol who claims that "[s]ubjectivity, postmodernism asserts, is always changing, always 'in process' rather than stable" (2009: 118). In his own way, in fact, Tony Webster by awkwardly examining his past actions and relationships, tries to re-define his own spaces, and shapes a story that insists on the confusing nature of identity. In addition, a novel that, like so many others in our contemporaneity, makes its way in relation to the rules and whims of memory cannot but challenge and subvert the traditional chronology, offering instead "a non-linear narrative with temporal fragmentation and frequent flashbacks and flashforwards" (Vecsernyés 2014: 35). Furthermore, as I mean to demonstrate in this paper, Tony Webster's fiction artfully, if gently, plays with the modes of a parodic form of a narration seemingly inspired by a confessional novel.

Linda Hutcheon is the scholar who has worked most widely on the reverberations of parody in postmodern literature and she has substantiated her theory by arguing that "[o]n the surface, postmodernism's main interest might seem to be in the processes of its own production and reception, as well as in its own parodic relation to the art of the past" (1987: 179). Barnes's novel, then, offers an outstanding example of how the narrative process in the late modern age is the product of a manipulative action endorsing any kind of strategic approach and/or artifice in order to simulate reality. Finally, in order for us to fully understand *The Sense of an Ending* within the wide frame of postmodern fiction and, by implication, infer its entire corollary, it is also important to briefly allude to the centrality of pastiche, defined as "the mixing of styles and genres, and the juxtaposition of 'low' and 'high' culture" by Nicol (2009: 2), and that Barnes appropriates without reserve. For instance, House finds in it affinities with the detective fiction of "Ruth Rendell" (2011: online), Jordan discusses a possible correspondence with the sensational plotlines of "Roald Dahl['s]"

(2011: online) short fiction, while Kakutani argues that it "manages to create genuine suspense as a sort of psychological detective story" (2011: online). If Carroll writes about it in terms of "a novella" (2015: 157), Greaney confidently locates it within the tradition of "the romance of the archive" (2014: 238). Alternative perspectives possibly include the psychological novel and the Bildungsroman: in this paper I will mainly adopt the stance of confessional fiction.

The confessional novel is an odd literary genre that, in recent times, has experienced a remarkable revival. Basically, it works on the splitting of the self, with a persona staging two distinct roles and identities in strict relation with the flow of time. In the past, in his younger years (most of the protagonists of confessional novels are male) he is described as a sinner, whereas in the present, after achieving maturity and a higher ethical perspective, he overlays a new image of himself as a penitent. The confession is the rite of passage enabling him to have access to a superior principled life that his current expectations and inner balance now require of him as a crucial step in his evolution. In terms of narratology, this duality becomes evident in the splitting of his persona into two separate narrative entities: narrator and protagonist, in fact, appear to be in dialogic opposition, and this explains why this literary genre shows an enhanced narrative distance enabling the chronicle to keep the two ends under control. More in detail, in some cases the narrator may wish to increase the distance and the dissociation from his past self, while in others he may desire to reduce the space from his past self and share his emotions. This will lead him to atone for his iniquity and achieve the cathartic stage of soul cleansing that, when he starts his narration, is precluded to him. If the splitting of the self appears to be a pre-requisite of the confessional novel, *The Sense of an Ending* openly brings this issue to the very surface of the narration, creating a psychological case. The manifestation of his division occurs at various times in the plot and the following is but an example: "My younger self had come back to shock my older self." (Barnes 2011: 92) Of course, the paradox – and the fascination – of the genre lies in the fact that the same individual is subject to a powerful polarization of his own self, in terms of ethical judgment, age and narrative roles. In his insightful essay on the repetition of oddness in the fiction of Julian Barnes, Greaney (2014) writes about the importance of the number three, invariably regulating the life of a man-woman relationship in Julian Barnes's literary output, but in particular in *The Sense of an Ending*, where the creation – and multiplication – of love triangles markedly characterizes the story. While this theory retains a certain fascination, I claim that *The Sense of an Ending* seems to display a thematic structure, creating a system with elements displayed in a binary opposition instead. My proposal to view the novel as referring to a polarized antinomy of two elemental components soon finds confirmation in the structure of the plot, divided into two macro-sections no better qualified than 'One' and 'Two'. These narrative fragments, however, mainly refer to the two time units in which the tale is narrated, the past and the present. *The Sense of an Ending* further develops this systematic polarity by creating a motivating opposition between the truth of the present clashing with the truth of the past. The already mentioned splitting of Tony Webster into narrator vs. protagonist also originates an additional contrast between youth vs. older age, which spices the fictional account. The moral re-assessment on which the confessional novel creates its assumption, in addition, produces counter discourses between candour and guilt, earnestness and unreliability, University of Bristol and University of Cambridge, as well as forgetfulness and memory. Along these lines, one cannot help but notice that the all-pervading duality between past and present also constructs two imaginary roles for the young and the elderly Tony, featuring alternatively as a villain or as a magistrate in their respective time-layers within a recurrent trope alluding to a trial. What seems to be relevant to stress at this point is that this complex set of opposed dichotomies exists in conformity with the rules of narration in confessional fiction. Nonetheless, *The Sense of an Ending* creates further oppositions also outside of the perimeter of the confessional tale, as it polarizes the perspectives of normalcy vs. disability, as well as those pertaining to gender.

Within this set of antagonistic attitudes, the splitting between the two stages of the narrator's life – youth vs. elderliness – provides a particularly prominent context from which the whole plot of *The Sense of an Ending* continuously draws life. In consonance with how the remaining key elements in the story are analysed, Tony Webster's age identification is never actually clarified, but remains a blurred issue throughout the narration. In part, we can easily ascribe this vagueness to the intrinsic characteristics of the problem, since:

Age identity embodies more than just recognition of chronological age. In large measure, personal assessments, regardless of age, reflect a complex set of socioeconomic or lifestyle factors, perceived age norms and age-appropriate behavior, social and anticipated timetables, health and physical limitations, and interaction patterns in both formal and informal networks. (Hendricks 2001: 37)

Having said this, it remains a fact that Tony cautiously avoids tackling the issue directly but disseminates a number of apparently irrelevant details that the reader ought to find and assess appropriately. Among other important factors, *The Sense of an Ending* is a charming reading exactly because we are demanded to fittingly ponder not only what Tony candidly confesses, but also what he omits, shuns, ignores, or forgets in the course of his monologue, with the result that one may also come to the conclusion that his oversights and exclusions generally occupy the very core of the narration. A discourse about his age needs to be contextualized in this frame: indeed, not only is his age in the present time never determined, but also his classification either as a 'middle-aged', 'elderly' or 'old' man is skilfully eluded. In a crucial passage, however, he identifies himself as a 'pensioner':

I'm retired now. I have my flat with my possessions. I keep up with a few drinking pals, and have some women friends – platonic, of course. (And they're not part of the story either.) I'm a member of the local history society, though less excited than some about what metal detectors unearth. A while ago, I volunteered to run the library at the local hospital; I go round the wards delivering, collecting, recommending. It gets me out, and it's good to do something useful; also, I meet some new people. Sick people, of course; dying people as well. But at least I shall know my way around the hospital when my turn comes. (Barnes 2011: 54)

To start with, it is meaningful that one of the very first characterising elements of his age is lack of sexual activity, which in his chauvinistic frame of mind is never irrelevant: in his youth it was also the main factor to determine up to what extent his relationship with Veronica could be said to be satisfying. Another interesting aspect in this phase of his life is that he admits that death is among his preoccupations, a common concern for people of advanced age. The rest of the plot clearly illustrates that he is a character who suffers from isolation and who is alarmed at his likely mental deficiencies, in particular in relation to his frequent lapses of memory. This clearly responds to an old person's identikit, however confident and reassured about one's expectations, and is in keeping with many observations made by the Mass Observation Project in their research on age-defining issues. In a way, Tony seems to be part of the group of volunteers who "showed a powerful resistance towards the idea of considering themselves as 'older' or 'ageing'" (Bazalgette et al, 2011: 53) and who rejected the idea of age advancement since "ageing is something that is always on the horizon, rather than imminent" (Bazalgette et al, 2011: 53). Since Tony's inclination towards avoiding taking the risk (and the responsibility) of showing a definite opinion regarding any matter in life seems a constant in his persona, one may be surprised about his sudden decisiveness and clear-cut identification of age in a lifetime when he comes to one of his sharpest and most memorable declarations: "when we are young, we invent different futures for ourselves; when we are old, we invent different pasts for others" (Barnes 2011: 75). This binary system that the narrator uses in order to categorize the natural development of the ageing process in two subsequent stages clearly recognizes his age identification along the two time layers that concur to form the plot of *The Sense of an Ending*.

Matters in relation to ageing are seldom straightforward, in this novel as elsewhere. If these appear to be negative connotations of ageing, advanced age also brings with itself a number of positive counter-effects. The 1992 Mass Observation Project made reference to subjects who claimed to have experienced "greater confidence, peace and self-acceptance" (Bazalgette et al 2011: 11) in old age, with the scholars explaining such beneficial effects both in terms of a diminished weight of responsibilities and as an increased sense of wisdom and experience. If Tony is a witness of many debilitating ageing processes, he also shows the typical self-confidence and sense of judgment that securely drive him to face an assessment of his young self. Even if his story repeatedly turns on his alleged dim-wittedness, the reader cannot fail to notice that he also narrates his autobiography elevating his conscience up to the level of a judge, and uses the trope (and the authority) of the magistrate when needed. The narration of *The Sense of an Ending* stems from this contradictory ambience, but it is most evident that Tony's attitude as a narrator largely benefits from both the sense of wisdom and freedom in judgment that his old age ensures him.

If, however, due to its own intrinsic characteristics the confessional novel originates a split in the subject, Julian Barnes's confessional novel exasperates the range between the contrasting elements to the utmost. A comparison between narrator and protagonist may offer a particularly intriguing result in terms of characterization and reveal (part of) the finesse with which this work of fiction has been conceived. As a protagonist of the story, Tony Webster can hardly be said to have contributed to the appeal of this short fiction, if assessments of the novel describe him as "a not very attractive man" (Cartwright 2011: online) when the reviewer is well-inclined to it, but also as "perhaps the most boring and least likable protagonist in years," (Martino 2012: 56) when the reviewer uses a more severe yard-stick. If not attractive, however, he remains an interesting and puzzling figure. His baldness seems to allude gently to a couple of literary models: Tony in fact incarnates both the ideal of Philip Larkin's 'ordinariness,'[1] and Prufrock's quintessential indecisiveness and procrastination. Accused by his ex-girlfriend of being "cowardly," (Barnes, 2011: 34) he retorts that he is "peaceable" (Barnes 2011: 34) instead, takes shelter in a noncommittal passivity, avoids having expectations and hurries to dismiss others' inattention to him. Around him, Julian Barnes constructs a myth of slow-wittedness that echoes throughout the plot and that brings the narrating voice – his alter ego – to jollily mock him, imagining the inscription on his tombstone: "Tony Webster – He Never Got It." (Barnes 2011: 137)

On the other hand, Tony Webster the narrator possibly shares with him his name only. Whereas as a character he always remains cautiously unconcerned, as a narrator he gains much more self-confidence. He leads his way, skilfully – sometimes unpleasantly – avoiding other people's interferences, deciding – apparently on the spur of the moment – what to tell, what to leave out, what to abridge and what to leave unfinished. Even if he pretends to share a sense of awkwardness and lassitude with his own homonymous self, one cannot miss that he shows a complete mastery of the situation. With his own peculiar ways of telling his story, he invariably manages to drive the reader toward irritation, frustration, sympathy,

---

1 Colm Tóibín (online) and Michael Greaney (2014) show a number of affinities between the English poet of Hull and the dull protagonist of *The Sense of an Ending* share.

distress, rage, pity, reproach, conspiracy and numberless other reactions. In this sense, it is his unreliability – even if seemingly candidly confessed from the very beginning of the plot – that shows the spectrum of his artfulness and his deceitfulness. In his role as a narrator, Tony is a histrionic play-actor, a creative entertainer and a vicious deceiver so that Greaney hits the mark when he claims that "Webster is a narrator who won't stop talking about himself even though he insists there is nothing to know" (2014: 233). Therefore, while his 'writer' self always shows a resourceful activity, his 'written about' self helplessly displays his irritating passivity: while the former reaps successes, the latter whines about his failures. The narrator's cunning lies in avoiding making his behaviour just too visible, and remaining safely hidden behind the mask of a boring protagonist. This strategy sometimes pops up in his discourse, and this is one of its transparent manifestations: "I was determined to be polite, unoffendable, persistent, boring, friendly: in other words, to lie." (Barnes 2011: 78) Hence, it is their joint action as a couple, made up of one dull and one smart component – like Don Quixote and Sancho Panza, for instance? – who secures the story success and liveliness.

It is evident then that in this novel one of the main challenges facing the reader is to make a selection from the constant flow of material that the narrator floods him with. By alternating gross lies with candid revelations, he manages to blur the boundary between fact and fiction, cajoling his audience to believe every single word he says. For this reason, I support the view that *The Sense of an Ending* "has an 'ambush' in place for any naive reader who takes Webster at his word as a decent if dull narrating voice" (Greaney 2014: 239). Webster's self-centredness, turning into various forms of conceitedness and self-absorption, in fact, not only edits his own memory in order to cut a nice figure, but also his memories of other characters, whose portraits appear to be deformed under the narrator's lens. Tony has evidently a score to settle, in particular with Adrian, yet for most of the narration he pretends to remain captivated by his friend's intellectual charm. Of the two, Tony is certainly the least alluring, with Adrian therefore crediting the role of the villain in the situation. Adrian, however, seems to me to be a real champion of heartlessness and selfishness: he does not hesitate to start a relationship with a friend's ex-girlfriend as soon as their story is over (but the time of the switch is not clear), he then betrays her with her mother and, on discovering that the woman is pregnant, he quits his responsibilities and commits suicide. Neither of the two excels in sympathy. Nonetheless, unsympathetic as he may be, Tony Webster could hardly be said to be as insensitive to ethical matters as his best friend. Of course, one may claim that Tony's unreliability as a narrator is mirrored in Adrian's way of managing relationships. Of course, the focus on the relationship between Tony and Adrian is crucial for a correct reading of the plot because (an unfavourable) comparison with the intellectually-gifted friend echoes throughout the plot and becomes a real obsession for the narrator. His fixation even reaches peaks of pure paroxysm, since his form of mania with his brilliant school-friend does not end with Adrian's suicide: in a Hamlet-like fashion, the protagonist is haunted by the ghost of Adrian's intellectual stature throughout his life. In a curious passage, Tony's mother concedes to him that, even though "a clever boy," (Barnes 2011: 47) he would not dare to stage anything like Adrian's suicide. It is not a coincidence, therefore, that shortly afterwards Tony makes one of his typical sharp-tongued and cynical comments that, on the one hand, reveals his regard for his defunct friend but, on the other, shows a creeping malice: "first-class degree, first-class suicide" (Barnes 2011: 48). The invisible link creating this conflicting friendship and connecting the two boys can be explained if we think of Adrian as Tony's double: both of them have a relationship with Veronica, they become targets of her mother, are clever and fond of philosophy, express the will to be cremated, display a shyness tending to a marked form of self-centredness. Adrian has "clarity and logic," (Wilhelmus 2012: 706) though, as well as a more practical and unswerving attitude regarding his objectives. I will shortly return to this important issue but in the meanwhile I will switch my attention to an analysis of the confessional novel in *The Sense of an Ending*.

Although criticized for its brevity – a number of commentators[2] were left somewhat perplexed when it received the Man Booker Prize in 2011, – *The Sense of an Ending* does not seem to lack in imaginary power, nor in material for a discussion. In terms of the rhetoric adopted and discourse practice, it shows more than a simple affinity with the confessional novel. Furthermore, its artful narrator shrewdly blends what Gill identifies as the main ingredients for the genre: "subjectivity, truth, authority, representation." (2006: 8) This notwithstanding, its author seems to be even

---

2   Cp. for instance Rachel Carroll 2015: 157.

shrewder than its narrator in creating a blurring motive around this "elegant, careful, and stylish" (Tóibín 2012: online) novel, so that its classification as confessional fiction is not always linear or granted. In her seminal work devoted to this literary genre, Susannah Radstone has analysed the evolution of this narrative pattern starting from Augustine's Confessions, written around 400 A.D., and has argued that if the literary form has obviously undergone modifications in the course of time, a great part of the structure has remained unaltered since then. The unravelling of the plot in a confessional tale goes through a development in four main stages (I will number them in order to better discern them) that the scholar spots as: "(1) recognition that some change is required; (2) distanciation from that which is causing difficulty; (3) articulation of the problem and of the projected future self; (4) and finally appropriation of a new way of life." (Radstone 2007: 22) As for points number 1 and 4, Tony Webster's evolution seems to follow the normative path. A mystifying aura invests *The Sense of an Ending* as one tries to verify a possible association of points number 2 and 3 of Radstone's outline with its plot. This is not to say that there is not a connection, but rather that it is not as straightforward as one may wish it to be.

Tony's progress, in fact, simultaneously matures on two parallel paths. Morality, as one may surmise, is an important field of development crossed by the protagonist-narrator in this fictional account. Actually, Tony needs to fight against his memory, and against his need to neglect episodes and reactions that involved him in the past. However, since the postman always rings twice, he receives two crucial letters – one from "a firm of solicitors" (Barnes 2011: 59) forwarding him the effects of the will of Veronica's mother, and another from Veronica herself, who after 40 years mails him back his letter to Adrian and herself with his rancorous comments about them – that start a long re-evaluation of his own youth and life. Tony does not suspect having any dealings with the will of Mrs Ford, while memory has erased any trace of his enraged reaction to the news that Veronica had started a new relation with Adrian. As a consequence, this double surprise makes the reading of the missives particularly intriguing. If, then, the first of the two letters piques his curiosity, it is the second that for a number of hazy reasons flares his sense of guilt. This message originally came in response to "the hypocrisy of a letter" (Barnes 2011: 40) from Veronica and Adrian, who had informed him of their new relationship, and contained some vituperative statements about the young couple. Whether he actually feels guilty about this after forty years seems a little hazardous to believe in such a rational subject, but his unrestrained confession returns to his regret at various times in the plot. He better qualifies his feelings declaring that "it wasn't shame I now felt, or guilt, but something rarer in my life and stronger than both: remorse" (Barnes 2011: 93). This sorrow is further amplified at his discovery that Adrian's natural son is disabled and, since his venomous letter to him and Veronica contained an ominous prophecy about their possible child, he seems to feel responsible for having had such an evil purpose. Afraid of seeming superstitious, however (maybe more than causing evil to the couple), he hurries to distance himself from this belief, arguing: "Of course I don't – I didn't – believe in curses. That's to say, in words producing events." (Barnes 2011: 131)

Now, although realistically Tony cannot claim to have had a crystal-clear conduct to Veronica and Adrian in the past, the motives that would now create such a consistent pang in his conscience seem a little too weak to support the entire structure of a piece of confessional fiction, that involves a complete transformation of a subject on the basis of the adherence to a new moral system. His sense of responsibility, in fact, appears to have been hardly involved in the chain of dramatic events which occurred following his reproachable behaviour. Gill's questions about modern confessional fiction seem to address the case in hand appropriately:

On turning our attention to modern confessional writing, we are faced immediately with a sense of its complexity, its indeterminacy and its apparent incomprehensibility. We are faced with numerous questions: who confesses? Why do they choose so to do? Is there an element of choice or is confession coerced in some specific and individual or general and social way? What, if anything, distinguishes confessional writing from other forms of confession (psychoanalytic, legal, religious?). (2006: 1)

Therefore, if modern confessional writing can be said to be characterized by the choice of a somewhat cloudy purpose, I argue that *The Sense of an Ending* possibly goes further than this. Of course, critical accounts devoted to this work could not underrate the weight of Webster's conscience in this story, and scholars have dealt with this knot. Many, however, have cautiously discussed his moral evolution and his noticeable sense of guilt in terms of the real engine to the story. Vecsernyés, for instance, claims that

"Tony demonstrates considerable reluctance to remember, presumably out of guilt and remorse," (2014: 32) whereas McAdams summarizes the end of the story in these terms: "Adrian's son – is not her son. He is instead her (half) brother, born of the affair that Adrian had with Veronica's mother. The affair, the deepest secret in the story, is revealed in the end. And Tony realizes that he may, in a sense, be culpable for the affair." (2015: 303)

If not in connection with the adoption of a superior moral system, Tony's evolution can alternatively be understood as intellectual growth. The whole plot has in fact Tony the narrator describing Tony the character as the personification of dullness: this drives characters around him – his ex-wife Margaret and Veronica in particular – to experience various degrees of amusement, irritation and exasperation, due to their incredulity at his lack of understanding. The question, as rhetorical as it seems, "You don't get it, do you?" (Barnes 2011: 59, the first time) rings in the plot no less than five or six times and contributes to the reader's figuration of Tony in terms of a thick and brainless character. This image, however, is removed at the very end of the novel when Tony finally grasps the truth about the disabled Adrian, and evenly claims: "And later, at home, going over it all, after some time, I understood." (Barnes 2011: 141) His switching to a higher intellectual level – from someone who never got it to someone who does – certainly elevates him, but hardly on a moral stage. Therefore, even if the novel seems to have the typical frame of a confessional novel, in this perspective *The Sense of an Ending* might not be eligible as such, but, in line with the standard in postmodern fiction, it may constitute a parodic use of confessional fiction.

It is needless to say that the shift from confessional fiction to a parodic use of this genre does not involve a mere problem of classification, but formally shows that the narrator is not offering a confession. Or, rather, his pleading guilty seems to be a mask used to cover a different activity. This feeling may possibly find confirmation if we focus our attention on another important element in confessional fiction: the narratee. The fictional persona to which a narration is addressed in a confessional fiction acquires an importance that seems to be inversely proportional to its presence in the text. In fact, this literary genre produces a discourse that magnifies subjectivity, self-centredness and, at times, even forms of narcissism, on the grounds that not only should its narration be seen as the result of a psychological torment met by the narrator, but also – and mainly – that his act of narration is intended as a salvific and soothing power for him. In these conditions the readers acquiesce in – and sometimes endure – the omnipresent selfhood of the narrator, who splits his persona into two distinct entities, who moves back and forth in his narration on the wave of his own emotions while possibly disregarding the readers' needs, and who makes use of melodramatic rhetoric. In the course of his narration, it is clear that the excessive presence of his selfhood is an artful strategy of the representation of his pain. It is true, however, that he actually shares the stage with another subject, the narratee, who happens to be a collaborative, friendly, kind but – most importantly – a silent figure. Whereas in the text the space assigned to the narratee shows a remarkable disproportion in favour of the narrator, the former is a figure of great magnitude since, by simply listening – sometimes even talking – to the narrator, he manages to have the narrator purified of his impurity, and cured of his malaise. Despite confining him to a (limited) space, *The Sense of an Ending* designates the narratee with a moderately sizeable place so that his presence is realistically felt: yet, his voice is never heard, but only echoed in Tony's long soliloquy. Below, I quote a meaningful example of this strategy:

You might think this is rubbish – preachy, self-justificatory rubbish. You might think that I behaved towards Veronica like a typically callow male, and that all my 'conclusions' are reversible.
For instance, 'After we broke up, she slept with me' flips easily into 'After she slept with me, I broke up with her.' You might also decide that the Fords were a normal middle-class English family on whom I was chippily foisting bogus theories of damage; and that Mrs Ford, instead of being tactfully concerned on my behalf, was displaying an indecent jealousy of her own daughter. You might even ask me to apply my 'theory' to myself and explain what damage I had suffered a long way back and what its consequences might be: for instance, how it might affect my reliability and truthfulness. I'm not sure I could answer this, to be honest. (Barnes 2011: 44)

While this mode of narration is widely used in confessional fiction, what seems to be a little uncommon is the clouding around the narratee's identity that invites us to wonder who the (fictional) entity is to whom this entire tale is addressed.

Of course, the immediate answer one is tempted to offer is that the narratee is the implied reader because he adopts the same manner of approach. However, no textual evidence in the plot drives us to a clear identification of this persona in terms of the implied reader, nor is there any allusion to the fact that the story we are reading is in a book-form; that would create the assumptions for a recipient in the text as an implied reader. In Graham Swift's *Waterland*, for instance, another English postmodern novel that may be interpreted along the lines of a confessional novel, the narratee has a clearer identification with Tom Crick's pupils and, at times, with one of them in particular, Price. What I am arguing here is not that the recognition of the addressee of the narration in *The Sense of an Ending* cannot be an implied reader: he may seem to be coincident with the narratee, but since we have no proof in the text, we cannot be sure about it.

Alternatively, one may imagine that the fictional 'you' to whom the narration is addressed is not someone different from Tony, but simply a projection of Tony's personality. Considering that the narratee is intended to help the narrator in his trip toward an inner liberation, I would suggest viewing him in terms of what Sigmund Freud called the 'superego,' a part of our self that represents our conscience, briefly defined as "that moral judgment which will be used in determining future behaviour" (Strickland 2001: 637). Interpreted in this way, *The Sense of an Ending* would be a tale that a troubled narrator is only pretending to tell to a listener, since the text would actually be the recollection of an entire lifetime narrated to his own double. Tony Webster is arguably not a very sociable person and one of his main difficulties in relating with others lies in his bar to communications, a limit he thinks he can overcome with a fervid imagination. He has a penchant for creating identities to whom he fancies he talks about his problematic past and who severely judge his conscience: one such imaginary persona is what he calls "the barrister in my head" (Barnes 2011: 114), with whom his tortured self creates a fascinating confrontation.

At least, that's how I remember it now. Though if you were to put me in a court of law, I doubt I'd stand up to cross-examination very well. 'And yet you claim this memory was suppressed for forty years?' 'Yes.' 'And only surfaced just recently?' 'Yes.' 'Are you able to account for why it surfaced?' 'Not really.' 'Then let me put it to you, Mr Webster, that this supposed incident is an entire figment of your imagination, constructed to justify some romantic attachment which you appear to have been nurturing towards my client, a presumption which, the court should know, my client finds utterly repugnant.' 'Yes, perhaps. But –' 'But what, Mr Webster?' 'But we don't love many people in this life. One, two, three? And sometimes we don't recognise the fact until it's too late. Except that it isn't necessarily too late. Did you read that story about late-flowering love in an old people's home in Barnstaple?' 'Oh please, Mr Webster, spare us your sentimental lucubrations. This is a court of law, which deals with fact. What exactly are the facts in the case?' I could only reply that I think – I theorise – that something – something else – happens to the memory over time. For years you survive with the same loops, the same facts and the same emotions. (Barnes 2011: 112)

The possibility that Tony Webster is therefore telling the story of his life to a part of his self – whether the fictional barrister, or any similar creation of his imagination is trivial – exists, even though, as in the previous case, this cannot be properly documented but remains on the level of pure hypothesis. However, the switch in interpretation is not inconsistent here. Again, the idea that Tony Webster is not making amends in front of an authoritative figure who may clean his conscience, but simply pretending to do so, while actually simply waiting for his own approbation, reinforces the possibility that the entire narration is shaped in terms of a parody rather than of a frank confession. This in fact would dismantle the entire architecture of a confessional fiction, the foundations of which directly respond to a relation of power engaging the penitent to the confessor. In a revealing passage, Michel Foucault argues:

The confession is a ritual of discourse in which the speaking subject is also the subject of the statement; it is also a ritual that unfolds within a power relationship, for one does not confess without the presence (or virtual presence) of a partner who is not simply the interlocutor but the authority who requires the confession, prescribes and appreciates it, and intervenes in order to judge, punish, forgive, console, and reconcile. (1978: 71-72)

If, then, confessional fiction does not solve all the problems concerning a correct interpretation of *The Sense of an Ending*, we should look for an alternative solution that fully gives sense to this complex, if brief novel. Although the narrator illustrates a dramatic story, burdened by a pervading sense of disorientation, remorse, anguish, frustration and dealing with suicides and broken relationships, the conclusion at least seems to offer a sense of relief and to remove a pessimistic aura from above the main character, so that Carroll has argued that it ends in an unconcealed note of triumph.[3] This should be possibly read less in relation with his final access to a superior understanding than with his discovery that his friend Adrian had a disabled son (named after him). Constructed as his own Doppelgänger, Adrian (the father), in fact, with his intellectual appeal has more than simply disturbed Tony, and his relationship with Veronica, Tony's ex-girlfriend, has further hurt the narrator's male ego. As in ordinary tales dealing with the double, therefore, a final balance is reaffirmed only on the condition that one self prevails over the other, in a solution typical of Stevenson's fiction. However, in Julian Barnes's hands the terminal duel between Doppelgänger extends further than to the lives of the two challengers, since Tony, as we have seen, still feels Adrian's pressure choking his sense of liberty after he has committed suicide. In a way, for Tony, Adrian has not yet died after cutting his veins "diagonally" (Barnes 2011: 48). Since the whole story – both the perspective and the chronicle – is subordinate to the narrator's subjectivity, the duel between the counterparts reaches its conclusion only when Adrian's image in Tony's mind has been definitively suppressed. In this sense, the homonymy of father and (disabled) son is not a mere coincidence. Wuthering Heights displays a parallel situation where the main character Catherine has a daughter who has the same name as her mother: in a famous essay, Linda Gold claimed that this is a strategy enabling the multiple narrator to create a connection between the two women, because "the youthful and passionate Catherine Earnshaw both dies and lives transformed in the person of her daughter and namesake, Catherine Linton" (1985: 71). It is meaningful that Catherine Earnshaw dies in childbirth when Cathy is born, whereas in *The Sense of an Ending*, Adrian Finn possibly commits suicide when he becomes aware that Sarah Ford, mother of his 'official' girlfriend, is pregnant with his child. Both stories seem to represent an ideal switching of identity between parent and child. As a result, Adrian Finn and his son are not necessarily to be seen as two distinct characters (only), but can also be

---

3 "Webster's narrative does conclude with a revelation which prompts him to declare triumphantly: 'And later, at home, going over it all, after some time, I understood. I got it.'" (Carroll 2015: 160)

interpreted as two distinct projections of the same identity. Adrian the father is the impeccable intellectual, whose image remains confined to the past, whereas his disabled son corresponds to Tony's representation in the present of his ex-school-friend, a representation that is obviously tinged with hate and revenge. In this perspective, Carroll's observation that "[t]he juxtaposition of Finn's exceptional intellect with Adrian's learning disability seems designed to deliver a decisive narrative irony" (2015: 168) appears particularly acute. More explicitly, the description of the disability in Adrian's son is equivalent to a murder of (the image of) Adrian Finn, in the mind of the narrator so that, after this crucial revelation, the story can swiftly reach its conclusion. Tony appears to be a little less "peaceable" (Barnes 2011: 34) than he claims, but Tóibín in his inspired review of *The Sense of an Ending* warns the readers that "it is easy to misread it" (2012: online).

I was amused to read in a note to Greaney's article on the oddness in the English novelist that "Barnes, in interview, has said that when he was writing *The Sense of an Ending*, he wasn't aware that the novel-in-progress shared its name with one of the twentieth century's most celebrated works of narrative theory" (Greaney 2014: 232). If one cannot trust Julian Barnes how can one trust his narrators, one is tempted to ask. Tony Webster is in fact one of those captivating postmodern storytellers who will swear to tell the untruth, the whole untruth and nothing but the untruth.

BIBLIOGRAPHY

Barnes, Julian (2012 [2011]): *The Sense of an Ending*, London: Vintage.
Bazalgette, Louise/Holden, John/Tew, Philip/Hubble, Nick/Morrison, Jago eds. (2011): *Coming of Age*, London: Demos.
Callus, Ivan (2012): "'There is great unrest': Some Reflections on Emotion and Memory in Julian Barnes's *Nothing to Be Frightened Of* and *The Sense of an Ending*." In: *Prague Journal of English Studies* 1/1, pp. 55-70.
Carroll, Rachel (2015): "'Making the blood flow backwards': Disability, Heterosexuality and the Politics of Representation in Julian Barnes's *The Sense of an Ending*." In: *Textual Practice* 29/1, pp. 155-172.

Cartwright, Justin (2011): "*The Sense of an Ending* by Julian Barnes – Review." In: *The Observer*, Sunday 31 July, last accessed February 26, 2018 (https://www.theguardian.com/books/2011/jul/31/sense-ending-julian-barnes-review). Web.

Foucault, Michel (1978): *The History of Sexuality. Vol. 1: An Introduction.* New York: Pantheon Books.

Gill, Jo (2006): "Introduction." In: Jo Gill (ed.), *Modern Confessional Writing: New Critical Essays*, London: Routledge.

Gold, Linda (1985): "Catherine Earnshaw: Mother and Daughter." In: *The English Journal* 74/3, March, pp. 68-73.

Greaney, Michael (2014): "The Oddness of Julian Barnes and *The Sense of an Ending.*" In: *English* 63/242, pp. 225-240.

Hendricks, Jon (2001): *The Encyclopedia of Aging. A Comprehensive Resource in Gerontology and Geriatrics*. (Third Edition) In: George L. Maddox (ed.), New York: Springer Science+Business Media.

House, Christian (2011): "*The Sense of an Ending*, by Julian Barnes." In: *The Independent*, Sunday 7 August, last accessed February 26, 2018 (http://www.independent.co.uk/arts-entertainment/books/reviews/the-sense-of-an-ending-by-julian-barnes-2333068.html). Web.

Hutcheon, Linda (1987): "The Politics of Postmodernism: Parody and History." In: *Cultural Critique* 5, *Modernity and Modernism, Postmodernity and Postmodernism,* Winter, 1986-1987, pp. 179-207.

Hutcheon, Linda (1989): *The Politics of Postmodernism*. London: Routledge.

Jordan, Justine (2011): "*The Sense of an Ending* by Julian Barnes – Review." In: *The Guardian*, Tuesday 26 July, last accessed February 26, 2018 (http://www.guardian.co.uk/books/2011/jul/26/sense-ending-julian-barnes-review1). Web.

Kakutani, Michiko (2011): "Life in Smoke and Mirrors." In: *New York Times*, October 16, last accessed February 26, 2018 http//www.nytimes.com/2011/10/17/books/Julian-Barnes-Sense-of-an-Ending-Review.html).

Martino, Andrew (2012): "Review." *World Literature Today* 86/1, January/February, pp. 56-57.

McAdams, Dan (2015): *The Art and Science of Personality Development*, New York: Guilford. Nicol, Bran (2009): The Cambridge Introduction to Postmodern Fiction, Cambridge: Cambridge University Press.

Radstone, Susannah (2007): *The Sexual Politics of Time: Confession, Nostalgia, Memory*, London: Routledge.

Ramsey Wallen, James (2017): "The Evils of Banality: Shallowness, Self-Realization, and Closure in Julian Barnes's *The Sense of an Ending* and Oscar Wilde's De Profundis." In: *Critique: Studies in Contemporary Fiction* 58/4, pp. 325-339.

Shields, David (2010): *Reality Hungers. A Manifesto*, London: Penguin.

Strickland, Bonnie R. (2001): *The Gale Encyclopedia of Psychology*. In: Bonnie R. Strickland (ed), Farmington Hills: Gale.

Tóibín, Colm (2012): "Going Beyond the Limits". In: *The New York Book Review of Books*, May 10, 2012 Issue, last accessed February 26, 2018 (http://www.nybooks.com/articles/2012/05/10/julian-barnes-going-beyond-limits/). Web.

Vecsernyés, Dóra (2014): "With His Watch on the Inside of the Wrist: Time in Julian Barnes's *The Sense of an Ending*." In: Tory, Eszter/ Vesztergom, Janina (eds.), *Stunned into Uncertainty: Essays on Julian Barnes's Fiction*, Budapest: Department of English Studies, pp. 29-40.

Wilhelmus, Tom (2012): *The Hudson Review* 64/4, Winter, pp. 705-711.

"Making Sense or No Sense of Existence"
The 'Plot' of Thomas Kinsella's *Late Poems* in the Light of Norberto Bobbio's *De senectute*

DONATELLA ABBATE BADIN, UNIVERSITY OF TURIN

Cyclicality has always characterized the poetry of Thomas Kinsella, one of the major Irish poets of the second half of the 20th century. It is not surprising then that in his more recent poetry, the poetry of *Late Poems* (2013), written in his seventies and eighties and initially published as pamphlets of his own Peppercanister Press,[1] he should not only be taking up familiar themes but indeed revisiting old poems whose titles are

---

[1] Peppercanister Press was established by Kinsella in 1972 to allow the divulgation of the polemical *Butcher's Dozen* and was operated from his home in the neighbourhood of the landmark church thus nicknamed. Most of his subsequent production first appeared in the form of pamphlets containing one long poem or gathering a few texts held together by a common theme, providing him thus the chance to take "another look at the work before publication – a final draft in published form" (Deane 1987, 87). Since 1988, John Deane's Dedalus Press has been issuing and distributing the Peppercanister series retaining the same logo. The titles of the pamphlets published in Kinsella's seventies and eighties, in other words in his old age, are *The Familiar* (1999), *Godhead* (1999), *Citizen of the World* (2000), *Littlebody* (2000), which are all part of *Collected Poems* (2001), and *Marginal Economy* (2006), *Man of War* (2007), *Belief and Unbelief* (2007), *Fat Master* (2011), and *Love Joy Peace* (2011), collected as *Late Poems* (2013).

proposed again with subtle variations. In doing so he completes a circular pattern going back to his beginnings and confirming some considerations on old age put forward by the Italian *maitre à penser*, Norberto Bobbio,[2] who, in his essay *De senectute* (1996) – an obvious allusion to Cicero's *De senectute* – suggests that old masters are so much "in love with their own ideas that they bring them up again and again." Many of the things they write are "variations on a single theme" (Bobbio [1996] 2001: 3).[3]

MEMORY AND UNDERSTANDING

As Bobbio puts it, since there is no future for the aged, the past is "the dimension in which the old live" (ibid: 12) so that, as a consequence, they "live on memory and for memory" (ibid: 31)[4] which is not necessarily a sterile or pathetic exercise for, as Bobbio writes, "by remembering you rediscover yourself and your identity, in spite of the many years that have passed and the thousands of events you have experienced" (ibid: 13).[5] Indeed, the inclination of ageing artists, who, at the end of their career, tend to dwell on the past and produce variations on the themes of their youth, far from being a sign of senile prattle or, simply, of lack of inspiration, lends itself to a different, more positive interpretation. Bobbio reminds us that old people "prefer to reflect on themselves and turn in on themselves where,

---

2 Norberto Bobbio (1909-2004) was a highly influential Italian philosopher of law and politics, an antifascist and a socialist. *De senectute*, his acceptance speech of an honorary degree at the University of Sassari, was translated into English by Alan Cameron as *Old Age*, 2001. All English quotations from *De senectute*, unless otherwise stated, are from Cameron's translation while the Italian quotations are from the Einaudi edition of his essays (1996).
3 "I vecchi professori sono tanto innamorati delle proprie idee da essere tentati di tornarci su con insistenza. Mi sto accorgendo io stesso che molte cose che scrivo in questi ultimi anni sono spesso variazioni sullo stesso tema" (Bobbio 1996: 17).
4 "Il vecchio vive di ricordi e per i ricordi." (ibid: 49)
5 "Nella rimembranza ritrovi te stesso, la tua identità, nonostante i mille anni trascorsi, le mille vicende vissute." (ibid: 29)

according to St. Augustine, truth is to be found" (ibid: 6),[6] and he recommends that, since the time ahead is so short because "old age doesn't last long [...] you have to use your time not for making plans for a distant future that is no longer yours, but in trying to understand, if you can, the meaning of your life or the lack of it" (ibid: 12).[7]

The original Italian words, "il senso o il non senso della tua vita," correspond exactly to Kinsella's "making sense or no sense of existence," which, in the interview he granted Andrew Fitzsimons in 2004, he indicated as being the 'plot' of the poetic production of his seventies and eighties (Kinsella 2004: 75). Like Bobbio who opines that in old age it is essential to try and understand, Kinsella, too, explains that he tries to "achieve some kind of understanding. Looking into the process and making what sense we can; extracting order if possible; assembling some sort of structure to resist the effects of time; with the power to articulate, connecting the generations" (ibid: 76). The importance of understanding also appears, poetically, in the longing for it in such verses as "I [...] allow / my arms to fall open in resignation, / desiring an understanding" (Kinsella 2013: 28). This is confirmed by the title of a section of Peppercanister 24, *Marginal Economy* (2006), called "Songs of Understanding." The poet expresses frustration at the vain aspirations of his life and art, between "waste" and "excess," but still asserts "the illusion, to a self-selected few, / of their positive participation / in a communal endeavour / with a final meaningful goal [...]. Through a fault in the outermost rim / left open for the length of a lifetime / a glimpse of preoccupied purpose" (2013: 28-29). This is how far one can hope to go in terms of giving a meaning to one's life and doings – finding a glimpse of purpose which, moreover, is communal. In this light, much of his late poetry could be termed 'songs of understanding.'

The focus on understanding, however, has always been for Kinsella the substance of poetry and all the more so in recent years when taking stock of

---

6   "Il vecchio rimane indietro, si ferma o perché non ce la fa o perché preferisce riflettere su se stesso, per tornare in se stesso, dove, diceva Sant'Agostino, abita la verità." (ibid: 21)

7   "Ma proprio perché [la vecchiaia] dura poco impiega il tuo tempo non tanto per fare progetti per un futuro lontano che non ti appartiene più, quanto per cercare di capire, se puoi, *il senso o il non senso della tua vita* [my emphasis]" (ibid).

one's whole life appears as a necessity in front of its impending end. "It is not easy to take stock" writes Bobbio but looking into the past, remembering, is one of his recipes to achieve it: "When you are old, and what is more, feeling old, you cannot suppress the temptation to reflect on your own past." ([1996] 2001: 80)[8]

This understanding comes, for Kinsella, by examining and acknowledging the "whole" and its "individual parts" despite "a fundamental inadequacy / in the structure" (Kinsella 2013: 28) – the "individual parts" being moments of one's whole life salvaged through memory in all their "waste" and "excess" – and discovering that

> There is still an ongoing dynamic
> in the parts as they succeed each other
> and in the assembling record,
> that registers as positive.
>
> This can be thought of as purposeful
> permitting the illusion,
> to a self-selected few,
> of the positive participation
> in a communal endeavour
> with a final meaningful goal
> [...]
> but sufficient to give the feeling
> of advancement toward an End.
>
> Accepting out of the past
> the Gift of the offered good
> add all of thine own best
> and offer the Gift onward. (Kinsella 2013: 28-29)

The fact that there is a Gift (and a capitalized one) and that it can be offered onward is what gives sense to individual and collective life, present and

---

8 "Quando si è vecchi, e per di più anche invecchiati, non si riesce a sottrarsi alla tentazione di riflettere sul proprio passato. [...] un bilancio non è facile." (ibid: 163)

past. As David Lynch (2015) writes in the latest book published about Kinsella: "Although it is important in the Kinsellian world view to evaluate honestly humanity's bleakest and most evil attributes, the best of his work may not redeem humanity, but it does bring a level of understanding to our actions." (Kindle. Chap. 3)

Many of Kinsella's compositions, often in a Peppercanister sequence *ad hoc*, hail back to his own personal past in respect to the belief that understanding comes by taking in the whole of one's life through memory. *The Familiar* (1999), celebrates his long relationship with the woman of his life, Eleanor, married in 1955 (and lost in 2017) by evoking various of their moments together, their courtship, her moving in with him in the digs of Baggot Street and, interspersed throughout *Late Poems* a variety of other scenes of their married life such as having breakfast together, attending a wedding or a jazz concert. Houses and neighbourhoods play an important role in many poems. The graffiti seen in the first neighbourhood where he lived ("Love Joy Peace inside the white sign of a heart") provide the title of his latest Peppercanister (2011). Some poems bring back to life city characters met in pubs, boxing matches, funerals. Even the Department of Finance, where he had his first job, is evoked through memories of a hated colleague, now met and acknowledged in a graveyard. Indeed, as Bobbio writes: "The great wealth possessed by the old is the marvellous world of the memory, an inexhaustible source of reflections on ourselves, the universe in which we have lived, and the persons and events that have caught our attention along the way." ([1996] 2001: 31)[9]

"The Gift of the offered good" of "Songs of Understanding" (Kinsella 2013: 28) could be the gift of memory and what it brings about. Taking stock, interrogating life, understanding its sense and finding some good in it happen mostly by immersing oneself in this "marvellous world" and looking back at the past, and Kinsella has always been a poet of the personal as well as of the archetypal memory.

---

9 "Il grande patrimonio del vecchio è nel mondo meraviglioso della memoria, fonte inesauribile di riflessioni su noi stessi, sull'universo in cui siamo vissuti, sulle persone e gli eventi che lungo la via hanno attratto la nostra attenzione." (ibid: 49)

The Past in Kinsella's Early and Late Poetry

Kinsella's whole career has been bent on the past which, he says, is part of his totality. The national and cultural past on the one side and, on the other, his own personal past are part of his poetry of memory through which he hopes to find some enlightenment not to say truth.

A salient characteristic of Kinsella's production as a retriever of the past was the work he did to repossess ancient Irish sagas and poetry through translation (the epic poem *The Tàin* (1970) and many other old Irish poems), anthologies such as *An Duanaire. Poetry of the Dispossessed 1600-1900* (1981) and *The New Oxford Book of Irish Verse* (1986) adding also seminal critical essays on the loss of a language and culture and the trauma of the broken tradition of Ireland (*The Irish Writer* (1970), *The Divided Mind* (1972), *The Dual Tradition* (1995)). In his most creative era (the 1970s and 1980s) it had also meant re-appropriating the foundation myths about the legendary invasions of Ireland to bare the original scar inscribed in the subconscious memory of each member of the community – a Jungian exploration of his own psyche that brought together mythical and individual history mirroring and enriching each other – a palimpsest of texts and time-frames.

The movement backwards however, in the more recent phase of his production, is polarized on the Self and its "moment of moral knowledge," as defined by Harry Clifton (2007), a prominent Irish poet, in a review of Kinsella's oeuvre in *The IrishTimes*. The recovery of the Irish material, in fact, is no longer part of his poetic project nor is he any longer preoccupied with healing the old wounds of the loss of language and tradition. He has long since come to terms with that, as he announced in his acceptance speech of an honorary degree from the University of Turin, in which he tried to define the aims of his recent poetry in relation to the ancient concerns.[10] Exploring the mythical past had only been a form of probing the self, animated, as Badin wrote, "by a process of self-investigation and by the search for a point of stability in the face of erosion" (1996: 12).

---

10 On May 9, 2006 the University of Turin granted Thomas Kinsella an honorary degree. His acceptance speech was first published in *Omaggio a Thomas Kinsella*, Torino: Trauben and then was included in Kinsella (2009). *Prose Occasions 1951-2006*, Manchester: Carcanet.

While the method now has changed, as it is no longer going through myth, he is still sifting the past in a process of self-understanding and search of a structure. In an early poem, "A Lady of Quality," he had suggested that communicating "recovered order to [his] pen" (Kinsella 2001: 8), was the aim of his poetic project and it continues to be so in spite of the fact that, especially after his move to the States and the publication of *Notes from the Land of the Dead* (1972), he broke away from the formal style of his early works that in itself had communicated clarity and order. In the poetry written in his late seventies and eighties, which continues being fragmentary and modernistic, we still find him intent on a search for a 'plot' or a 'structure' – terms he frequently used throughout his career – and which in Turin he called "the substance of a life expressed with understanding as best one can," (Kinsella 2009) and in his more recent poetry a form of "good."

In the poem, "Blood of the Innocent," contained in Peppercanister 24, *Marginal Economy*, he affirms that "we should gather in each generation / all the good we can from the past, / add our own best and [...] leave to [...] those behind us [...] a growing total of Good (adequately recorded)" (Kinsella 2013: 20). Another short poem from "Songs of Understanding" in the same Peppercanister sequence reiterates his position towards the past with a view to the present and the future: "Reclaiming out of the past / all the good you can use, / and all the good that you can / and offer it all onward." (ibid: 29) The search for 'good' – a term he uses repeatedly – may mean acceptance, peace, finding a 'structure,' an 'order' in the universe, realising "That the life-form as we have it / is inadequate in itself; but that / having discovered the compensatory devices / of Love and the religious and creative imaginations" (ibid: 21) one has reached understanding for oneself and the generations to come and added a sense to what one has been doing. The search is incremental, including new material, and, at the same time, cyclical as it embraces the past. Its final purpose is that of reviewing and recording his findings transmitting them to the generations to come. Therefore, Kinsella cannot be catalogued as a griever of times past, as many old people are: the past is present for him, lively and to be used. Its loss is not bemoaned and its retrieval celebrated not only as a personal gift, but as a contribution to the community. A cyclical taking stock of past concerns and experiences is the hallmark of Kinsella's late poetry.

Thomas Kinsella's attachment to the ideas he had been "in love with," to quote Bobbio's ironical phrase, and which had yielded a sense of a structure, an understanding, is clearly displayed in his latest Peppercanister pamphlets in which he distils "a lifetime of writing" as poet and critic Harry Clifton (2007) wrote in *The IrishTimes*. Although remembering and "sifting and reconfiguring of a few archetypal elements" (ibid) is the favourite pastime of the elderly, including Kinsella, there are times, however, when he rebels against his continuous ruminations on the past. In the poem "Novice," a chilling vision of old age, the persona of the poet finds a moth on his path and recognizes it as an insect that he had seen in a childhood book, an insect belonging to a "species that sucks and swallows / only while it is growing; that cannot eat / once it reaches maturity" (Kinsella 2013: 51). The suspicion that there might be an analogy between this insect and the old poet who can no longer feed on anything new but must go back to what he absorbed or intuited in the past is so troubling that the speaker of the poem viciously crushes the "death moth" with his foot. The gesture reads as a rebellion against what old people mostly do, according to Bobbio, and what Kinsella himself has been mostly doing.

There are, however, many exciting inroads in contemporary territory, compositions that are not repetitive or backward-looking but on the contrary rooted in the present. Asked by John F. Deane to write a poem about war, after some hesitation Kinsella produced Peppercanister 27, *Man of War* (2007) launched at the Gate Theatre in Dublin on June 17, 2007 at a celebration of his career and his upcoming eightieth birthday.[11] The sequence deals with "the brutal basis in the human species" which is displayed not only in war – "the willed, and mass, occasional destruction / of others, face to face, of the same kind" – but also in human relations, at work, in sports, in the hunt, "in dealing with the lesser forms of life"

---

11 On the evening of 17 June 2007 a group of poets, writers and critics gathered at the Gate Theatre in Dublin to celebrate the long and influential career of a poet and scholar who had long been neglected and would be reaching briefly his 80th birthday (Kinsella was born in 1928). At that same time, the poet also received the prestigious Freedom of the City award, in other words the symbolic keys to Dublin, his native city which had played such an important role in his work. An *Irish Studies Review* special issue (edited by Derval Tubridy) dedicated to Kinsella followed in 2008 gathering the homages of friends and colleagues.

(Kinsella 2013: 33). In this philosophical and indignant sequence, Kinsella speaks not as a recriminating old man but as a human being fully involved in the present, a man that would "sign / all protests and appeals for abolition / of warfare in the world" if he could "find / where to send them" (ibid: 39). In John F. Deane's words (2007) "[i]t is, perhaps, Kinsella's fullest response to society's current urges towards wars and self-indulgent immorality" although we cannot ignore that in 1962 he had already made the voice of a pacifist heard, with equal graphic horror, in his "Old Harry" describing nuclear war and the attack on Hiroshima.

"Marcus Aurelius," too, a long philosophical poem from *Marginal Economy* (2006), comments on the present world "threatened by outer and inner forces hard to define" through the "uncommitted and marginal voice" of a ruler who incarnated "modern qualities," Marcus Aurelius, "one that had access to the bureaucratic world as well as the sensual, a figure that was alienated and involved at the same time" (Kinsella 2009: 128). Through his involvement and his stoic vision of the world, the emperor becomes an alter-ego for the speaker's vision of the world.

CIRCULARITY AND REPETITION

These sallies into the problems and evils of the present, are, however, an exception. In Kinsella's *Late Poems* (2013) we find the artist repeatedly turning, as we have seen, to "the good that came from the past" (especially the "good" he produced himself) and feeding, like the insect in "Novice," on what he had "swallowed" before. Old people do tend to repeat themselves, as Bobbio said. What Badin wrote about his production in the last century still applies to his twenty-first century production: "Similar situations, characters, and thematic concerns reappear in each phase [of his long career] enriched each time by the significance they have acquired within the macro-text. […]. A number of internal quotations from his own poems, in fact, underline their interdependency." (1996: 12) Adrienne Leavy (2016), in an article in *The IrishTimes*, confirms this assumption for Kinsella extending it to his more recent production: "[r]ecurring imagery and motifs are a hallmark of his poetry (especially his late poetry) […] with entire sequences and individual poems frequently and deliberately incorporating situations and language from earlier work."

Kinsella's probing the self by going back to the beginnings of his poetic questioning, to the tentative answers he found then, reminds one of Eliot's defence in "East Coker" of possible allegations of repetitiveness: "You say I am repeating / Something I have said before. I shall say it again. / Shall I say it again?" (Eliot 1963: 23). Kinsella "says it again" even to the point of picking up old titles of early poems. In searching for understanding which, in Bobbio's opinion, is what the elderly must urgently look for, Kinsella rehearses old approaches and terminology – "finding," as Leavy (2016) writes, "new aesthetic meaning in experiences and poems from decades earlier" and intentionally echoing creatively old poems of which "he retains (or slightly modifies) the titles and content." Two such pieces are "Into Thy Hands" and "Elderly Craftsman at his Bench," both from *Late Poems* (2013) that engage with antecedents from much earlier times. "Into Thy Hands" (2011) reiterates a title from one of his first collections, *Moralities* (1960). "Elderly Craftsman at his Bench" (2011), answers "Worker in Mirror at his Bench" from the collection *New Poems* of 1973.

In both pieces dealing with craftsmen / artists, the speaker contemplates his act of creation, and through it, of understanding, but with different reactions. The self-regarding "artist in mirror" of the earlier poem, apparently a craftsman talking to some visitors about his production, declares publicly that his work of art, which, privately, he had defined a "Self-Reflecting Abstraction," has no practical application:

> I am simply trying to understand something
> – states of peace nursed out of wreckage.
> The peace of fullness, not emptiness.
>
> [...]
> Often the more I simplify
> The more a few simplicities
> go burrowing in their own depths
> until the guardian structure is aroused. (Kinsella 2001: 124)

The reader, however, tends to mistrust this optimistic declaration. Once alone, his visitors gone, the 'peace of fullness' feigned as resulting from finding the guardian structure is revealed to be, in fact, the peace of a blank 'emptiness', a fake: "Blackness – all matter / In one polished cliff face / Hurtling rigid from zenith to pit / Through dead" (Kinsella 2001: 126).

The elderly craftsman appears more positive. After all, despite his "bent body," the worker of the poem included in the pamphlet *Fat Master* is still at his "worn bench," (Kinsella 2013: 67) as was his counterpart in the earlier poem who, decades before, was searching "truth as tinkering / easing the particular of its litter" (Kinsella 2001: 124-125). The more recent impersonation of the artist is still searching by using the tool of memory, "think[ing] [his] way back / into the depths, beyond their origin" (Kinsella 2013: 67). His "serious efforts," however, are no longer so compulsive and he allows himself to pause, meditate and look back as a response to a surreal beckoning arm ("a soft arm reaching toward me / out of nowhere, / the fingers closing and opening") (ibid). This "signal reaching unfulfilled from somewhere in the past" (ibid), another of the poet's reminders to look back far enough to the prime source, leads however to the finding that "there is no peace here" (Kinsella 2013: 67). Although Kinsella writes to find clarity, his "efforts are always unfulfilled," writes his friend and prominent critic Maurice Harmon (2012: 14).

Although admitting failure, the older artist, unlike his desperate predecessor, hopes that "there will be a like thoughtfulness / for me and my concerns when the time comes" (ibid). Thus, the craftsman does find peace in the reminder of approaching death and the vague promise that his findings and concerns will not be unattended by those that will follow him. His is not the "peace of fullness" that his colleague pretended to have found but a peace of questioning, "a serviceable calm / so that I can attend to my work again" (ibid). In this beautiful statement of intimations of mortality and immortality in old age, the elderly craftsman, although he has no new input, can, like the mature insect, make new sense of what he had fed on before, by thinking his "way back" and experiencing at least acceptance if not understanding or truth.

This almost mystical peace is confirmed by the two other poems bearing the same title of "Into Thy Hands." A religious frame of mind is suggested by the title itself which resonates with Christ's words on the cross "Father into thy hands I commit my spirit" (Luke 23:46). The words are also to be found in psalms and prayers of the Catholic Church. The earliest "Into Thy Hands," included in *Moralities*, 1960, is part of a sequence entitled "Faith" presenting three different attitudes to belief thus summarized by Badin (1996): "that of the skeptic, who finds nurture for his doubts in contemplating a polished seashell, a symbol of relentless erosion; that of the unconditional believer, whose total yielding to God's will is expressed through the metaphor of the diver [...]; and that of the opportunist, a Lucifer whose 'puckish rump' is inscribed 'Do good / Some care and a simple faith will get you on'" (Badin 1996: 44).

The 1960 "Into Thy Hands" (the middle piece of "Faith") describes the "salty joy" of the start of "our dreadful journey into being" which involves hurling "the Present at the Past" and soaring confidently "into the azure chasm."

>Diver, noting lightly how the board
>Gives to the body, now with like intent
>I watch the body give to the instant, seeing
>In risk a salty joy: let accident
>Complete our dreadful journey into being.
>
>Here possessed of time and flesh at last,
>I hurl the Present bodily at the Past.
>
>Outstretched, into the azure chasm he soared. (Kinsella 2001: 24)

The more recent poem, first published in Peppercanister 28, *Fat Master* (2011) deals with a handicraft shaped by a careful, thoughtful worker (as do the two companion twin poems about artists at their benches) and is a common topos for a poet always interrogating himself on the sense of his art:

>The whole and all its parts
>made of a given substance.
>The parts self-selected,
>tried along the senses,
>founded on hard practice.
>The whole shaped and corrected
>To stand unsupported. (Kinsella 2013: 68)

In the last lines of the 2011 poem, the perfected object, like the body of the diver in the 1960 "Into Thy Hands", is "offered to an intimate, / wayward in acceptance, / self-chosen and unknown" (Kinsella 2013: 68). The oxymoron of "intimate" and "unknown" might refer either to a lover or to some divine entity. The man who has crafted it and the diver of the earlier poem both yield to a mysterious power, putting themselves into the hands of another entity, whether human or divine. The musician of *Fat Master* (possibly Bach) is also presenting his "orderly offering / of new discoveries [...] / to the one adequate reflecting Other" (Kisella 2013: 77).

The two pairs of poems show that Kinsella's sifting his past production is not due to his having something new to say but to his wanting to return to the past, to his own words, in a new spirit, close, at times, to a mystical view of the world or at least to a position of acceptance and peace. Being unable to "suck and swallow" new food does not mean that a poet cannot feed on what he ate earlier to produce something new and valuable. There is a continuous refining and simplifying, in search of new answers to the old familiar questions. "Taking stock of one's life," Bobbio's advice, consists mostly in chewing on things of the past even if one can no longer "suck and swallow" and, starting from there, proposing new solutions and foraying in different directions knowing that "[t]he search for meaning and order will always be provisional" as Adrienne Leavy (2014), points out in a review of *Late Poems*.

The cycle of sifting and distillation seems to be one of the possible benefits of old age that, as Kinsella said in his Turin "Acceptance Speech", means, essentially, bearing in mind "what has been done before, by the same few human types, with slight variations" (Kinsella 2009: 127). As Kinsella suggests, "Everything [...] will happen again" (ibid). In the background we can hear the words framing "East Coker": "in my beginning is my end" and "in my end is my beginning" (Eliot 182 and 190). The same circular trajectory describes Kinsella's poetic endeavour, interpreting now as in his youth, his present situation by going back to the personal, national, mythical and metaphysical beginnings. More pointedly, the latter verse points to how, in the case of Kinsella, the awareness of last matters approaching prompts him to try once again to give an answer to questions put before, in his beginnings, even by tentatively approaching religion, as the title of one of his recent publications, *Belief and Unbelief*, suggests.

But with a difference: it is now done in the awareness of last matters.

DISEASE AND THOUGHTS OF DEATH

In the general perception of old age, the consciousness of a decaying body, increasingly tormented by aches and disease, and the *memento mori* this brings about, are attendant to the final stage of life. This is certainly true about Bobbio who acknowledges being "increasingly tottery on feeble legs" and crossing "the road leaning on my stick and holding my wife's arm" (Bobbio [1996] 2001: 18). His essay gives voice to the experiences and fears of many old people confronted everyday by the miseries of ageing:

[T]the descent into the void is long, much longer than I would have ever imagined, and slow, so slow as to appear almost imperceptible (although not to me). The descent is continuous and, what is worse, irreversible: you descend one step at a time, but having put your foot on the lower step, you know you will never return to the higher one. I have no idea how many more downward steps are to follow. I can only be sure that their number is steadily decreasing. (Bobbio [1996] 2001: 17)

Many diaries and fictional works dwell on ageing and the feelings of approaching death either, as Virginia Woolf suggests, because it is an interesting literary subject to be dealt with, or to dispel the anguish of the process by understanding and accepting it:

Oh & I thought, as I was dressing, how interesting it would be to describe the approach of age, & the gradual coming of death. As people describe love. To note every symptom of failure: but why failure? To treat age as an experience that is different from the others; & to detect everyone of the gradual stages towards death which is a tremendous experience, & not conscious at least in its approaches, as birth is. (Woolf 1977-1984: 230)

At that time, she was still not considering giving herself death. It was an abstract topic she was curious about. Such a curiosity does certainly not pertain to Kinsella. Unlike Bobbio, who examines in detail what it means to grow old and enfeebled, and Woolf who would like to examine it (and partly does in many of her novels), Kinsella in his old age shuns, at least publicly, such preoccupations and his poetry rarely reflects directly the slow and painful process of ageing although publicly he at times wryly hints at his approaching end. Before his reading at the Gate Theatre celebration of his career on 17 June 2007, for instance, he remarked that the occasion "has been slightly painful because I know that such an experience is granted only toward the end of one's life" (Tubridy 2008: 232). On the same occasion he quipped: "I think it was Yeats who said, 'Best of all is never to have been born. Second best is to die soon.' I've failed on the first but I am hoping to succeed on the second." (Byrne 2009. online) Apart from such occasional sallies, Kinsella mostly directs his concerns and fears towards what happened in the past and what is happening in the outer world, with its crises and decline, but pays no attention to his own diminishing powers. The subject is too urgent and painful to be addressed head on although his frequent mention of waste acts as a powerful euphemism.

On the contrary, when he was a relatively young man, an awareness of decay was central to Kinsella's view of man and made him "particularly responsive to failing powers or outright disease," as Badin (1996: 53) wrote in relation to some poems in the collection *Nightwalker and Other Poems* (1968). "[He] seemed morbidly obsessed with deteriorating physical forms and loss of power" (ibid: 53). In "Soft Toy," a battered teddy bear, or some similar soft toy, becomes a fitting persona for the poet – a "soiled," "crumpled," "beaten," "ragged," heaped" thing, "limp with use and re-use" with "a cold pitted grey face" (Kinsella 2001: 75). In "Mirror in February," a poem he wrote in his thirties, he straightforwardly expresses an awareness of ageing:

Under the fading lamp, half dressed
[...]
I towel my shaven jaw and stop, stare,
Riveted by a dark exhausted eye,
A dry downturning mouth.
[...]
Now plainly in the mirror of my soul
I read that I have looked my last on youth.
[...]
And how should the flesh not quail, that span for span
Is mutilated more? In slow distaste

> I fold my towel with what grace I can,
> Not young, and not renewable, but man. (Kinsella 2001: 53)

The compositions of the last twenty years rarely dwell so graphically on signs of physical deterioration, actual illness or death. There are a few exceptions, nonetheless, such as "Delirium," describing the awakening in hospital form an operation and drifting back into a daze, "Will drained bare / back to the dark / and the depths that I came from" (Kinsella 2013: 52). The nightmarish poem "Free Fall" is another symbolic representation of illness and approaching death "I was falling helpless in a shower of waste, / reaching my arms out toward the others / falling in disorder everywhere around me" (Kinsella 2013: 75).

Another piece, untitled, opens the collection *Late Poems*, with the account of a much too realistic dream of the indignities of old age, which lingers in mind as one reads the other poems. "*Wandering alone / from abandoned room to room / down the corridors of a derelict hotel, / searching for the lost urinal…*". The use of italics and the words "I woke" indicate this is a nightmare but one that announces the coming of "the waste" that will sink the active days of the speaker into night. The second part of the poem starts with an invocation to the Fates or Moirai, or, much closer home, to Banshees, asking them that all may not be lost: "Nightwomen, / picking the work of my days apart, / will you find what you need / in the waste still to come?" (Kinsella 2013: 13). The poem, set at the beginning of *Late Poems*, appears as an invitation to approach the whole collection *sub specie aeternitatis*, or rather, since expectations of eternity are doubtful in Kinsella's universe, under the perspective of an ending, in other words, *in substantia nostrae mortalitatis*.

Rather than of ageing and mortality, Kinsella prefers to talk about 'waste,' a term he has been using amply since the beginning of his career to indicate the unescapable outcome of all forms of existence. In Kinsella's stoic view of life, physical deterioration and the human indignities awaiting the ageing are, consistently with his past positions, to be seen as part of a general design and, therefore, to be endured. As in his past production, in *Late Poems* there is a constant talk of the waste marking our society at all times. Several poems contained in Peppercanister 24, *Marginal Economy*, deal with situations of difficult survival and risk of extinction of waning civilisations:

> We worked farther out toward the edge
> while anything could still be found.
> Bringing back less and less,
> until it was time to move again.
> The need for care increasing.
>
> We accepted things as they were,
> with no thoughts of change.
> The only change was in ourselves:
> moving onward, leaving something behind each time.
>
> There were ten years at most
> even in the good places. (Kinsella 2013: 27)

The condition of the primitive society of gatherers or of the stranded wanderers alluded to in "Songs of Exile" as "your tired tribe" awaiting the word "in dust of the desert" (ibid: 26) lend themselves to be seen as metaphors of the waning conditions of ageing humans. Surviving in a weakening body is also a form of "marginal economy" as is the condition of the people in the sequence bearing the same name.

Death is also part of the process of waste and it, too, is not addressed directly in *Late Poems* nor does it play a great part there. This is surprising not so much because it is an event which should occupy the minds of old people as it looms so near, but because Kinsella's past production was rich in meditations on death and accounts of public and personal loss: there were elegies ranging from the loss of a family member to that of a public figure (Sean O Riada, John Kennedy, Valentin Ironmonger, but also the fisherman in "The Shoals Returning"); poems dealing with tragic events in the history of the Irish nation such as Bloody Sunday, Vinegar Hill, Robert Emmett's death at the dock, but also about foreign massacres (Hiroshima, for one). The concern and indignation for the horror of man-willed death, however, is still present in the 2007 sequence *Man of War*.

The explanation for the avoidance of the topic of one's individual end is simple. There is little to say about it apart from expressing fear about the way and the time it will happen or entertaining hopes of an afterlife. "By its very essence the manner of our destiny is unknown and shrouded in mystery" as Bobbio (1996) explains. "Only other people can speak of my death. I can give an account of my life using my memories and the memories of those who are close to me [...] I can speak of it up to my very last minutes. But I can never speak of my death. That is up to others." (Bobbio [1996] 2001: 17)[12] The stoic Kinsella, who does not complain about declining powers nor gives voice to fear, shows by his silence that he is in full agreement with Bobbio's privileging memory over meditations on death.

BELIEF AND UNBELIEF

Theologians, philosophers as well as the common man have endlessly discussed what will happen once our destiny is fulfilled, advancing all sorts of speculations about an afterlife. Believing that there is one would undoubtedly help reveal the meaning of life that Kinsella, like all people, especially ageing people, has been seeking. *Belief and Unbelief* is the title of one of his most recent publications (2007) signalling the importance this binary opposition has for him in the late stages of his life and underlining his wavering position. "In these poems," said Kinsella at the Gate Theatre ceremony, talking about two of his *Prayers* contained in the sequence, "the growing doubts and certainties of that lifetime are trying to live together" (Turbidy, 2008: 234). The chink of hope left open by his wavering represents his own version of Pascal's wager.

Total belief in the "transition to another form of life perceived and defined in different ways according to the individual, religion or

---

12 "Del proprio destino che è per essenza ignoto ed è quindi avvolto nel mistero [...] si può parlare a ragion veduta soltanto quando è compiuto. [...]. Della mia morte possono parlare solo gli altri. Io posso raccontare la mia vita attraverso i miei ricordi e i ricordi di coloro che mi sono stati vicini [...]. Posso raccontarla sino agli ultimi minuti. Non posso raccontare la mia morte. Solo gli altri lo possono fare." (Bobbio 1996: 34)

philosophy" (Bobbio [1996] 2001: 17)13 cannot be accepted by confirmed agnostics such as Bobbio and Kinsella. Andrea Byrne (2009) in an article in *The Independent* quotes the Irish poet as saying: "I believe now, with a certain nervousness, that you simply go back from where you came from which is nowhere. We are phenomena, we are biological freaks, we simply come to the end of a given ordeal and go back to nothing." (22 March 2009) All this endorses the opinion of Maurice Harmon (2012) who maintains that "The awareness of the meaninglessness of the world [...] underlies all his recent work. [...] *Godhead* measured the Divine and found it wanting. *Marginal Economy* faced the truth that there is no redemption from outside. *Belief and Unbelief* that if there is no expectation, there is less disappointment" (2012: 14).

It is true that in "Love Joy Peace" Kinsella rejects the answers offered by traditional religions: "That the select only, the chosen few, / should enter effortless into the Kingdom / to meet a Maker wasteful on high / as in His worldly works. / Unacceptable." (Kinsella 2013: 89) The poem also criticizes the official Church: "a growing waste of ornament / [...] / the waste increasing through the centuries / into what had been bothering me / – the hierarchies, councils of elders / [...] / The Temple clattering with worldly goods" (ibid: 88). He has, however, sympathetic words for "the beliefs of the first Church," for the historical figure of Christ, and elaborates his own theory of Grace. Even Harmon concedes that "[t]he final poem 'Love Joy Peace,' is a statement of personal faith" (2012: 14).

The disbelief in an afterlife, in fact, does not close the door to all forms of religiosity and the sense of the divine. As Kinsella is walking the last stretch of his long life, there have been some signs of his searching the consolations of faith after for several decades refusing to see a source of understanding and of meaningfulness in God. He often uses, though gingerly, more explicit terms such as Belief, Faith, God and refers to the symbols of Christianity. The title of the two Peppercanister sequences, *Godhead* (1999) and *Belief and Unbelief* (2007), and the presence of several poems bearing the title of "Prayer" make one suspect that Kinsella besides trying throughout his career and especially in his latest years to take

---

13 "Che la morte [...] sia il passaggio ad un'altra forma di vita diversamente immaginata e definita secondo i diversi individui, le diverse religioni, le diverse filosofie, non è un fatto, è una credenza" (Bobbio 1996: 35).

stock of life (as the ageing should), is also trying to find God. His condition is that of the women in "Songs of Exile": "In soiled survival, / awaiting the Word, / we are here assembled." (2013: 26)

Indeed in the latest publications, *Fat Master* and *Love Joy Peace*, the speaker gives voice both to the temptation and the refusal to believe. Other forms of faith are given a possibility and John F. Deane (2007) rightly sees some of these poems as "'prayers' to an unnamed but guiding force behind nature and human being." There is a sense of acceptance although, in Harmon's opinion, "understanding, even partial, is the most we can hope for" (2012: 14).

In the poem "Ceremony" the speaker goes through the motions of yielding "to an impulse" of entering a church, "kneeling before the altar / under the bowl of blood," raising his "palms together / before the hidden Host." All to no avail: there is no revelation and he returns disappointed to the awareness of his body and back, through Westland Row, "into the world" (Kinsella 2013: 59). "Religion has disappeared, but ceremony has not" he tells his interviewer Fitzsimon (Kinsella 2004: 79) and he finds in it some form of consolatory structure.

More importantly, in this phase of his career Kinsella elaborates what Harmon (2012) calls "his personal faith" (14): he surmises that a sparkle of divinity, an inkling of the meaning of life, may only be communicated by art – music and poetry especially – and by the contemplation of nature. "At a time like the present, when religion has more or less vanished, poetry can almost act as a substitute" he told Fitzsimon (2004: 74). The purpose of art becomes a kind of prayer or sacrificial offering. Both the artist of the second "Into thy Hands" contemplating the self-standing object of his craft, and the musician of "Fat Master" drawing powerful chords from the organ offer religiously the product of their art, the former to an "intimate," "unknown" being (Kinsella 2013: 68), the latter "to the one adequate reflecting Other" (ibid: 77). Bach reaching into "the heart of matter" (ibid: 77), Michelangelo "manipulating immensities of mind and matter" (ibid: 90) come closer to intimations of divinity than the speaker of the poem in his shows of religiousness. Nature also offers some glimpses of the divine. An ocean sunset provokes the poet into writing "In the face of God's creation / our last doubts fall silent," but the title "Rhetoric of Natural Beauty" disavows the emotion of the poem revealing it for what it is, a rhetorical figure (ibid: 30). Finally, there is the "Joy of the flesh. / Saying all it can of love. Peace and nothingness of the last end" (ibid: 91). Like religion, art, and especially poetry "can contribute a view of the 'process' as a whole" (Kinsella 2004: 74). The glimpse one obtains from nature, art or sex is, indeed, nothing but a glimpse but it provides peace, the easing of the ache of life like the grace that comes by producing a carefully crafted object:

> Grace as routine.
> The lone artificer loosening the charged facts
> from an imagination arguing with itself
> until the ache is eased – by the will, in tedium;
> and the ache object eased in its correctness
> out of the containing inexactness. (Kinsella 2013: 90)

Moreover, while Kinsella does not seem to believe in a caring God that will welcome humanity into His bosom after death, he concedes, however, the existence of a creating god and of a god immanent in the universe. Answering Fitzsimon who had asked him whether he believed in God, Kinsella cryptically replied: "From the imagined vantage point distant overhead, it would be very difficult. And yet, there is a drive making things happen down there. And when you push back into the past, into the first microsecond of time, physics and poetry intersect in a kind of religion." (Kinsella 2004: 76) By going back to that instant, and to the many minor 'big bangs' of prehistorical and historical times, and by often recognizing a presence in the universe, the cycles of belief and unbelief are set into motion.

The persona of Marcus Aurelius, epitomises fittingly Kinsella's beliefs and scepticism:

> accepting established notions of a cosmos
> created and governed by a divine intelligence
> – while not believing in an afterlife;
>
> proposing exacting moral goals, with man
> an element in that divine intelligence
> – while pausing frequently to contemplate

the transient brutishness of earthly life,
our best experience of which concludes
with death, unaccountable and blank. (Kinsella 2013: 23-24)

CONCLUSION

Taking stock of one's life seems to be the first and most obvious imperative for the ageing. It is an endeavour requiring lucidity and courage. "Senility needs the energy and intuitions of youth," says Bobbio. (Bobbio [1996] 2001: 19) Kinsella's *Late Poems* display this sort of courage and energy for his constant attempts to understand and to share his understanding, his going through memory to the past even to the point of repetition in order to find new meanings in what has been done before. Yet he also often sounds ironical about the attitude he shares with people his own age. In *Fat Master*, written in his eighties, he is talking about "a dysrhythmia in some among you / the watchful and the partly fulfilled / A worrying for evidence of purpose / [...] Trusting there will be / an easing of the disorder at a time to come" (Kinsella 2011: 13). In spite of such apparent distrust that the disorder may be eased and some purpose found, Kinsella displays in these poems a level of understanding and peace in contrast to his earlier production, as illustrated by the poem "Reflection" from *Fat Master* dedicated probably to Bach but staging a generic elderly artist "retiring homeward" but still questioning his beliefs and his achievements and grateful for the "minimal understanding" he has reached:

I pray You to remember me, as I retire
Homeward across a darkening Earth,

And still curious at my contaminated conception,
Not convinced that my existence
Might ever have been of relevance
[...]
but thankful, on the whole, for this ache
for even a minimal understanding. (Kinsella 2013: 74)

This "minimal understanding" in Kinsella's view is the only thing one can achieve by the backward look, the cyclicality in one's thoughts and works, the attempt to give fresh answers to old questions, in other words by the process of ageing.

BIBLIOGRAPHY

Badin, Donatella Abbate (1996): *Thomas Kinsella*, New York: Twayne.

Badin Donatella / Cataldi Melita eds. (2006). *Omaggio a Thomas Kinsella*, introduction by Liborio Termine, Torino: Trauben.

Bobbio, Norberto (1996): *De senectute e altri scritti autobiografici*, Torino: Einaudi.

Bobbio, Norberto (2001 [1996]): *Old Age and other Essays*, Translated by Alan Cameron, Cambridge: Polity.

Byrne, Andrea (2009): "Kinsella's Wife Reveals Her Hurt." In: *The Independent*, March 22, accessed March 16, 2018 (http://www.independent.ie/irish-news/kinsellas-wife-reveals-her-hurt-at-the-poets-words-of-love-26522803.html). Web.

Clifton, Harry (2007): "Finding a late excellence." Review of Thomas Kinsella's *Selected Poems*. In: *The IrishTimes*, August 11, accessed March 10, 2018 (http://www.ricorso.net/rx/az-data/authors/k/Kinsella_-T/comm.htm). Web.

Deane, John F. (2007): "'The Rough course': Celebrating Thomas Kinsella." In: *Poetry Ireland News*, July-August, Accessed March 10, 2018 (http://www.poetryireland.ie/writers/articles/the-rough-course-celebrating-thomas-kinsella). Web.

Eliot, T. S. (1963): *Four Quartets*, London: Faber and Faber.

Harmon, Maurice (2012): "The Rhythms of the Real. Review of *Fat Master* and *Love Joy Peace* by Thomas Kinsella." In: *The Poetry Ireland Review* 106, pp. 14-18, accessed March 10, 2018, retrieved from (http://www.jstor.org/stable/41583509).

Kinsella, Thomas (1987): "A Conversation with John Deane." In: *Tracks*, 7, pp. 86-91.

_____ (2001): *Collected Poems 1956-2001*, Manchester: Carcanet.

_____ (2004): "Interview with Andrew Fitzsimons." In: *Journal of Irish Studies*, IASIL, Japan 19, pp. 71-82.

_____ (2009): *Prose Occasions,* edited by Andrew Fitzsimons, Manchester: Carcanet.

_____ (2013): *Late Poems,* Manchester: Carcanet.

Leavy, Adrienne (2014): "Review of Thomas Kinsella's *Late Poems.*" In: *The Poetry Porch,* accessed February 28, 2018 (https://www.poetryporch.com/leavyonkinsella14.html). Web.

_____ (2016): Thomas Kinsella: "eliciting order from significant experience." In: *The IrishTimes* 13 January, accessed February 28, 2018 (https://www.irishtimes.com/culture/books/thomas-kinsella-eliciting-order-from-significant-experience-1.2495241). Web.

Lynch, David (2015): *Confronting Shadows: An Introduction to the Poetry of Thomas Kinsella.* In: *Stillorgan*: New Island Books. Kindle edition.

Tubridy, Derval (2008): "'Keep us alert / for the while remaining': Kinsella at eighty." In: *The Irish Studies Review* 16/3, pp. 231-234.

Woolf, Virginia (1977-1984): *The Diary.* Vol. 5. Edited by A. O. Bell and A. McNeillie, London: Hogarth.

A Voice Fit for Winter

Seamus Heaney's Poetry on Ageing in *Human Chain*

IRENE DE ANGELIS, UNIVERSITY OF TURIN

In August 2006 Seamus Heaney and his wife, Marie, had gone to Donegal to celebrate the 75th birthday of Brian Friel's wife. Many old friends were there beside the Friels – the singer, film-maker and broadcaster David Hammond, the Northern Irish politician John Hume, the writers Tom Kilroy and Desmond Kavanagh, who had known Seamus since the days of high school in Derry. When Heaney woke up the following day, he tried to get out of bed and suddenly felt strange. "I didn't know what was wrong with me," he told Robert McCrum in an interview, "I made to move, but I couldn't move, and I felt very odd. My speech wasn't affected. When Marie came over to help me, she saw my leg was twisted, and she began to cry out" (2009). At that point Heaney realised there was something seriously wrong, and asked his wife to go and call the Kavanaghs, who alerted the medical services. Soon an ambulance was on its way, and Kavanagh and the poet Peter Fallon helped to carry Heaney downstairs. Even on that occasion, Seamus did not lose his typical sense of humour: since most of the friends who were there had in some way been involved in the Field Day Theatre Company, and many had recently experienced some illness, he made a joke about the 'curse of Field Day'. Although Heaney told McCrum that he remembered Marie sitting in the back of the ambulance with him, and he felt that the bumpy ride through the countryside to reach the hospital had renewed their love, the stroke suddenly made him aware of his frailty. The collection *Human Chain*, published in 2010, is Heaney's last creative response to illness and old age.

This essay will take into consideration a selection of these poems, showing how they are spoken in the voice of someone 'fit for winter'.[1]

An Unexpected, Almost Dangerous Wind

Human Chain opens with "Had I Not Been Awake", a meditation on the serious illness that caught Heaney off-guard, leaving him both shaken and at the same time deeply aware of having been miraculously offered a second chance in life. It seems particularly apt that the following analysis should start with this evocative poem, because, as will be shown, the sudden gust of wind "that rose and whirled until the roof / Pattered with quick leaves off the sycamore" (Heaney 2010: 3) closes the collection in a circular pattern, with the image of a kite that finally takes flight, breaking free of its string ("A Kite for Aibhín"). As the first poem of *Human Chain* begins, lying in bed, the speaker hears the howling wind: "It came and went so unexpectedly / And almost it seemed dangerously" (2010: 3). Something has changed forever, and the poetic "I" is both physically and spiritually reawakened: "the whole of me a-patter, / Alive and ticking like an electric fence" (ibid). The image of newly rediscovered vitality corresponds to the creative impetus that has not abandoned the poet, despite his weakness and fear. Although with the advancing of old age Heaney is resigned to the ephemerality of life, which he elsewhere defines *as mono no aware*[2] or *lacrimae rerum*,[3] he is determined to treasure the moments of delight that the future, however short, still has in store for him. As John Banville has commented, "Had I Not Been Awake" "does stand at the head of the collection like the compact but elaborate first letter of a medieval codex"

---

1 I owe this definition to Luke Smith's 2011 online review "A Portrait of the Artist as An Old Man".

2 *Mono no aware* refers to a central ideal of Japanese aesthetics, literally the "tears of things" or *lacrimae rerum*. It is usually associated with a feeling of melancholy which is caused by the contemplation of the impermanence or the ephemeral beauty manifested in nature, human life or a work of art. For further reference cp. Heaney 2007: 15.

3 *Lacrimae rerum*, literally "the tears of things", is an expression derived from *Aeneid* I, l. 462: "*sunt lacrimae rerum et mentem mortalia tangunt*".

and "crackles with the force of a presentiment that seems as dangerous as it is exciting" (2010). It sets the atmosphere for a "book of grief and pain" (Lewison 2010), "of shadows and shades" (Tóibín 2013), "of ghosts and goodbyes" (Lordan 2011).

FAMILY MEMORIES AND MISSED EMBRACES

Heaney's brush with death, which, as already said, is symbolised by the unexpected, dangerous wind of the first poem, leads the poet's imagination to linger on the figures of his loved ones, in a collection which, as will be shown, is also and above all a celebration of human bonds and solidarity. This section of my analysis will focus on three poems in particular, all of which concentrate on the intergenerational parent-child relationship: "Album", "Uncoupled" and "The Butts". "Album" is a sequence of five pictures from the past, which are filled with remembrance and regret. The first part takes the reader back in time, to a period the poetic voice is struggling to recall. The reference to "the timed collapse / Of a sawn down tree" (2010: 4), in the first stanza, clarifies from the outset that the poem is about severed relationships and demise, while at the same time reminding the reader of the chestnut tree in "Clearances",[4] associated by the poet with a dead aunt, who left behind a void later turned into a creative space, "utterly empty, utterly a source" (Heaney 1987: 26). In "Album" the first person pronoun "I" is coupled in the poet's fervid imagination with "them", a reference to his parents, and his memories are set into motion: "I imagine them // In summer season, as it must have been, / And the place, it dawns on me, / Could have been Grove Hill" (ibid). Heaney's friend and translator Marco Sonzogni[5] comments that the depth and nature of the parents' relationship is revealed by their "steady gazing / Not at each other but in the same direction" (ibid.), a quotation from Antoine de Saint-Exupéry's *Terre des hommes*.

However, it is "Too late, alas, now" to retrieve the moments when he would "stand with them on airy Sundays / *Shin-deep* in hilltop *bluebells*" (ibid, emphasis added). This reference may call to mind a similar image in

---

4   First published in *The Haw Lantern* (1987).
5   Cp. Heaney 2014: 1120.

a poem by Sligo-born Joan McBreen, titled "The Broken Swing", which also deals with memory, the advancing of old age and death: "Come with me / through the rusting gates / [...] into this high-walled garden / and move ankle deep in *bluebells*" (2003: 55, emphasis added). McBreen's poetic voice is reminded of her dead mother, as she seems to hear the sound of a piano coming from the now abandoned family home, surrounded by the "garden with the broken swing" where she used to play as a child. The last two stanzas of her poem offer a hopeful image of continuity between generations, with a new, closing reference to the flowers which are also dear to Heaney:

> [...] bring
> your children here.
>
> Take them in from the town
> to pick bluebells in the garden.
> Stay near the house with the shuttered windows
> from where you first saw the stars. (McBreen 2003: 55)

Heaney's "Album" of family memories includes a second picture of his parents, this time as they leave him on his first day as a boarder at St Columb's College, in Londonderry, in the 1950s:

> Seeing them as a couple, I now see,
>
> For the first time, all the more together
> For having had to turn and walk away, as close
> In the leaving (or closer) as in the getting. (2010: 5)

An old Heaney appreciates, in retrospective, the inner strength of his parents, who despite the wrench of imminent separation and their consequent emotional upheaval, managed to dutifully conceal their feelings, thus confirming their solidarity as a couple. Dipping into the past, age has added a new perspective to the emotions that, as a child, he did not possess.

The third section of "Album" is characterized by a further flashback in time, as the poetic voice describes the parents' "wedding meal" (2010: 6).

Heaney is "uninvited" but "ineluctable" (ibid), non-existent but an inescapable future reality, an integral part of their destiny. The poem may be read as a commentary on the detachment and stern aloofness of Heaney's parents, particularly on his father's part, as that side of the family was graver and far less convivial than his mother's (McCrum 2009). An allusion to this can be found in the reference to "all the anniversaries of this / They are not ever going to observe // Or mention even in the years to come" (2010: 6). As Fawbert acutely observes, "[t]his reluctance to show and respond to emotions of love will resurface in [Heaney's] father-son poems" (2010).

The father figure and the difficulty of communicating with him emotionally resurface in the penultimate section of "Album", an autobiographical meditation on lost chances. Heaney evokes the painfully vivid memories of three attempted embraces with his now dead father, which call to his mind the sixth book of Virgil's *Aeneid*,[6] in which Aeneas, after his descent into the Elysium, longs for one last meeting with Anchises. The first attempt Heaney remembers was "on the riverbank / That summer before college, [his father] in his prime" (2010: 7). The son's desire to hold his father was unfulfilled, and with hindsight Heaney evokes the inhibition he felt, as an eleven-year-old, in that attempted contact. The second opportunity happened years later, "When [his father] was very drunk and needed help / To do up trouser buttons" (ibid). Heaney's embrace came as an answer to his parent's helplessness and undignified state. The third, final hug was during his father's "last week", when he was reduced to his most basic needs and unable to hold himself up: "Helping him to the bathroom, my right arm / Taking the webby weight of his underarm." (ibid) This image of the elderly father, now physically impotent and completely

---

6   Heaney had shown a deep interest in the *Aeneid* since the publication of *Seeing Things* (1991), which includes "The Golden Bough". Other references to Virgil can be found in *Electric Light* (with 'Glanmore Eclogue'), and in *Human Chain* itself, particularly in "The Riverbank Field" and "Route 110". Before his death, in the summer of 2013, Heaney completed an integral translation of *Aeneid* Book VI, which was published posthumously by Faber in 2016. For further references cp. *Virgilio nella Bann Valley*, edited by Giorgio Bernardi Perini and Chiara Prezzavento, with a contribution by Massimo Bacigalupo (2013).

dependent on the family for support, closely anticipates "The Butts", which will be dealt with further on in this essay.

"Album" closes with a reflection on generational differences:

> It took a grandson to do it properly,
> To rush him in the armchair
> With a snatch raid on his neck,
>
> Proving him thus vulnerable to delight. (2010: 8)

In his spontaneous gesture of love, the grandson ignores the emotional inhibition of his grandfather. The use of the adjective "vulnerable" emphasizes the grandfather's lack of strength, his fragility and unsteadiness. Heaney seems to imply that the new generations are allowed to break the rules of formal behaviour and it is easier to forgive them, because they can melt the ice of even the most hardened souls. The poet himself was fortunate enough to experience the blessing of becoming a grandparent,[7] and among many poems *in memoriam*, he also celebrates new lives and new beginnings in the three poems he dedicated to each of his beloved granddaughters, Anna Rose, Aibhín and Síofra.[8]

As has been shown, the series of snapshots from Heaney's family album takes the now aged poet and his readers on a walk down memory lane. A similarly nostalgic mood also dominates "Uncoupled", "a diptych in memory of his parents", with "all the placid beauty of a Dutch painting or a Schubert song", as Colm Tóibín noted in a 2010 review. "The first part describes his mother carrying a tray of ashes from the house to the ash-pit", offering "a picture of immense, distant dignity" (Tóibín 2010), while the second part is a picture of his father "not much higher than the cattle /

---

7   For a poem about Heaney's own grandfather, cp. "In the Attic" (2010: 82).

8   To Síofra Heaney dedicated the poem "In Time", which he wrote twelve days before his death in 2013. The poem celebrates the encounter between an old man and a newborn child, and it is essentially a contemplation of time, suspended between the memory of the past, the fleeting present and a hope for the future to come.

Working his way towards me through the pen, / His *ashplant*[9] in one hand" (Heaney 2010: 11, emphasis added). The father is captured in a moment of everyday life, but he is "Waving and calling something I cannot hear", because of "all the lowing and roaring, lorries revving / At the far end of the yard, the dealers // Shouting among themselves" (ibid). Once again, the poet's memory lingers on the useless attempt at communication between father and son, but the parent's figure turns into a shade dissolving in the past. As becomes apparent in the last two lines, "time has passed and death has intervened" (Tóibín 2010): "So that his eyes leave mine and I know / The pain of loss before I know the term." (Heaney 2010: 11)

The "pain of loss" is equally crucial in "The Butts", another poem about the winter of life, the sense of longing and the unbearable loneliness after the demise of his parent. In this case, the pain "is caused by the unshakable certitude that his father is no more" (Kędzierska 2016: 34). As the poem opens, an adolescent "I" delves "past flap and lining / For the forbidden handfuls" (Heaney 2010: 12), the cigarette butts his father kept in the pockets of his suit. Even "this last hopeful moment of intimacy brings only a kind of empty-handedness" (Kędzierska 2016: 34), a sad foreboding of what remains of his father's life. In the second part of the poem, a mature son assists his father, at his most helpless, with the other members of the family, learning how:

[...] to reach well in beneath
Each meagre armpit
To lift and sponge him,
On either side,
Feeling his lightness,

Having to dab and work
Closer than anybody liked

---

[9] The symbol of the father's ashplant also recurs in "The Strand", one of Heaney's haiku-like poems, which was published in *The Spirit Level*: "The dotted line my father's ashplant made / On Sandymount Strand / Is something else the tide won't wash away." (1996: 62) Also cp. "1.1.87" from *Seeing Things*: "Dangerous pavements. / But I face the ice this year / With my father's stick." (1991: 20)

> But having, for all that,
> To keep working. (Heaney 2010: 13)

As Kędzierska perceptively observes, "The Butts" "registers an unwavering, familial respect for the elderly, as well as the preciousness of human life in general", celebrating "the frail and ailing people as gifts to be cherished" (2016: 34). The poet realises how the presence of his father has enriched him, even *in hora mortis*, when the test of love was most arduous. At the same time, the inevitability of death leads him to ponder on his own mortality: to quote Nicole O'Driscoll, Heaney "leaves it to us to make the connection that he is now the most vulnerable link in the chain" (2012).

ILLNESS, THE RENEWAL OF LOVE AND SOLIDARITY

In *Human Chain* three poems deal with various degrees of explicitness with Heaney's stroke in 2006, an experience he faced with utter courage and strong determination: these are "Chanson d'Aventure", "Miracle" and the title poem. "Chanson d'Aventure" takes its title from an Old French type of lyric, "a framing device, where the singer (or poet) wanders into a wild, rural setting and has a chance encounter usually of an erotic or amorous nature" (Fawbert 2010). As emerges from the 2009 interview with McCrum, Heaney kept the latter aspect of the original genre: "The trip in the ambulance I always remember, because Marie was in the back with me ... To me, that was one of the actual beauties of the stroke, that renewal of love in the ambulance." The jolting ambulance ride, the hospitalization and the gradual recovery are an occasion for reflection on the relationship between the body and the soul, as made clear by the epigraph from John Donne's "The Extasie".[10] As Fawbert comments, "the soul seeks outward expression through the body, inhibited at this point by stroke-induced paralysis" (2010). The patient recalls being "Strapped on, wheeled out, forklifted / Locked in position for the drive" (Heaney 2010: 14), a process described by the language of trade inscribed in a series of past participles. The memory of his wife Marie's loving presence mitigates the feelings of

---

10 "Love's mysteries in souls do grow, / but yet the body is his book." (Donne 2014: 181)

extreme vulnerability and impotency that are nestled in the image of "me flat on my back" (ibid).

The first poem in the sequence directs the reader's attention to the tense electricity of the silence between husband and wife ("Everything and nothing spoken", ibid): there is no need for outward communication. The critical circumstances heighten the couple's spiritual union and their mutual understanding, which find expression in their interlocked gazes ("Our eyebeams threaded laser-fast", ibid.). From the eyes, the second part of the sequence shifts the attention to the hands. "Recalling how strong he once was, he realizes that his hand is no longer 'capable' and 'warm', and that he could not even feel Mary lift and hold it" (Kędzierska 2016: 35). In its numbness, "it lay flop-heavy as a bellpull" (Heaney 2010: 15). However, the unforeseen illness helps the poet rediscover the bond of love, and the deep feelings shared by the couple as they travel at full tilt along the roads of Donegal are only disrupted by the medical paraphernalia on the ambulance: "our gaze ecstatic and bisected / By a hooked-up drip-feed to the cannula." (ibid)

The third and final poem in the sequence describes a further stage in Heaney's recovery, expressing his determination to recuperate physical strength. The poet compares his own condition to that of the charioteer at Delphi, a well-known icon of ancient Greece, which depicts, "in its incompleteness, a man striving onwards despite incapacities that would appear to render progress impossible" (Fawbert 2010) – "[h]is left hand lopped / From a wrist protruding like an open spout" (Heaney 2010: 16). The sculptor has created a figure that emanates unwavering determination: "his gaze ahead / ...His eyes-front, straight-backed posture" (ibid.). Heaney shows a similar "almost heroic struggle with his impotence and weakness" (Kędzierska 2016: 36), as he learns how to walk again, "[d]oing physio in the corridor, *holding up*" (Heaney 2010: 16, emphasis added), this last verb alluding to both his regained capacity to stand erect and his single-mindedness. The poem closes with the image of the physiotherapist, who, like Heaney's father teaching him the art of ploughing, now teaches an elderly man how to move again.

If "Chanson d'Aventure" makes an explicit reference to Heaney's struggle for physical recuperation, the poem "Miracle" expresses with highest dramatic intensity the poet's tribute to the 'guardian angels' who came to his aid on the day of the stroke, the invaluable friends and dedicatees of the collection, Desmond and Mary Kavanagh and Peter and Jean Fallon, whose support "helped bring about the miracle of recovery" (Fawbert 2010). The poet alludes "to the disorientating experience of being carried, helpless, to an ambulance, and of feeling the support of those bodies doing the lifting" (Fawbert 2010). This emotionally charged, painful memory is associated with the gospel story of the paralytic who is carried to be healed by Jesus, an episode narrated in three of the four Evangelists: Matthew (9:2-8), Mark (2:1-22) and Luke (5:17-26). Heaney does not commemorate "the beneficiary of a biblical miracle", "but rather, his own 'stretcher-bearers' whose solidarity took up the challenge however daunting of moving him" (Fawbert 2010):

> Not the one who takes up his bed and walks
> But the ones who have known him all along
> And carry him in –
>
> Their shoulders numb, the ache and stoop deeplocked
> In their backs, the stretcher handles
> Slippery with sweat. (Heaney 2010: 17)

Although the poem is written in the third person, it is clear that it was inspired by personal experience. The repetition of the sibilants, in the last two lines of the second stanza ("stretcher handles / Slippery with sweat", ibid.), emphasizes the lack of grip, which makes the task of delivering a sick man for healing even more difficult. Heaney invites his readers to "be mindful" "of those who had known him all long" (ibid), who tried to help in the best way possible, with their resilience and strength (the body is "strapped on tight, made tiltable / And raised ... then lowered", ibid), sparing no effort ("no let-up", ibid.). Without their assistance, "his illness might have met with a less felicitous outcome"[11] (Fawbert 2010).

The imagery of "Miracle", with its crucial theme of the shared burden, is recalled and amplified in the title poem of the collection, where Heaney compares the sadly familiar televised image of aid workers passing sacks of food "hand to hand / In close up" (2010: 18), in emergency assistance to the victims of social and political disaster, to his own experience of lugging

---

11 Cp. O'Driscoll 2008: 461-462.

bags of grain on a trailer, during the harvests of his rural youth. The experience of loading these heavy bags is described in terms that recall a confrontation between two assailants ("eye-to-eye", ibid), the quick, rhythmical movements evoked by the expression "one-two, one-two upswing" (ibid), while the repetitiveness of the action is suggested by "the stoop and drag and drain / Of the next lift" (ibid). In the last two lines, Heaney lingers on the sense of relief that is felt after a weight is released: "Nothing surpassed / That quick unburdening, backbreak's truest payback." (ibid)

If the expression "A letting go" literally refers to the release of grip, it may also be read as a metaphor for the final liberation of the body through death, which will come again "once / And for all" (ibid). Andrew J. Auge argues that the "unburdening" of the body in death can be interpreted as "both welcome release from and meagre recompense for the pain endured in life" (Auge in O'Brien 2016: 35). However, the poem "Human Chain" and the collection as a whole seem to express Heaney's great gratitude for the precious gifts life has reserved for him, above all the consolation of human solidarity, which, thanks to his own extraordinary generosity and warm-heartedness, he treasures most in the winter of life. However, as Kędzierska has argued, "The proximity of death, as well as the poet's response to it, weaves its elegiac patterns throughout the collection, preventing oversimplifications and naïve sentimentality" (2016: 33).

GHOSTS AND GOODBYES

In *Human Chain*, old age and approaching death inspired Heaney to write a series of poems *in memoriam*, many of them celebrating the lifelong friendship of artists and intellectuals. "Loughanure" is dedicated to Colin Middleton, an Irish artist and friend of the Heaneys, who is immortalized "with tenderness and regret" (Lordan 2011) with his inseparable cigarette, "nodding" and "grunting" (Heaney 2010: 61) as he would stand in front of a picture he had sold them, gazing at it. Similarly, in "Death of a Painter" Heaney bids a last farewell to Nancy Wynne-Jones, "working to the end" (2010: 60). Perhaps the most touching of these portrayals is in "The Baler", which recalls the figure of the aged painter Derek Hill. The speaker's perception of the beauty of sunset, the "dusk Eldorado" he is enjoying, is contrasted with the artist's refusal to watch this spectacle:

> But what I also remembered
> [...]
> Was Derek Hill's saying,
> The last time he sat at our table,
> He could bear no longer to watch
>
> The sun going down
> And asking please to be put
> With his back to the window. (Heaney 2010: 24)

Heaney describes "the feelings and responses of a man" who "was already wheel-chair-bound" and "knew that he was dying" (Fawbert 2010). Smith emphasizes how the definite article in the expression "[t]he last time" evokes a "terrible finality" (2011). In this image, the artist turns away from the world, "abandoning a vital part of himself ... defeated" (Smith 2011). Yet the poem may be interpreted as an affirmation, through suffering, of "art's power to look at death unblinkingly – to keep a chair facing the window" (Smith 2011).

Sonzogni has rightly noticed (2014: 1126) that the figure of Derek Hill in "The Baler" is in stark contrast with the old woman of "Field of Vision", from *Seeing Things*:

> I remember this woman who sat for years
> In a wheelchair, looking straight ahead
> Out of the window [...]
>
> She was steadfast as the big window itself.
> [...]
> She never lamented once and she never
> Carried a spare ounce of emotional weight.
>
> Face to face with her was an education
> Of the sort you got across a well-braced gate. (Heaney 1991: 22)

The poem celebrates the old woman as a positive, living example of patient acceptance of the ageing process. "Looking straight ahead", she invites the poet and the readers alike to embrace wider horizons, beyond the thresholds of that window and the gate, which so recurrently feature in Heaney's poetry.

Another moving dedicatory piece from *Human Chain*, which stands out in a collection "of ghosts and goodbyes" (Lordan 2011), is "The Door Was Open and the House Was Dark", written in memory of Heaney's close friend, the Irish musician David Hammond:[12]

> The door was open and the house was dark
> Wherefore I called his name, although I knew
> The answer this time would be silence
>
> That kept me standing listening while it grew
> Backwards and down and out into the street
> [...]
> I felt, for the first time there and then, a stranger,
> Intruder almost, wanting to take flight
>
> Yet well aware that there was no danger,
> Only withdrawal, a not unwelcoming
> Emptiness, as in a midnight hangar
>
> On an overgrown airfield in late summer. (Heaney 2010: 82)

Hammond was a refined connoisseur and practitioner of traditional Irish music. In the *Guardian* obituary Heaney devoted to him on 28th August 2008, he affectionately defined him as "a natural force masquerading as a human being", remembering how, "For all his love of Belfast, David was

---

12 One is reminded, by contrast, of an earlier poem Heaney wrote for Hammond, "The Singer's House", published in *Field Work*: "his song / A rowboat far out in the evening. // When I first came here you were always singing" (1979: 27). There, too, he celebrated Hammond's inspiring friendship and his essential encouragement in the 1970s, when they both collaborated with the Field Day Theatre Company.

equally at home in his 'singer's house' by the sea in west Donegal", where "he exulted in being head of a loving household and acted as host to a veritable court of music and poetry" (Heaney 2008). The situation and the atmosphere evoked by Heaney in "The Door Was Open" are the opposite: David's house is dark, silent, empty, and his friend's familiarity with the place makes it even harder to accept his absence, especially when Heaney calls the friend's name but receives no answer. Feeling like "a stranger, / Intruder almost, wanting to take flight" (Heaney 2010: 82), he is reminded of a visit by night to a place not far from his parents' home, the airfield at Creagh. He had always found it mysterious and oddly fascinating (cp. Dennis O'Driscoll 2008: 358), even when it was not in use any longer, like Hammond's house, now deprived of its lively owner's presence, which used to be associated with his singing and his warm hospitality. As Kate Kellaway insightfully observes, in "The Door Was Open" "Heaney explores the silence after a death. It is a wonderful idea that silence should develop a life of its own, journeying through the second stanza and retiring into the street. The strangeness rings emotionally true, a reaction to a new relationship with silence. And the last line is an extraordinary release: 'On an overgrown airfield in late summer'" (2010).

Conclusion: Kites Taking Flight

Human Chain closes with "A Kite for Aibhín", a poem which celebrates the birth of Heaney's second granddaughter, born to his eldest son Michael and his wife. The title significantly recalls an earlier composition included in *Station Island* (1984), "A Kite for Michael and Christopher", in which he, the father, teaches his two sons how to launch a kite and keep it flying up in the air:

> Before the kite plunges down into the wood
> And this line goes useless
> Take it in your two hands, boys, and feel
> The strumming, rooted, long-tailed pull of grief.

You were born fit for it.
Stand in here in front of me
And take the strain. (Heaney 1984: 44)

In *Stepping Stones*, where Heaney spoke about "the mysterious gulf between childhood and old age ... that I can only now put into words" (2008: 27), he told Dennis O'Driscoll that the poem was triggered by the childhood memory

of an afternoon when my father came out to a field at the back of the house and launched a kite. What was surprising and what I still remember most vividly was the powerful drag in the kite string ... The more string you could pay out ... the higher and more spectacular your flight; although often ... because of that mighty strain, the string would break and you would lose the kite. (2008: 254⁻255)

From the kite of his own childhood, made by his father "of lath and pasted newspaper" (ibid), the poet moves to the one "made of nylon" that he bought for his two adolescent sons, whom he encourages to follow in his path. Gabriella Morisco talks about "[a] metaphorical lesson for life based on a constant attention and the capacity never to give in; to have the strength to endure even the pain caused by the taut, thin, cutting string in one's hands" (2013: 36). In *Human Chain* it is an elderly Heaney, now a grandfather, who makes the kite fly for his beloved granddaughter: in this case, the symbol so dear to the poet's imagination blends with an image he derived from Giovanni Pascoli's "L'aquilone". Pascoli was inspired to write this poem during a period he spent in the Italian city of Urbino, where, still today, in the month of September, the local people hold a traditional kite challenge. In her essay Morisco recounts how Heaney first heard about Pascoli's "L'aquilone" during a visit he made to Urbino in 2007, when he was awarded a honorary degree. On that occasion, Morisco had given him a postcard of a painting that showed a boy flying his kite outside the city gates, "a postcard he kept long afterwards, because he told [her]" "I had not finished with the image of that boy and his plaything" (ibid). In "A Kite for Aibhín", Heaney replaces the countryside surrounding Urbino with the hills of Anahorish. While the opening lines are written after Pascoli, in the part which follows, Heaney's voice takes over and echoes Yeats and his own poem written twenty-five years earlier. "But this time", Morisco emphasizes, "[i]t is he himself, the poet, who, with his feet well-planted on the ground, gazes up with a sense of waiting, until ... the line breaks and the kite flies away, light and elated, a separate and free being" (2013: 38):

> Rises, and my hand is like a spindle
> Unspooling, the kite a thin-stemmed flower
> Climbing and carrying, carrying farther, higher,
>
> The longing in the breast and planted feet
> And gazing face and heart of the kite flier
> Until string breaks and – separate, elate –
>
> The kite takes off, itself alone, a windfall. (Heaney 2010: 85)

As Troy Jollymore acutely comments in *The Washington Post*, the "transformative wind" that opened *Human Chain* returns in the final poem, a symbol of the poet's wish "that death might represent a liberation, a passage to a higher state of being", a feeling which "is ubiquitous in this collection, and ... infuses these meditative poems with a spiritual buoyancy, a subtle and reassuring joy" (2010).

BIBLIOGRAPHY

Auge, Andrew J. (2016): "Surviving Death in Heaney's *Human Chain*." In: *"The Soul Exceeds Its Circumstances". The Later Poetry of Seamus Heaney*, edited by Eugene O'Brien, Notre Dame: Notre Dame University Press.

Banville, John (2010): "Living ghosts. *Human Chain* by Seamus Heaney." In: *The New York Review of Books*, accessed March 14, 2018 (http://www.nybooks.com/articles/archives/2010/nov/11/living-ghosts/). Web.

Bernardi-Perini, Giorgio/Prezzavento, Chiara, eds. (2013): *Virgilio nella Bann Valley*, Mantova: Tre Lune.

Donne, John (2014): *The Poetry of John Donne*, edited by Robin Robbins, New York: Routledge.

Fawbert, David (2010): "Connecting with Seamus Heaney." Accessed March 17, 2018 (http://fawbie.com/category/human-chain/). Web.

Grennan, Eamon (2010): "Seamus Heaney's book of resurrections." In: *The IrishTimes*, accessed March 14, 2018 (https://www.irishtimes.com/culture/books/seamus-heaney-s-book-of-resurrections-1.644008). Web.

Heaney, Seamus (1979): *Field Work*, London: Faber and Faber.

_____ (1984): *Station Island*, London: Faber and Faber.

_____ (1987): *The Haw Lantern*, London: Faber and Faber.

_____ (1991): *Seeing Things*, London: Faber and Faber.

_____ (1996): *The Spirit Level*, London: Faber and Faber.

_____ (2007): "Afterword." In: Irene De Angelis/Joseph Woods (eds.), *Our Shared Japan. An anthology of contemporary Irish poetry*, Dublin: The Dedalus Press.

_____ (2008): "David Hammond Obituary", *The Guardian*, accessed March 14, 2018 (https://www.theguardian.com/world/2008/aug/28/ireland.folk). Web.

_____ (2010): *Human Chain*, London: Faber and Faber.

_____ (2014): *Poesie scelte*, edited by Marco Sonzogni, Milano: Mondadori.

Jollimore, Troy (2010): "*Human Chain*: A new collection of poetry by Seamus Heaney." In: *The Washington Post*, accessed March 14, 2018 (http://www.washingtonpost.com/wpdyn/content/article/2010/09/20/AR 2010092005533.html). Web.

Kędzierska, Aleksandra (2016): "In the Autumn of Life: Seamus Heaney's *Human Chain*." In: *British and American Studies*, pp. 31-40.

Kellaway, Kate (2010): "*Human Chain* by Seamus Heaney." In: *The Guardian*, accessed March 14, 2018 (https://www.theguardian.com/books-/2010/aug/22/seamus-heaney-human-chain-faber). Web.

Lewison, Janet (2010): "Seamus Heaney: 'Had I not been awake' in *Human Chain.*" In: *Sheer Poetry*, accessed March 14, 2018 (http://www.sheerpoetry.co.uk/forums/general/seamus-heaneyhad-i-not-been-awake-in-human-chain). Web.

Lordan, Dave (2011): "*Human Chain* by Seamus Heaney." In: *The Stinging Fly*, accessed March 14, 2018 (http://stingingfly.org/sample/dave-lordan-reviews-human-chain-seamus-heaney). Web.

McBreen, Joan (2003): *Winter in the Eye*, Cliffs of Moher, Co. Clare: Salmon.

McCrum, Robert (2009): "Seamus Heaney: a life of rhyme." In: *The Guardian*, accessed March 17, 2018 (http://www.theguardian.com/books/2009/jul/19/seamus-heaney-inter-view). Web.

Montague, John (2015): "The Big Splatter. *Human Chain* by Seamus Heaney." In: *Dublin Review of Books*, accessed March 17, 2018 (http://www.drb.ie/contributorsarticles/the-big-splatter). Web.

Morisco, Gabriella (2013): "Two Poets and a Kite: Seamus Heaney and Giovanni Pascoli." In: *Linguae et. Rivista di lingue e culture moderne* 1, pp. 35-45.

O'Brien, Eugene, ed. (2016): *"The Soul Exceeds Its Circumstances." The Later Poetry of Seamus Heaney*, Notre Dame: Notre Dame University Press.

O'Driscoll, Dennis (2008): *Stepping Stones. Interviews with Seamus Heaney*, New York: Farrar, Straus and Giroux.

O'Driscoll, Nicole (2012): "Review of Heaney's *Human Chain.*" In: *Emerging Writer*, accessed March 14, 2018 (http://emergingwriter.blogspot.com/2012/01/review-of-heaneys-human-chain.html). Web.

O'Riordan, Adam (2010): *"Human Chain* by Seamus Heaney: Review." In: *The Telegraph*, accessed March 14, 2018 (http://www.telegraph.co.uk/culture/books/7963969/Human-Chain-by-Seamus-Heaney-review.html). Web.

Smith, Luke (2010): "Seamus Heaney: *Human Chain.*" In: *Agenda Ni*, accessed March 14, 2018 (http://www.agendani.com/seamus-heaney-human-chain/). Web.

—— (2011): "A Portrait of the Artist as an Old Man." In: *The Oxonian Review*, accessed March 14, 2018 (http://www.oxonianreview.org/wp/a-portrait-of-the-artist-as-an-old-man/). Web.

Tóibín, Colm (2013): "Seamus Heaney's books were events in our lives." In: *The Guardian*, accessed March 14, 2018 (http://www.theguardian.com/books/2013/aug/30/seamus-heaney-bookspoetry-colm-toibin). Web.

"The Mark on the Floor"
Alice Munro on Ageing and Alzheimer's Disease in *The Bear Came Over the Mountain* and Sara Polley's *Away From Her*

CARMEN CONCILIO, UNIVERSITY OF TURIN

In Italy, as well as in most European countries, alarm over Alzheimer's does not seem to be as obsessive as it is in North America, perhaps with the exception of the UK, where echoes of the medical research and media campaign conducted in Anglophone cultural contexts are certainly wider: "Americans now fear Alzheimer's more than any other disease, even cancer, according to a survey from MetLife." (Goldman 2017: 4)

In spite of the fact that ageing studies are gaining attention and are gathering academic strength and rigorous scientific scrutiny, the main preoccupation in Italy/Europe seems to be about the increasing number of elderly people, also due to a decreasing birth rate, and the general sanitary, sociological and political consequences of such a demographic turn:

It seems reasonable to assume that the growing numbers of very old people will increase the numbers of physically dependent people, with a resultant increase in costs, especially arising from their need for care due to ill health. (Thane 2000: 483)

The Bear Came over the Mountain by the Canadian short story writer Alice Munro (*The New Yorker* 1999), taken as an emblematic literary representation of such a social change and its consequences in the Canadian context ("by 2021 the number of Canadians with dementia will rise to

592,000" – CSHA, 1994) (Johnson & Krahn 2010: 1), was translated into Italian in 2003. After the release of its film adaptation by the Canadian director Sarah Polley, *Away from Her* (2006), the short story, almost a novella, became popular and even more so after Munro received the Nobel Prize in 2013.

The ascending success of this literary/cinematic work shows how the new millennium is indeed the temporal frame for our becoming more and more conscious of ageing-related social consequences.

A close, textual scrutiny of this carefully constructed short story with reference to its film adaptation can help detect whether this masterful representation of old age, Alzheimer's disease and disability, still grants agency, free will and dignity to the ageing person and what kind of responsibility it places on the care-giver.

"THE MARK ON THE FLOOR"

The temporally layered short story *The Bear Came over the Mountain* (*New Yorker* 1999; 2001) by Alice Munro opens with a flash back, a short paragraph written in the past tense and by an extradiegetic, omniscient narrator, briefly describing Fiona in her youth, in her parents' house, in her University years, including Grant's courtship. Fiona is the first word in the story, the subject of the first paragraph. She is the protagonist, although Grant has a similarly relevant role, for this is a story about a married couple. She is the one who proposed to get married, at Port Stanley, Ontario, on Lake Erie's beach, and Grant eagerly accepted for "he wanted never to be away from her. She had the spark of life" (Munro 2001: 274). Thus, from the very beginning Fiona appears as a woman of will and agency, capable of freedom of choice and initiative. It is also interesting to notice that Southern Ontario and provincial life have always been at the centre of Munro's literary representations. Fiona and Grant live there, near Georgian Bay.

After a few lines, although the narrative insists on the past tense, the action moves to a moment closer to the present. Past and present, analepsis and prolepsis, are only the first of a long series of binaries and opposites on which the plot structurally stands. Time, moreover, is a much more flexible category in the text, due to ellipsis, time-shifts, and various other strategies.

Among other parallels, there are the things that Fiona forgets or cannot forget and the things that Grant forgets or pretends to forget. Moreover, sometimes the binaries create a cross over and Marlene Goldman rightly observes that chiasmatic reversals rather sustain the short story (2017: 294).

Just before they left their house, Fiona noticed a mark on the kitchen floor. It came from the cheap black house shoes she had been wearing earlier that day.

"I thought they'd quit doing that," she said in a tone of ordinary annoyance and perplexity, rubbing at the grey smear that looked as if it had been made by a greasy crayon.
She remarked that she'd never have to do this again, since she wasn't taking those shoes with her.
"I guess I'll be dressed up all the time," she said. "Or semi-dressed up. It'll be sort of like in a hotel." (Munro 2001: 274)

At this stage, the reader does not know yet where Fiona and Grant are going. Thus, what seems to be the present moment, reveals itself, in fact, as a flash forward. For this passage alludes to the very moment Fiona leaves their house and moves to a private clinic to spend there her last days, for she suffers from Alzheimer's and she is still in the stage when she can decide about her own future. Above all, she does not want to be a burden to Grant. In this respect, Fiona shows a strong agency and seems to incarnate the values which were the rule in ancient times. The point Cicero made in 44 BC is a timeless one:

"Ita enim senectus honesta est, si se ipsa defendit, si ius suum retinet, si nemini emancipate est, si usque ad ultimum spiritum dominatur in suos."
Old age will only be respected if it fights for itself, maintains its own rights, avoids dependence on anyone, and asserts control over its own to the last breath. (Johnson & Thane 1998: 38)

In the film, Fiona's strength and firmness of mind is stressed by her attempt to reassure Grant that he is not taking this decision alone. In fact, they are deciding together, or better, she has made up her mind, also thanks to the specialized medical literature she is reading: quite scary about the burden cast on the care-giver, it must be added (Mace 1982; Shenk 2001). Grant feebly protests that this solution might be considered only temporary, a sort of experiment, a rest cure.

Yet, the passage about the mark on the floor is interesting also for another reason. What is relevant is that Fiona engages herself in erasing the mark her slippers left on the floor. That mark is a clear sign of her presence in their house. Symbolically, then, it is a sign of her treading on the ground, on this Earth, in her house as well as in Grant's life. What she is doing is erasing not only the trace of herself (a metonym), but her whole self from the very house she has inhabited with Grant for a life. She is un-writing her own life-story, her physical presence, for the mark looks like a sign made by a crayon on a board, like the written sign on a page. Thus, while Alice Munro starts writing the first paragraphs of her story, Fiona is starting erasing it, for she is about to leave her story/house/life. In passing, it is worth mentioning that to Virginia Woolf "The mark on the wall" became the pre-text to figure out and conjure up a whole short fiction, by recollecting how she shaped that mark with her observer's phantasies and conjectures, till war is cursed, right before pronouncing a final trivial revelation: "Ah, the mark on the wall! It was a snail" (Woolf 1991: 89).

In Munro's story, the first iconic image we have of Alzheimer's – for the metaphor of the erasure of the mark on the floor has more layers – is an erasure of signs, marks, traces, as if the illness could bring us back to a tabula rasa, a blank board, first deleting our signs, then ourselves. Fiona's absence will be the absence of her signs.

Fiona will then be leaving the house. She might have ignored that mark or indulged with it, leaving it behind for Grant to clean, or for time to erase it. On the contrary, she deliberately erases it after her passage, not to leave traces of her self behind her and beyond her. Once accomplished that gesture, the gesture of a housewife, Fiona dresses up, puts on her red lipstick and leaves the house: "She looked just like herself on this day – direct and vague as in fact she was, sweet and ironic." (Munro 2001: 275) These four epithets, like a painter's touches of colours, characterize Fiona. Yet, irony is her most striking feature. Indeed, she always faces her illness with irony, playing with words, answering "flippantly" as she admits to the doctor and to the policeman who diagnose and ascertain her status. Quite strikingly, Fiona has always the last word, she is never intimidated by questions, and she has answers that do make sense in a way.

The film – which is by no means considered here in terms of "faithfulness" – by the Canadian director Sarah Polley, *Away from Her* (2006), is the short story transposition and adaptation for cinema. It starts with a brief sequence on a close-up of Grant driving his car towards an address scribbled on a piece of paper: "Paris, Ontario". From that moment onwards, the film patently shows its agenda of Canadianness. Another crucial example of the film as a Canadian cultural product is the intimate moment when Grant is reading the poem by Michael Ondaatje's *The Cinnamon Peeler* to Fiona. From a well-recognizable paperback edition, he quotes the well-known stanza: "This is how you touch other women ... ." (Ondaatje 1989: 157) It alludes to infidelity, another important theme in the plot, hinting at the momentary diversions of Grant's life from Fiona's side (Rodríguez Herrera 2013: 110). It is true, however, that other intertextual references are relevant as well, as the reference to Auden's *Letters from Iceland*, for Iceland is an elsewhere all through the narrative (Szabó 2008). Indeed, Iceland does not only provide a background to Grant's profession, as professor of Nordic mythology and skaldic poems, but it is Fiona's ancient motherland, the land of love and be-longing for "love is homesickness", in Freudian words, that is, the land/body of the Mother (1919: 15). It is also a young land, geologically speaking, still 'sparking' with volcanic life, yet incapable of giving Fiona eternal youth. In the film, Grant complains with the nurse that his wife is far too young for Alzheimer's. This reference to Iceland calls to mind what the American scholar, Robert Pogue Harrison writes:

My body is at once sixty years old and several billion years old, since all of its atoms originated a few seconds after the Big Bang, hence are as old as the universe itself. Moreover, a body does not age uniformly in all its parts. The age of a weak heart is not that of a sound kidney. One may turn old in one part of the body and stay young in another over the course of years. (Harrison 2014: 8)

As for Fiona, her belonging to a young Land, makes her young, from a geological point of view. Yet, she is also very old, for her origins date back to the Vikings and their legends. Fiona is also as old as the Goddess Friia, as Héliane Ventura writes (2010: 8), for we are as old as "the archetypes of prehistoric myth" (Harrison 2014: 8). She is getting older in one part of her body, before slowly declining physically. This does not prevent her from being an inspiring Muse all her life.

At the beginning of the film, there is a close up of Fiona's face as a young girl, with Grant's voiceover, reminiscent of when she proposed to him. Then, there follows a long sequence with Fiona and Grant cross-country skiing, while the titles start appearing. This sequence is particularly meaningful and symbolic, for it seems to lyrically translate and refer back to the opening of the literary text.

On a flat, white, unlimited expanse of snow, Fiona and Grant go skiing at first following parallel paths. Then, Fiona keeps on skiing straight on, while Grant – once left behind – diverges from her for a while, and they both move separately towards a far-away horizon of silhouetted, low and black hills. Subsequently, they re-unite and go back skiing towards their house.

What can be taken for an afternoon spent practicing sports is, in fact, a symbol of life itself. Grant and Fiona have proceeded together as husband and wife in their parallel life, yet an unexpected destiny has crossed their paths, and soon Fiona will have to leave, her path will diverge from that of Grant, as in the past Grant had distracted himself from her, luckily without consequences for their married life. The tracks they leave in the snow, well-marked as if on a white board, are symptomatic of their paths/passage in life.

Our field of vision, as film spectators, as well as the two actors's field of vision, coincide with the snowy field, and the field is a clear metaphor for life itself. "Field" is a key term in psychoanalysis: it implies a shared space, a game to play together (to "dream together"), a place to be cultivated, but also to be transformed constantly. It is the space of the analytic relationship. "The field in front of one", Berger claims, "seems to have the same proportions of one's life" (Berger 1980: 262; Lingiardi 2016: 83-84).

This white expanse of snow – an oblique reference to Iceland – might also be considered a metaphor for memory, where our life experiences are stored as traces, signs, marks that Alzheimer's might affect, for these memories can easily be deleted. The skiing sequence placed at sunset is also symbolic, for it alludes to the ending of life, and to the coming of dusk that erases the landscape by slowly enveloping it in darkness. In the film,

Fiona and Grant stop for a moment to admire, absorb and ponder on the fading light of the day, and perhaps on the ending of their lives.

There is a further reference in the story to a swampy place the couple drives by while on their way to the clinic, and Fiona suddenly remembers: "She was talking about the time that they had gone out skiing at night under the full moon and over the black-striped snow." (Munro 2001: 278) Here, too, the moon projects its light on the white expanse and the tracks on the snow are like black marks on a white board. In this way, the text creates a consistent net of recurrent references, all insisting on the memory of signs and on the erasing of those same signs.

On the contrary, the film here takes a different turn, for Fiona reminds Grant of the Brant Conservation Area and the flowers they saw there, as if they visited the place in spring, while the text says that only in winter, with thick ice, it is possible to walk there. The flowers, skunk lilies, are typical of that latitude and it is indictment of the film purpose to strictly relate to an Ontario imaginary and a strong sense of Canadianness, for it aims at distancing itself from American and Hollywood productions. In the film, Fiona's irony reaches its peak when she answers to the doctor: "we don't go very often now to the movie theatre, all those multiplex showing all that American garbage" (my transcription), when asked what she would do in case she spotted a fire in a cinema.

It must be said that flowers, too, like animals, constitute one among many leitmotifs in the text; when Grant goes to visit Fiona for the first time, in February, he buys some Narcissus while pondering that it is the first time in his life he buys flowers to Fiona, like one of those husbands who have reasons to make themselves forgiven. As soon as he arrives at the clinic, he is met by the nurse's comment – in the film it is the hateful supervisor's comment: "Wow. Narcissus this early. You must have spent a fortune." (Munro 2001: 286) The cost of Narcissus must be nothing if compared to the fees due to the clinic, and to add more irony, it is perhaps not too early, but too late for Grant to bring flowers to his wife. She might not recognize either him or his gesture. The bluebirds painted on the nameplate at the door look kitsch to Grant and, indeed, he does not even find Fiona in her room and is compelled to roam through the corridors with Narcissus in his hands, till the nurse puts them in a vase. Grant could even be identified with the mythical figure of Narcissus, while Fiona, once in the clinic transforms herself into the nymph Echo, for she repeatedly insists on offering Grant "a cup of tea", or on claiming he is "persistent".

"On this day" (Munro 2001: 275) is the deictic indicating the present moment in the story, when Fiona takes the final decision and all arrangements have already been made for her retirement and her separation from Grant. Thus, the story must once again go back to the past, through a flashback.

Over a year ago, Grant had started noticing so many little yellow notes stuck up all over the house. That was not entirely new. Fiona had always written things down [...] The new notes were different. Stuck onto the kitchen drawers – Cutlery, Dishtowels, Knives. Couldn't she just open the drawers and see what was inside? (Munro 2001: 275)

In this passage Fiona is still described by the extra-diegetic, omniscient narrator – who nevertheless adopts an internal focalizer: Grant. Sticking up notes on kitchen drawers has been suggested by Fiona's fear of forgetting where things are, but they also show how she is having problems in connecting signifier and signified. The graphic symbols which also correspond to sonic signifiers, need to be attached to the signified, to the real, material objects they represent, in order to be recognized by Fiona. On the one hand, this might be an intertextual literary reference, for in *One Hundred Years of Solitude* by Gabriel Garcia Marquez, Aureliano Buendia marks every single object with its name for the sake of his father who is forgetting everything. However, he starts thinking that perhaps one day people will only know inscriptions but lose the sense of the objects' function and use. Thus, the final question asked at the end of the quoted passage – "Couldn't she have just opened the drawers and seen what was inside?" (Munro 2001: 275) – seems to allude to a similar situation, where the use of the object is lost and not only the word that names it. Moreover, the question is asked in a neutral tone that seems to embody Roland Barthes's "middle voice" (1989: 18-19), for the narrator speaks with the voice of Grant.

Thus, Fiona is ill, she does not necessarily forget, but above all she cannot match signifier and signified, she cannot reach the unity of the linguistic sign anymore. Now, if the connection between signifier and signified is arbitrary and artificial, Fiona's loss of words would not be a problem. For, after all, if we exchange the names of forks and spoons, the two objects would continue to operate as tools with inverted functions. The problem lies in the usage and social conventions to which we all should conform. Apparently, every coupling of concept and sound-image is a word. It follows that language, as a system of relations between words, is internal to the mind. This is what Ingold writes about Saussurre's linguistic theory (2016: 120). Thus, Fiona's illness becomes problematic not so much because it allows her to take some freedom in arbitrary re-combinations of words and objects, signifier and signified, but because it is an illness of the mind, which breaks socially and historically established (linguistic and cognitive) conventions. As Derrida would say, by visualising Saussurre's notion of the sign as a page with two faces (signifier and signified), Fiona has stopped living within the logocentric / phonocentric logic. She cannot coordinate her mind with her voice (Derrida 1976: 12).

In the short story, immediately after the question about the cutlery, there is a passage that does not seem to fit into the narrative. In fact, it corroborates the signifier vs signified split:

He remembered a story about the German soldiers on border patrol in Czechoslovakia during the war. Some Czech had told him that each of the patrol dogs wore a sign that said *Hund.* Why? Said the Czechs, and the Germans said, Because that is a *hund.*
He was going to tell Fiona that, then thought he'd better not. They always laughed at the same things, but suppose this time she didn't laugh? (Munro 2001: 275)

This anecdote is completely out of place in this context. The only reason why it might fit, is exactly the endorsement of the arbitrary relationship between signifier and signified, for we perfectly know from linguistics that to the same signified a different signifier is matched in the various languages (eng. "dog", fr. *"chien"*, it. *"cane"*, ger. *"hund"*). Later on, we learn that Fiona had two dogs as a substitute for the children she could not have. Thus, dogs are a recurrent element giving cohesion to the story.

A problem arises from the subsequent question. Why should Fiona laugh or not laugh at this anecdote? Who are those "some Czech" Grant refers to? The short story is characterized by ellipses and elisions, much remains unsaid, not only between husband and wife, but also between the narrator – who seems to speak through Grant – and the reader.

In contrast, the film produces an explanation for these interrogatives, by re-proposing the anecdote. It is Fiona telling the little story to Grant. She claims she heard it from Veronica, a former Czech student of his, with whom he might have flirted or even have had an affair. Thus, in the film, the director seems to underline how Fiona is perfectly conscious of what is happening to her. She has to watch the word-label in order to identify the object/signified. More dramatically, in the film Fiona affirms she fears she is going to disappear.

A similar split of the linguistic sign occurs in the novel *Dogs at the Perimeter* (2012) by the Cino-Canadian novelist Madeleine Thien, which is partly dedicated to Alzheimer's. A young Cambodian researcher and her Japanese boss work in a research lab for the study of Alzheimer's. A woman comes to Dr. Hiroji:

Elie was fifty-eight years old when she began to lose language. She told Hirogji that the first occurrence was in St. Michael's Church in Montreal, when the words of the Lord's Prayer, words she had known almost from the time she had learned to speak, failed to materialize on her lips. For a brief moment, while the congregation around her prayed, the whole notion of language diminished inside her mind. Instead, the priest's green robes struck her as infinitely complicated, the winter coats of the faithful shifted like a collage, a pointillistic work, a Seurat: precision, definition, and a rending, rending beauty. The Lord's Prayer touched her in the same bodily way that the wind might, it was the sensation of sound but not meaning. She felt elevated and alone, near to God and yet cast out.
And then the moment passed. She came back and so did the words. A mild hallucination, Elie thought. *Champagne in the brain.* (Thien 2012: 10-11; original emphasis)

Elie is a retired biomechanical engineer and she now dedicates herself to painting. Her final, ironic consideration about "champagne in the brain" is very similar to Fiona's initial playful awareness that she is only "losing her mind". This apparent light heartedness, or irony, in defining one's symptoms has to do with what Marlene Goldman reminds us:

The oldest known appearance of the term "dementia" – which is primarily a group of symptoms, rather than a disease – was in Roman texts, where it meant "being out of one's mind." (Goldman 2017: 13)

Loss of language, seen here as a momentary failure, does not widen the distance from God, for any form of prayer might be acceptable in a church, but it does widen the distance from men – "near to God and yet cast out" – for words are a social convention not a private religious act. As we know from Ferdinand de Saussurre:

If the Frenchman of today uses words like *homme* ('man') and *chien* ('dog') it is because these words were used by his forefathers. Ultimately there is a connection between these two opposing factors: the arbitrary conventions, which allow free choice, and the passage of time, which fixes that choice. It is because the linguistic sign is arbitrary that it knows no other laws than that of tradition, and because it is founded upon tradition that it can be arbitrary. (Saussurre 1983: 85-86)

In the film, Fiona produces a couple of slips of the tongue. The first time, this happens during a dinner in the company of another couple. Fiona takes the bottle in her hand and when she is about to pour its content in the glasses, she asks: "Would you like some wane, wine, ween?" The embarrassed guests think they have to indulge with her, and answer back "Why not, some wane!" (my transcription).

Another relevant moment, actually the most touching in the whole story, and literally re-proposed in the film, occurs when Grant goes to visit Fiona and brings Aubrey – an ex temporary patient – back to her, in the hope that she might benefit from re-enacting their affective relationship and so improve her conditions. She embraces Grant and says: "You could have just driven away. Just driven away without a care in the world and forsook me. Forsooken me. Forsaken." (Munro 2001: 321)

This almost childish attempt at reciting the paradigm of an irregular verb, according to the basic English mnemonic approach to conjugations, shows how Fiona knows exactly what she wants to say, only she does not find the right sonic signifier, the right word. But she has recognized Grant, to the point of pinching his earlobes, a loving gesture they only know too well from their married life.

After "Discipline and Punish": The New Institution

The clinic where Fiona choses to retire, Meadowlake, is known to her and Grant for in the past they used to pay visits to an old neighbour there, but now the newly restored building looks completely rehabilitated. Thus the short story deploys the strategy of comparing a past gothic-like description of an institution dating back to the fifties (pre-anti-asylum movement) were old people were dumped and disposed of, to a present institution modelled on new standards:

[Past:]
There had been some unnerving sights: wiskers on old women's chins, somebody with a bulged-out eyed like a rotten plum.
Dribblers, head wagglers, mad chatterers.
[Present:]
Some people were sitting along the walls, in easy chairs, others at tables in the middle of the carpeted floor. None of them looked too bad. Old – some of them incapacitated enough to need weelchairs – but decent.
Now it looked as if there'd been some weeding out of the worst cases. (Munro 2001: 287)

Definitely, the gothic sights of illness, of which Marlene Goldman gives a precise historical and cultural scrutiny, has been turned into a decent image of human beings in a new phase of their life. Only the narrator/Grant's allusion to "weeding out the worst cases" remains attached to the gothic vision of people disposed of against their will. In fact, it is said later on that the worst cases are hidden behind locked doors, on the second floor of the building, where Fiona, too, is threatened to go, should her conditions worsen. That is the place for mentally disturbed people, too. Thus, in the text the new clinic, in spite of its luminous appearance, its greenery, its efficient staff manager, seems only a white-washed copy of the old one. The narrator, through the internal focalizer, has Grant voicing his scepticism and his sarcastic comments on the clinic. He cannot forget what the clinic was like in the past and he remains attached to that stereotype.

First, the institution is characterized by rules, and they are particularly hateful: "nobody could be admitted to Meadowlake during the month of

December. The holiday season had so many emotional pitfalls." (Munro 2001: 278) Therefore, Fiona will be admitted in early January. The second rule concerns the fact that during the first month of permanence, patients cannot receive visitors, even close or loved relatives. After one month on their own, they are settled in, claims the efficient supervisor, and "they are as happy as clams" (Munro 2001: 279),[1] she adds in a matter of fact voice. The choice of this idiom unintentionally shows a certain lack of humanity pervading this clinic, where emotions and feelings are banned and where the happiness of clams alludes to invertebrates, whose happiness is perhaps limited if it is proportional to their lack of mobility.

Moreover, clams as mussels are imprisoned in their shells. Thus, the institution figuratively sees itself as a prison, limiting the movement, the emotional life and the freedom of its patients. In this respect the clinic is not different from the Foucaultian type of institutions for total control of bodies and souls (Foucault 1977: 135-169). In spite of appearances the biopolitics of total control remains substantially the same, although critics have different opinions, seeing the clinic as a positive 'elsewhere' (Jamieson 2014; Johnston & Rao 2018: 17).

Grant is then informed that Fiona's adaptation process is defined by the nurse as if she were "coming out of her shell. What shell was that? Grant wanted to ask [...]" (Munro 2001: 281).[2] Thus, the metaphor recurs here, too, textually reinforcing the idea that patients, once there, inevitably lose their vitality. Although, it must be said that animals are frequently mentioned all through the short story as Héliane Ventura claims by precisely mapping their presence (Ventura 2010: 4).

The film, quite successfully and also updating the story to the present, increases the gap between the supervisor or staff manager, Ms Madeleine Montpellier, with her French sounding surname and her super-efficient attitude, and Kristy, the kind and sympathetic nurse. In the short story, Kristy is a blond nurse with "voluminous, puffed-up hair" (Munro 2001: 286), coiffed according to the fashion of the seventies. On the contrary, but

---

1   "As happy as a clam": well pleased, quite contented. US colloq. *Oxford English Dictionary*, vol. III, 2nd edition, Oxford: Clarendon Press, 1989, p. 263.
2   "Out of one's shell": in figurative phrases referring to "emerge into life". *Oxford English Dictionary*, vol. XV, 2nd edition, Oxford: Clarendon Press, 1989, p. 230.

very realistically, in the film she is a modest black haired nurse, probably belonging to a minority ethnic group, with a problematic family life; thus showing the internal hierarchies in contemporary clinics or hospitals.

At a later stage, when Fiona's conditions seem to worsen and she does not recognize Grant any more, Grant notices that she is wearing a cheap pullover, not of the kind Fiona used to wear. Fiona used to be a very elegant woman with "hair that was as light as milkweed fluff":

> It must be that they didn't bother to sort out the wardrobes of the women who were roughly the same size and counted on the women not to recognize their own clothes anyway. They had cut her hair, too. They had cut away her angelic halo. (Munro 2001: 297)

When Grant has the chance to talk to his wife, he uses the subtler and accusatory expression "Why did they chop off your hair?", and Fiona answers nonchalantly "Why – I never missed it" (Munro 2001: 2097). Yet, the phrasal verb "chop off" alludes to a careless attitude, a rough and approximate gesture that does not take into consideration the dignity of a styled haircut for patients. It is clear that Grant has neither trust nor sympathy for such an institution, where patients are conceived of as passive by the staff. The latter seem to count on their inability to react and even to recognize themselves in a mirror, thus diminishing their sense of dignity. In the film, Grant's suspect is voiced when he sees nurses in the act of feeding the patients while listening to pop music. He complains that the music is not the choice of the patients', nor respectful of their tastes. Fiona and Grant, conversely, listen to and sometimes dance to the music by Neil Young, a Canadian-born musician and singer, once more, to underline the Canadian setting of this story. Neil Young's words "There is a town in North Ontario" will then close the film.

Yet, Fiona is not so completely lost. She knows things. Grant finds Fiona and her dear friend, Aubrey, at their worst, for Aubrey is about to go back home to his wife, Marian. Fiona asks Grant: "Do you by any chance have any influence around here? [...] I've seen you talking to them...?" (Munro 2001: 303). This is a sign that Fiona, too, sees the members of the staff as hostile and coalesced against patients. Both Grant and Fiona speak of "they/them" alluding to members of the staff almost as enemies.

Fiona's permanence in the clinic is described as a progressive deterioration, particularly after the separation from Aubrey. She does not recognize Grant any longer. She treats him as a newly arrived patient, someone she owes kindness to, as a "persistent" visitor or suitor, but her attention revolves around Aubrey, her new friend. Fiona's and Aubrey's attachment seems to match Grant's past infidelity to his wife, to the point that he imagines a revenge or a charade by his wife, as a sort of late punishment.

Yet, everything is more complex in this text. For Munro shuffles her cards only too frequently. Fiona's new engagement with life is a response to a natural need for socialization. Her presence is so benign as to get Aubrey out of his wheelchair. She becomes his nurse and she supports him while walking. She has found a new agency in the clinic. It is also possible that in her mind she is fantasizing about Aubrey as her once young and shy suitor. Thus, the story seems to echo Joyce's *The Dead*, where Gretta, too, reveals Gabriel of her once young suitor.

On the other hand, Grant's past flirts and love affairs with younger women are attributed to a misinterpretation of waves of feminism uniquely intended as emancipation through sexual transgression on the part of women, which once again, surprisingly, dissolves our too easy notion of Munro as a feminist writer. Gender here is discussed more subtly, through nuances, rather than through easy and clear-cut slogans. Grant is almost excused, he seems pursued rather than pursuer:

Married women had started going back to school. Not with the idea of qualifying for a better job, or for any job, but simply to give themselves something more interesting to think about than their usual housework and hobbies. To enrich their lives. And perhaps it followed naturally that the men who taught them these things became part of the enrichment, that these men seemed to these women more mysterious and desirable than the men they still cooked for and slept with. (Munro 2001: 299)

Aubrey mostly depends on Fiona. What is extremely important in the narrative is that Fiona's presence, her empathy, allows Aubrey to shortly abandon his wheelchair for short strolls. In spite of the fact that he needs support, he is able to slip out of his disability now and then. At the clinic, Grant learns of Fiona's almost miraculous effects on Aubrey, and this is an extremely interesting passage. Fiona did not want to be a burden to her husband. Moreover, it is normally assumed that elderly people – when they lose their autonomy – end up depending on the younger generations. Here, on the contrary, Fiona is given agency, she acts as a nurse to Aubrey, and this means that elderly people might be reciprocally supportive and might have a social role, till the very end. A similar highlighting of agency is authoritatively provided by Marlene Goldman:

within Canadian literary works people struggling with dementia are neither depicted nor perceived solely as non persons lacking in agency, ontological "black holes". In "The Bear Came over the Mountain" the narrative's ambiguous treatment of Fiona's dementia, specifically her capacity to remember fragments of her past, including Grant's affairs, makes it impossible for readers to perceive her as a powerless victim lacking in selfhood. (Goldman 2017: 295)

Both the narrative and the film show Aubrey's disability as permanent and irreducible, thus adding a new theme to old age and caring. His wife hints at his immobility, while Grant witnesses how Fiona has to prevent cards from slipping from his grasp. Yet, the film produces a more romanticised version of Aubrey, who can sublimate his lack of kinetic skills with a talent for drawing, which he expresses in a series of beautiful portraits of Fiona. The film, thus, seems to pick up Munro's major concern, that is to provide agency to the old. Meaningfully, Aubrey obsessively and serially portrays Fiona's head and profile: a sign that her head is still fascinating and interesting, still sparking beauty and intelligence, no matter how far it is affected by dementia or Alzheimer's. Reinforcing this idea of agency with Aubrey's artistic talent, while insisting on Fiona's beauty, is another feature that reverses the stereotypical, gothic idea of old women as ugly.

OVER THE MOUNTAIN AND BEYOND

The title of the short story sounds misleading, referring as it does to a children's lyric, although the critic Héliane Ventura builds an interesting intertextual interpretation of it. The bear and the mountain do not fit in that flat landscape proposed by the film. Yet, they are two unavoidable natural elements in classical Canadian literature. The bear and the mountain frequently represent the wrestling of man against nature. And in this case Fiona, too, has to fight against nature. The other side of the mountain that the bear has to face and confront with might be the declining or descending side of one's life, as ageing is traditionally thought to be. Yet, the text seems to resist this simple solution by leaving an open ended narrative, full of gaps and unsaid or silenced things (Casado-Gual 2013: 394-395).

Fiona-Grant and Aubrey-Marian represent two elderly couples with different life-styles. Fiona and Grant have neither relatives nor children and represent the typical, self-sufficient, mono-nuclear family of our modernity, now so typical in the capitalist North. Particularly, once left alone, Grant must face everything on his own, he drives a car, he takes care of the house, he cooks his own meals, he shovels the snow. His dependence on Fiona is hinted at when he admits that now his skiing exercise is reduced to just going round and round.

Marian, too, has to rely only on her own strength. She has a son, but he lives on the west coast and seldom comes to visit. He only provides new technological gadgets to his parents (an electric coffee pot and a satellite Tv sports channel to entertain his disabled father), thus substituting affection with money. This technology, including an answering machine, serves to date the short story to the late eighties or early nineties.

The main difference between these two nuclear families is economic, for Fiona and Grant are upper middle class and can afford to pay the fees of a private clinic. Conversely, Marian cannot afford to leave her husband permanently at the clinic, for that would mean selling her house, the only thing she possesses.

The difference between the two families creates an interesting linguistic pun around the word "quit", which becomes more and more relevant in the short story. The first time the verb "quit" is used, it refers to the mark on the floor: "I thought they'd quit doing that" (Munro 2001: 274), Fiona says, meaning that her slippers should have stopped leaving marks like that. And certainly after her quitting the house, they won't be used any more. Towards the end of the narrative, when Grant pays his first visit to Marian in order to try and convince her to bring her husband back to the clinic, for the sake of Fiona, Marian jokes about her habit of smoking. Since Grant says he does not smoke, she asks him if he never did or if he quit smoking. "Quit" (Munro 2001: 311), he answers and remembers that it happened when he started his affair with Jacqui. Thus, the verb "quit" seems to refer to Fiona rather than to smoking. Indeed, he quit Fiona in the past, and maybe now, too. Vice versa, Marian says she has quit quitting. She has willingly refused to stop smoking or pretending to stop. She has not quit her husband either, whom she takes care of, even though that means her individual sacrifice and renunciation. When she leaves her husband at the clinic it is only for a short vacation.

However, due to her routinely fatigue in taking care of her inert husband, keeping him bed-ridden and under the TV's hypnotic effect does not seem to produce positive effects. On the contrary, Fiona's influence on Aubrey's ability to walk had meant a slight improvement, Marian's attitude clearly shows the fatigue and frustration of care-givers, who inevitably end up exhausting their resources.

It is however most meaningful that Fiona's last words in the story as well as in the film hint at the fact that after all, no matter all the diversions in his life, Grant has not quit her:

"I'm happy to see you," she said, both sweetly and formally. She pinched his earlobes hard.
"You could have just driven away," she said. "Just driven away without a care in the world and forsook me. Forsaken me. Forsaken."
He kept his face against her white hair, her pink scalp, her sweetly shaped skull. (Munro 2001: 321)

The short story ends with a happy ending, a moment of recognition and acknowledgement on the part of Fiona. Her gratitude to her husband is moving, yet her condition might be only temporary and one of the last words in the story is "skull", an allusion to death. Ironically, however, Fiona recognises Grant, when he brings Aubrey back to her. As it happened with the Narcissus, here too, Grant is responsible for wrong timing. Perhaps, Fiona is no longer able to recognize Aubrey. She affirms that names elude her. This gift, like the flowers, might be spoilt or wasted.

Grant and Marian represent two different versions of care-givers, both affected in different ways by the grief and difficulty of taking care of disabled people who do not always show recognition or appreciation. Both of them hold fast on their beloved, out of marital duty, love and a life of shared propitious and hostile circumstances. What is striking is their absolute loneliness and the portrait of an individualistic society, where there is absolutely no sense of community.

Fiona's case is even more striking for her choice is exemplary of a free woman and a self-determining individual. Although the choice to leave her home and her husband might still look improbable and rare, particularly in Southern European countries where religion and tradition might prevent such a gesture. It must be said that a stronger sense of family bonds still characterises the Italian society, where elderly people, disabled people and also mentally disturbed people are taken care of at home, thanks also to new figures, the so-called "badanti". Earlier, in the eighties, they were mostly South American women, more recently they have been substituted by Eastern European house-workers. The Italian National Sanitary System nowadays also offers home assistance for medications and small interventions.

Both Munro's story and Polly's film show a possible path. In the story, Fiona has definitely agency till the very end (Lecker 2015). Grant, too, takes actions be they selfish or generous, and Marian – as Fiona did in the past – implicitly proposes to Grant by inviting him to the dance.

The film goes further, for even Aubrey is allowed agency as a painter, using his brain to coordinate his hand, particularly using his right brain (Bergland 1985: 1), which normally presides over the figurative skills, while Fiona is slowly losing her left brain, presiding over language skills. This inversion reminds us of what happens in Goethe's *Elective Affinities* (1809), where two couples exchange partners, and young Ottilie feels a pain in her head that is specular to mature and married Eduard's headache:

She [Ottilie] frequently suffers from pain in the left side of her head. (Goethe 1872: 28-29)
I have it frequently on the right. If we happen to be afflicted together, and sit opposite one another, – I leaning on my right elbow, and she on her left, and our heads on the opposite sides, resting on our hands, – what a pretty pair of pictures we shall make." (Goethe 1872: 49-50)

In this respect, the film also completes the series of the arts represented. It adds drawing – thus highlighting the visual arts – to reading and writing, which are the main activities of Grant and Fiona, as well as dancing and listening to music. The major implication is that elderly people are not excluded from the production, performance and consumption of various forms of art.

Moreover, the renewed clinic in both narrative and film might be exemplary of institutions that have been reformed after the abolition of asylums and such like places. A most applauded law was passed in Italy in 1981, abolishing asylums and this brought to the complete reformation of the sanitary system, including clinics for elderly and disabled people. Thus, Fiona's choice is in tune with these new possibilities of being cared for by professionally trained staff, in adequately furnished places, which also meant a relief to families.

The film however, for the sake of romanticising the plot, significantly diverges from the literary text. The short story ends on the recognition of the spouse and does not provide an answer on whether Grant will accept Marian's invitation to the dance.

Meanwhile, the film alludes to Grant's late affair with Marian – for, there is a hint at her moving to live with him – and this is certainly a cause for controversial interpretations. On the one hand, Grant might be blamed for he seems to betray Fiona now, as he did in the past, being incapable of marital faithfulness – "a philanderer", Munro writes (2001: 284).

In the film, he is portrayed as a new Orpheus, who pays his last visit to his Eurydice, then turns back and finds a substitute and a sublimation not so much in his own art – Grant is not a poet, but he likes reading poetry, being a professor of Nordic mythology and skaldic poems – but in a substitute female figure. This substitution of partners and exchange between the two couples is certainly a matter of questionable ethics if reduced to its literal meaning.

In the traditional elegiac model of Orpheus and Eurydice, for example, the hero seeks his beloved in the underworld, but inevitably relinquishes her and returns to the world of the living, where he is celebrated as a culture–hero. For Zeiger, such narrative frameworks doom women to death and silence. (Goldman 2017: 36)

On the other hand, Grant might be admired for his generosity, leaving space to his wife for a late relief from pain and depression when he offers Aubrey to her, as a gift. In the film, this idea is clearly introduced during one of Grant's visits to the care facility, when he becomes a sort of spectator in a film, where Fiona and Aubrey play the role of aged fiancés before his eyes. He observes them while sitting on a sofa, as if he were watching a film. This is an interesting shot for it introduces a meta-cinematic element, for we as spectators watch a film where Grant, too, is watching the actors performing their actions. A punk girl, who finds the spectacle of patients and relatives as "fucking depressing" (my transcription), asks Grant why he is sitting there, if his wife is with another man, only to realize immediately how lucky Fiona is to be allowed such space and such freedom.

The film is keener on showing how elderly people might find comfort in living together, having company, uniting their strengths and supporting and helping one another as long as they can. Considering old age as a moment in life when emotions, affections and even sensuality are still possible would certainly be a step forward in our cultural prejudices against the old, the so-called "ageism".

Thus, the Canadian short story and its filmic translation – through the typical ambiguities of artistic masterpieces, the ellipses and gaps implied in and applied by the two media – do provide a model and do provide answers, do suggest cultural challenges. The two works of art suggest a model of social engineering based on communal life and reciprocal support, on providing opportunities, rather than seeing the old merely as disposable, even those affected by dementia and Alzheimer's, as stressed by medical literature (Johnson et al. 2010).

The risks of a growing individualism, of a destiny of loneliness in old age is questioned in both the story and the film, when new forms of social life are suggested, even in the form of private clinics for the elderly, disabled and mentally disturbed people (Jamieson 2014). Alternatively, Grant and Marian keep company to each other in old age. While the story suggests their going out to dance on a Saturday night, the film more explicitly hints at their sleeping together. Their possible life together would be another way to mitigate the absence of extended families whose members might take care of their elders. In a recent survey in Sweden, the answer to the question about what people fear most was "to die alone". Neither the film nor the short story offer easy solutions to face a terrible disease like Alzheimer's, or suggestions for care-givers of disabled people. Yet, these two artworks show old age for what it is, a moment of agency, solidarity, sociability. When Grant expresses his dislike for Meadowlake,

Fiona answers that what one can aspire to at their age, if Alzheimer's has been diagnosed, is just "a little grace" (my transcription).

BIBLIOGRAPHY

Barthes, Roland (1989 [1967-1980]): *The Rustle of Language*, trans. by R. Howard, Berkeley: University of California Press.

Bergland, Richard (1985): *The Fabric of Mind*, New York: Viking Penguin.

Casado-Gual, Núria (2015 [2013]): "Unexpected turns in lifelong sentimental journeys: redefining love, memory and old age through Alice Munro's 'The Bear Came Over the Mountain' and its film adaptation *Away from Her.*" In: *Ageing & Society* 35, pp. 389-404, last accessed March 3, 2018 (http://doi.org/10.1017/SO144686X13000780). Web.

Derrida, Jacques (1976 [1967]): *Of Grammatolgy*, trans by G.C. Spivak, Baltimore: Johns Hopkins University Press.

Foucault, Michel (1977 [1975]): "Docile Bodies." In: *Discipline and Punish*, trans. by A. Sheridan, London: Penguin, pp. 135-169.

Freud, Sigmund. [1919]: *The Uncanny*, trans. by A. Strachey, pp. 1-21, last accessed March 3, 2018 (web.mit.edu/allanmc/www/freud1.pdf). Web.

Garcia Márquez, Gabriel (1992 [1967]): *One Hundred Years of Solitude*, New York: Harper Collins.

Goethe, Johann Wolfgang (1872 [1809]): *Elective Affinities*, trans. anonymous, New York: Henry Holt and Company.

Goldman, Marlene (2017): *Forgotten. Narratives of Age-related Dementia and Alzheimer's Disease in Canada*, Montreal: McGuill-Queen's University Press.

Harrison, Robert Pogue (2014): *Juvenescence. A Cultural History of Our Age*, Chicago: The University of Chicago Press.

Ingold, Tim (2016): *Evolution and Social Life,* London: Routledge.

Jamieson, Sara (2014): "Reading the Spaces of Age in Alice Munro's 'The Bear Came Over the Mountain'." In: *Mosaic* 3, September, pp. 1-17, last accessed March 3, 2018 (https://muse.jhu.edu/article/555659). Web.

Johnson L. Syd/Krahn M./Timothy M. (2010): "Intimate Relationship and Dementia – an extended commentary on *Away From Her.*" In: *Journal of Ethics and Mental Health* 5/1, pp. 1-11, last accessed March 3, 2018 (http://www.jemh.ca/). Web.

Johnson, Paul/Thane, Pat (1998): *Old Age from Antiquity to Post-Modernity,* London: Routledge.

Johnston, Christin-Lorre/Rao, Eleonora (eds.) (2018): *Space and Place in Alice Munro's Fiction. 'A book with Maps in it'.* New York: Camden House.

Lecker, Robert (2015): "'Like Following a Mirage': Memory and Empowerment in Alice Munro's 'The Bear Came Over the Mountain'." In: *Journal of the Short Story in English* 64, Spring, pp. 1-10, last accessed March 3, 2018 (http://jsse.revues.org/1583). Web.

Lingiardi, Vittorio (2017): *Mindscapes. Psiche nel paesaggio,* Milan: Raffaello Cortina.

Munro, Alice (1999): "The Bear Came Over the Mountain." In: *The New Yorker,* December 27, last accessed March 3, 2018 (https://www.newyorker.com/magazine/1999/12/27/the-bear-came-over-the-mountain). Web.

_____ (2001): "The Bear Came Over the Mountain." In: *Hateship, Friendship, Courtship, Loveship, Marriage,* London: Chatto & Windus, pp. 273-321.

Ondaatje, Michael (1989): *The Cinnamon Peeler and other Poems,* London: Picador.

Rodriguez Herrera, José (2013): *"Away from Her*? Sarah Polley's Screen Adaptation of Alice Munro's 'The Bear Came Over the Mountain'." In: *Brno Studies in English* 39/2, pp. 107- 121, (DOI: 10.5817/BSE2013-2-7). Web.

Saussurre, Ferdinand de (1983 [1916]): *Course in General Linguistics,* trans. by Roy Harris, Chicago: Open Court.

Szabó F., Andrea (2008), "Munro's Auden: 'Letters from Iceland'." In: *Hungarian Journal of English and American Studies* 14/1, Spring, pp. 105-115, last accessed March 3, 2018 (http://www.jstore.org/stable/41274411). Web.

Thien, Madeleine (2012): *Dogs at the Perimeter,* London: Granta.

Ventura, Héliane (2010): 'The Skald and the Goddess: Reading "The Bear Came Over the Mountain" by Alice Munro.' In: *Journal of the Short Story in English* 55, December 1, pp. 1-11, last accessed March 3, 2018 (http://jsse.revues.org/1121). Web.

Woolf, Virginia (1991 [1917-1921]): "The Mark on the Wall." In: *The Complete Shorter Fiction*, ed. S. Dick, London: Grafton Books, pp. 83-89.

Coming to Terms
Ageing and Moral Regeneration in J.M. Coetzee's *Age of Iron* and *Elizabeth Costello*

BLOSSOM FONDO, UNIVERSITY OF MAROUA, CAMEROON

INTRODUCTION

Both literary gerontology and postcolonial studies are becoming firmly established in the academia and both forms of critiques continue to grow and intersect with other disciplines and sub-disciplines. However, in spite of their interdisciplinarity there is an unfortunate dearth in dialogue between them. Ageing is the missing theme in postcolonial studies and at the same time, the postcolonial dimension is the silent area of ageing studies. Ageing studies is still firmly located in the West and represents Western experiences. Julie Twigg and Wendy Martin have noted the flourishing of studies on ageing:

Books and articles on ageing and literature proliferated throughout the 1990s and into the twenty first century, and there is no sign of a slowing of the pace. Literary gerontology has spread its net widely, taking in drama and performance, fiction, auto/biography and poetry. It includes attention to non-Western writers – though it is true that at the moment the balance is still tipped in favour of the US, Canadian, European and (to a lesser extent) Australian writers – and pays some attention to both the popular and the literary. Content-based studies draw close attention to representations of ageing within literature. Others look at ageing and creativity, genre or readership. More and more, intersectionality is invigorating literary studies of ageing, with a notable flood of work addressing age and gender and a more limited amount of research onto 'race' and age. (2015: 58)

This citation highlights the three main points with which I opened up this discussion: namely, the spreading of literary gerontology, its limitation to Western authors and its distance from the postcolonial question. What this means is that this vibrant area of studies runs the risk of representing a single perspective on the subject of ageing and there is the eventual danger of universalizing this perspective across cultures and experiences. Whereas as Margaret Morganoth Gullette (2004: 11) has noted " 'aging' even at the merely visual level cannot have a single, invariable, universal and ahistorical meaning." In this light, Twigg and Martin pursue their discussion by citing areas of weaknesses of cultural gerontology, one of which "concerns the character of cultural gerontology as a Western-dominated and arguably post-imperialist form of analysis. It is certainly the case that most of the work that has been done under this label focusses on the West" (2015: 7).

It is also important to note here that this accusation may as well be levied at postcolonial studies which continues to incorporate other fields such as feminism and environmentalism, but has made no significant attempt to address the subject of ageing in the postcolony. Yet through ageing studies, important insights might be had into the postcolonial condition as well as into the tensions between the colonizer and the colonized. Even though there have been some critical engagement (albeit few) with ageing in formerly colonized societies, these studies have in a general sense not adopted a postcolonial perspective whereby the interconnections particularly between questions of ageing and colonial agenda are addressed. Postcolonial studies have been understandably more interested in the colonial question that is the lasting effects of colonialism on colonized societies. What has seemingly gone unnoticed is the way a postcolonial approach to ageing might open up new ways of studying the effects of colonialism on the individual. Whereas one of the ways postcolonial studies has done this has been through genre studies and genre revision in the case of writers. The bildungsroman for example which in a way constitutes studies into the first stage of ageing has received much attention from postcolonial scholars who through this have revealed the ways in which colonialism deformed the development of the postcolonial child and consequently reshaped the bildungsroman genre in the hands of postcolonial writers. From a similar viewpoint, postcolonial ageing studies could provide the adequate critical platform from which to ascertain the effects of colonialism on the psychological evolution of the individual as s/he ages in a colonized or formerly colonized society. Brian J. Worsfold has advised that: "approaches to gerontology must focus on the microcosm, that is, focus not on the society, the nation or even the community at large, but on the individual and the human and social context of the individual." (2011: xix) Following this advice creates room for the study of the ageing individual in postcolonial societies.

Similarly, ageing studies might enrich its perspective by integrating the postcolonial element. Therefore in a nutshell, adopting a postcolonial perspective to ageing studies will accomplish two major things amongst others: first of all, it will decolonize ageing studies and secondly it will enrich the field by bringing to it other experiences from across cultures. Similarly, introducing ageing to postcolonial studies will open up possibilities within the field to engage with the question and meaning of ageing in the postcolony. It will equally trace the evolution of consciousness in the ageing process, which evolution is important to postcolonial studies. Thus the intersection of these two disciplines will doubtlessly result in mutual enrichment.

It is even interesting to note some of the ways and areas in which postcolonial studies and ageing studies conflate and how this might open up possibilities for greater dialogue and mutual enrichment.

Both postcolonial studies and ageing studies are interested in the interrogation and deconstruction of cultural and social constructs. Put differently, much of the discussions of these two forms of critique are animated by the question of representation. Talking for ageing studies, Roberta Maierhofer in the "Preface" to *Acculturating Age* notes that "by placing cultural representations in a social, cultural and political context, existing disciplines and traditional paradigms can be reconstructed" (2011: xv), while speaking for postcolonial studies, Homi K. Bhabha underscores that postcolonial studies "bears witness to the unequal and uneven forces of cultural representation involved in the contest for political and social authority within the modern world order" (1994: 171). This underpins an interesting intersection between these two forms of critiques which have sadly remained aloof with each other. Whereas, given their shared interest in cultural representation, some form of conversation would have opened up possibilities for collaboration.

Both forms of critique therefore play the political role of dispelling long-held myths about different groups of people: the aged and the colonized. Thus Twigg and Martin have stated that "much of the impetus behind cultural gerontology has come from a desire to get away from the dominant account of ageing in academic studies that has focused on problematic old age, emphasizing frailty and its consequent social burdens" (2015: 2). Similarly Bhabha whom I cited before further intimates that colonial discourse has as objective "to construe the colonized as a population of degenerate types on the basis of racial origin in order to justify conquest and to establish systems of administration and inclusion" (1994: 70). We therefore notice here that both studies are critically engaged in responding to the biases and distortions of master discourses.

These biases constitute both for the aged and the colonized a process of othering, whereby both groups find themselves on the wrong side of the binary divisions that serve to categorize human beings. These binarisms constitute an important concept in postcolonial studies and are of equal importance to ageing studies which seeks to uncover and therefore dismantle the ways old age is considered as the negative other of youthfulness. Bill Ashcroft, Gareth Griffiths and Helen Tiffin are of the opinion that:

The binary logic of imperialism is a development of that tendency of Western thought in general to see the world in terms of binary oppositions that establish a relationship of dominance [...]. Clearly, the binary is very important in constructing ideological meanings in general, and extremely useful in imperial ideology. (2000: 19)

Margaret Morganoth Gullette in reference to the Dalai Lama's (somewhat ageist) reaction to his own ageing faced with two older priests notes that "he used 'young' as everyone does – to mean a desirable state of being in opposition to the unwanted state of feeling 'old'." (2015: 21) These two aforementioned views underline the way postcolonial studies and ageing studies conflate. With these areas of convergence between these two forms of cultural studies, some shared sympathies would have been expected of them but this has unfortunately not been the case.

FROM PHYSICAL FRAILTY TO MORAL STRENGTH

Part of my aim in this paper is to attempt a formulation of postcolonial gerontology; and I think that for this project a good starting point would be the novels of eminent South African writer J.M. Coetzee. The role of literature in lending insights into human experience can neither be overstated nor underestimated. As concerns ageing studies, two of its prominent critics have said a word on this aspect. Hannah Zeilig argues that "Fictional stories can be invaluable for considering the various manifestations of age and ageing" (2011: 31), while Worsfold concurs by holding that:

Using works of literature – fictionalisation – as a source of knowledge and experience allows students of ageing to research perceptions and attitudes across frontiers, in other countries, other societies and other parts of the world. It also enables a diachronic vision of the ageing process, crossing not just the barriers of space but also the barriers of time. (2011: xxv)

This idea is further buttressed by Diana Wallace who notes that "artistic representations of older people both shape and have the potential to counter our ideas about age and ageing" (2011: 389).

J.M. Coetzee's *Age of Iron* is a good example of a novel that creatively paints such "manifestations of age and ageing" and this in the postcolonial context. The use of the epistolary device makes this more effective. The story focuses on the dying days of a retired university professor, who is battling cancer and the entire story is in the form of a letter she is writing to her grown-up daughter in the US. Through the letter-writing mode, the reader is granted access into her most intimate thoughts, fears, expectations as well as daily activities. Here the main question is how does Coetzee present ageing in the postcolonial context? Coetzee uses the technique of juxtaposition to portray the ageing process in this context. He juxtaposes two processes going on at the same time in the life of Mrs. Curren: On the one hand, she is physically degenerating into frailty, but at the same time there is a moral regeneration or reawakening. My use of the word "moral" here has to be understood in context and it actually refers to what I term "postcolonial morality" which I define as the recognition of the excesses of the dominant class, its dehumanization of the colonized and an informed choice to resist this dehumanization of others which is based on imagined or perceived cultural, racial or ethnic differences. Based on this definition therefore, Mrs Curren, although in physical decline, is indeed in moral rejuvenation. She moves from passive opposition of the inhuman Apartheid system in South Africa to become more politically engaged. She stands up to policemen when they hound a black youth and expresses unconcealed sympathy for the victims of this system. It is important to note that Mrs. Curren is a white lady who under the Apartheid regime was exempted from its myriad abuses. She would rather have been a beneficiary of this system. Nevertheless, she rejects this privilege, identifies with the downtrodden and adopts a subversive stance against the system.

Through this juxtaposition of the physical degeneration and moral regeneration of Mrs Curren, I read Coetzee as interrogating assumptions about later life. Ageing is not a process of hardening of the heart, of becoming inured to the pains of those around us but rather a time of rethinking long held values. So, when Mrs. Curren offers shelter to a homeless man, considered by others as a "vagrant" and a "rubbish man", she makes the following important statement: "There are no rubbish people. We are all people together." (Coetzee 1990: 47) In this statement, she overthrows the leitmotiv of not only the Apartheid system but also of every other system that makes rubbish out of people. She insists on our shared humanity and on the recognition of everyone's personhood. This is one of the aims of postcolonial studies.

When she witnesses the consequence of police brutality in a black township which kills several youths including the son of her servant Florence, her moral consciousness becomes more acute. She writes to her daughter: "we kill these people as if they are waste, but in the end it is we whose lives are not worth living" (Coetzee 1990: 104). We witness a continuous moral renewal in Mrs Curren even as her body degenerates towards death. It is in her later years that she finally comes to terms with the failures of the colonial society. In the aftermath of the police brutality she states:

Now that child is buried and we walk upon him. Let me tell you, when I walk upon this land, this South Africa, I have a gathering feeling of walking upon black faces. They are dead but their spirit has not left them. (Coetzee 1990: 126)

She acknowledges the wrong done to black South Africans and expresses the desire for things to be done differently in her society. This subversion is a form of resistance dear to the postcolonial project and so her activism deconstructs myths about the helplessness of the aged and punctures colonialist ideology. J.M. Coetzee creates a character who defies the untruths of colonialism as well as the untruths about ageing. Through Mrs Curren, Coetzee seems to suggest that the inevitability of physical degeneration in ageing does not necessarily imply a dimming of moral vision. That Coetzee successfully interrogate ageist and colonialist visions indicate a position beneficial to both ageing studies and postcolonial studies and opens up the possibility of postcolonial gerontology.

Coetzee adopts a similar posture in the novel *Elizabeth Costello* which chronicles the later years of the eponymous protagonist, a renowned Australian writer. Quite early in the novel Coetzee paints the picture of an old frail woman to indicate that his story is indeed about the intricacies of ageing. It is said of her that: "Elizabeth has become a little frail: without the help of her son she would not be undertaking this taxing trip across half the world" (Coetzee 2004: 21) and also "After the long flight, she is looking her age. She has never taken care of her appearance; she used to be able to get away with it; now it shows. Old and tired" (Coetzee 2004: 3). Once again, Coetzee acknowledges the physical degeneration that comes with ageing. However, Costello illustrates a sharpening of consciousness highlighted in the numerous talks she is invited to give. While Mrs Curren in *Age of Iron* fights for the rights and protection of blacks in South Africa, Elisabeth Costello is an activist for animal rights. She is adamant in her position against cruelty to animals and early in the novel, she expresses sympathy for the Penguins of Macquarie Island which were brutally killed for their oil by human beings.

In the chapter entitled "The Lives of Animals", Coetzee once again brings in his technique of juxtaposition but to this he adds the concept of the gaze. Through Michael, Elisabeth's son Coetzee is able to portray what society sees when looking at an older person: the degenerating exterior. So Michael notes of his mother as follows: "Two years have passed since he last saw his mother, despite himself, he is shocked at how she has aged. Her hair, which had streaks of grey in it, is now entirely white; her shoulders stoop; her flesh has grown flabby" (Coetzee 2004: 59). Even when she is about to deliver her lecture Michael sees only frailty "she looks old and tired" he says. He representing the society here perceives human personality and ability only through the physical aspect reason why he tries to will strength into her. But Elisabeth Costello is not lacking in strength – at least not moral strength. In spite of the opposition to her thesis on human cruelty to animals, she persists and makes her points with convictions. She implores human beings to extend their sympathy to animals with the words: "There are no bounds to the sympathetic imagination"(Coetzee 2004: 80). And she pursues her point with the statement:

I return one last time to the places of death all around us, the places of slaughter to which, in a huge communal effort, we close our hearts. Each day a fresh holocaust, yet, as far as I can see, our moral being is untouched. We do not feel tainted. We can do anything, it seems and come away clean. (Coetzee 2004: 80)

Her evocation on our moral being here is indicative of the fact that physical degeneration is in no way accompanied by moral decline. She resists the speciesism that has guided human/non-human relations and makes a call for more consideration to be granted to the non-human species. Bill Ashcroft, Gareth Griffiths and Helen Tiffin underscore the importance of the environmental question to postcolonial studies. They write:

One of the most persistent and controversial topics of contemporary politics is the issue of the environment. Global warming has demonstrated the devastating effects of the industrial revolution and the unfettered pursuit of capital expansion. The environment and attendant topics such as ecofeminism, ecological imperialism, environmentalism, and speciesism have all taken an increasingly prominent place in post-colonial thought because it has become clear that there is a direct connection between colonialist treatment of indigenous flora and fauna and the treatment of colonized and otherwise dominated subjects and societies. (2007: viii)

Costello's battles therefore conform to the expectations of both ageing studies and postcolonial studies. In refusing to occupy the state of helplessness and dependency attributed to the aged, she is making a statement against ageist doctrines. Even her son Michael is exasperated by her non-conformist attitude and complains "why can she not be an ordinary old woman living an ordinary old woman's life? If she wants to open her heart to animals, why can't she stay at home and open it to her cat?"

(Coetzee 2004: 83). In refusing to live this so-called old woman's life she displaces cultural misconceptions about ageing and the aged and in attending to the rights of animals, she aligns her moral struggle with one of the agendas of postcolonial studies.

Both postcolonial and ageing studies are interested in interrogating and deconstructing the process of cultural othering through stereotyping. They contest cultural representations and social constructs based on biased notions of what it means to be normal and acceptable. Ideologies are also born of humanity's cultural, ethnic, racial and national arrogance which considers all that is different or apart from self as inferior. Such thinking has resulted in many of the gross abuses of human rights such as the transatlantic slave trade, the holocaust, colonialism, environmental destruction and genocides. Within the context of colonialism, it was the constructed racial and cultural superiority of the West that led to the subjugation of the colonized. These colonized peoples were deprived of their humanity, culture and resources through the misguided and warped perceptions of the colonizer.

From a similar ideological standpoint, the physical and sometimes mental degradation that accompanies ageing has resulted in the popular construction of the process of ageing as well as the aged in negative terms. Ageing is represented in many cultures as the dulling of the emotions and hardening of perspectives. It is seen as the moment when the individual becomes unreceptive to new ideas and when change is consequently impossible. Thus both the aged and the colonized constitute categories of cultural constructs. As a consequence, just as postcolonial studies critiques Eurocentrism, so too is ageing studies a critique of ageism, the stereotyping of the ageing process and the aged. Both approaches question such popular consciousness by resisting such stereotypes. They are both engaged with the unthinking and displacing of the untruths inherent in cultural and social representations.

John Marx has noted of postcolonial writing as follows: "First, postcolonial writing is held to repudiate the canon. [...]. Second, postcolonial literature has been shown to revise canonical texts and concepts" (2004: 83). Marx's proposition here underlines two important aspects that I evoked in the formulation of postcolonial gerontology and these are 'repudiation' and 'revision'. I do not limit the idea of repudiation here to just the Western conception of the colonized but extend it to cover the process of rejecting as well the Western approach to ageing studies. Therefore, the repudiation and revision here call to mind a reworking or indeed the decolonization of ageing studies. It is no doubt that before now ageing studies have focused on the Western experience and so the postcolonial perspective comes in to serve as a check towards the universalizing or generalizing of this experience. The postcolonial approach infuses into ageing studies the vexed questions of racism, Eurocentrism, anthropocentrism, speciesism and sexism; while, concomitantly, ageing studies brings to postcolonial studies the question of ageing in a colonized land or ageing as a colonized individual or as a colonizer. This is the essence of postcolonial gerontology.

Coetzee's texts underline the idea that ageing in the postcolony far from being a process of moral degeneration is rather a time of awakening to moral consciousness. The transition from passivity to active resistance is a highly politically charged move that dislodges the belief that all there is to ageing is frailty. These novels underline the notion that physical frailty does not serve as an impediment to political engagement for the right reasons. This political commitment emphasizes the postcolonial dimension to ageing in Coetzee's texts. Both protagonists, Mrs Curren and Elizabeth Costello, reach out to and stand up for the downtrodden of their societies. Mrs Curren defends the outcasts and blacks who are the victims of the Apartheid system and Costello defends the rights of animals which are victims of human cruelty. They both rise up to the injustices and brutality of their societies even as they are faced with the spectra of ageing, frailty, sickness and death. Their activism debunks the consideration of old age as a period of helplessness and dependence. Thus in coming to terms with the untruths of the society and adopting a subversive stance, they legitimate Diana Wallace's view that "even in frail old age, there is the possibility of an opening up to life" (2011: 394). No doubt, even though she is faced with approaching death, Mrs Curren still expresses her love for life when she declares "Yet this first life, this life on earth, on the body of the earth – will there, can there ever be a better? Despite all the glooms and despairs and rages, I have not let go of my love of it" (Coetzee 1990: 13). Given the inevitability and imminence of her death, Mrs Curren still expresses this love for life which she manifests through the love she shows for the lives of others. She writes thus to her daughter:

The first task laid on me, from today: to resist the craving to share my death. Loving you, loving life, to forgive the living and take my leave without bitterness. To embrace death as my own, mine alone. (Coetzee 1990: 6)

Even in her sickness, she refuses to burden anyone but is ready to face death unaccompanied, yet she shares her love not only with her daughter but with the outcasts and downtrodden of her society.

CONCLUSION

Coetzee indicates that the ageing process can actually constitute a time of moral ripening where the ageing character has a rich stock of experiences from which to draw and come to terms with certain realities in the society. The later years of life have the benefit of these experiences which make greater room for informed positions on many issues. Within postcolonialism, recognizing the crimes of the oppressor and resisting them constitute important moral positions. Therefore, both gerontology and postcolonialism are critically involved in interrogating processes that hierarchize the world. The conflation of the concerns of ageing studies and postcolonial studies may be a good beginning of discussions on postcolonial gerontology.

In postcolonial societies, the question at stake is not only the othering of the aged but more importantly the relationship between this ageing process and the larger questions of colonialism. In this study, I have focused especially on the ageing of privileged individuals who nevertheless are discontented with the injustices of their respective societies whether these affect them or not. It has serious implications for perceptions of the aged as unbending, and unaccepting of new ideas, cultures or peoples. What we find in our texts are individuals who refuse the general flow and adopt "risky" postures faced with the excesses and abuses of systems of domination. The postcolonial gerontology which I propose here therefore is one which critically studies the nexus between colonialism and ageing. Such a perspective is beneficial in deconstructing some of the long held myths about old age and ageing. Through this approach, the ageing process is addressed not only in terms of frailty, sickness and death but also in terms of moral renewal and the maturing of what Coetzee terms the "sympathetic imagination". This confirms Wallace's view that "work on representations of age and ageing can continue to draw strength from its interdisciplinarity" (2011: 410), and this same assertion holds true for postcolonial studies. Thus, in thinking about ageing in the postcolonial context, certain questions seek answers such as: what has one learned and unlearned?, what versions of truth has one imbibed and accepted and which others has one rejected and fought against? It is in answering these questions that I have read Coetzee's two novels as portraying the different possibilities of old age and ageing.

Bibliography

Ashcroft, Bill/ Griffiths, Gareth/ Tiffin, Helen (2007): *Postcolonial Studies: The Key Concepts*, London: Routledge.

Ashcroft, Bill/ Griffiths, Gareth/ Tiffin, Helen (eds) (2000): *The Postcolonial Studies Reader Second Edition*, London: Routledge.

Bhabha, Homi K (1994): *The Location of Culture*, London: Routledge Classics.

Coetzee, J.M (2004): *Elizabeth Costello*, London: Vintage Books.

Coetzee, J.M. (1990): *Age of Iron*. London: Penguin Books.

Gullette, Margaret Morganoth (2015): "Aged by Culture" in Julia Twigg and Wendy Martin (eds). *Routledge Handbook of Cultural Gerontology*, London: Routledge, pp. 21-28.

Gullette, Margaret Morganoth (2004): *Aged by Culture*, Chicago: The University of Chicago Press.

Marx, John (2004): "Postcolonial Literature and the Western Literary Canon" In: Neil Lazarus (ed) *The Cambridge Companion to Postcolonial Literary Studies*, Cambridge: CUP, pp. 83-96.

Twigg Julia and Martin Wendy (eds) (2015): *Routledge Handbook of Cultural Gerontology*, London: Routledge.

Wallace, Diana (2011): "Life Writing: auto/biography, Memory and Reminiscence." In: Ian Stuart-Hamilton (ed). *An Introduction to Gerontology*, Cambridge: CUP, pp. 389-415.

Worsfold, Brian J. (ed) (2011): *Acculturating Age: Approaches to Cultural Gerontology*, Lleida: Edicions de la Universitat de Lleida.

Zeiling Hannah (2011): "The Critical Use of Narrative and Literature in Gerontology." In: *International Journal of Aging and Later Life* 6/2, pp. 7-37.

Imagi(ni)ng Ageing: Old Women in J.M. Coetzee and Virginia Woolf
Mrs Curren and Mrs Dalloway

CARMEN CONCILIO, UNIVERSITY OF TURIN

INTRODUCTION

In an exchange between Italo Calvino and Umberto Eco, Calvino wrote a dedication to the theorist that reads "To Umberto, *superior stabat lector, longeque inferior* Italo Calvino." The critic and semiotician claims that, if taken literally, the dedication "was making a major statement and was paying homage to the role of the reader"; if not, it was meant to be ironic (Eco 1995: 2).

Similarly, William Golding unleashed the reader's power, when he wrote "I no longer believe that the author has a sort of *patria potestas* over his brainchildren. Once they are printed they have reached their majority and the author has no more authority over them, knows no more about them, perhaps knows less about them than the critic who comes fresh to them, and sees them not as the author hoped they would be, but as what they are" (Golding 1965: 100).

Relying on this potentiality for the reader – that Calvino was undoubtedly echoing from Roland Barthes's idea of the death of the author and the birth of the reader (Barthes 1967) – I would like to appeal to Julia Kristeva's principle of intertextuality, in order to propose a comparative reading of J.M. Coetzee's *Age of Iron* (1990) and of Virginia Woolf's *Mrs Dalloway* (1925). This intertextuality is not explicit in J.M. Coetzee, who has not made reference to that novel in his text. Rather, he has hardly ever mentioned Virginia Woolf in his writings, nor has he dedicated critical comments to her works. Therefore, it might be possible to refer to Michel Riffaterre's concept of 'aleatory intertextuality', one that allows him to further claim that "the only requisite for [reading] may be a presupposition of intertext" (Riffaterre 1990: 26). In this essay, I feel I am in the position of a reader who is alert to the presence (however hidden) in the text of a foreign body which is the trace of an intertext. What follows is a reading of J.M. Coetzee's character of Mrs Curren through intertextual references to Virginia Woolf's women in *Mrs Dalloway*. The latter is not obviously a source-text, but rather live matter: absorbed, inherited, and transposed by a writer who inhabits the culture of letters of our World. 'Viscosity' is the euristic tool that, according to semiologist Cesare Segre, helps detect relations between texts. The intertextual game, no matter how loose references might be, is an aspect of that viscosity (Segre 1984: 109-110).

To begin with, one must admit that the most Woolfian character in all of Coetzee's fiction is Magda (*In the Heart of the Country* 1977). Magda claims she inhabits a green room: "My room, in the emerald semi-dark of the shuttered late afternoon" (Coetzee 1977: 1). We know from biographies, and particularly from the lately published volume *Virginia Woolf's Garden* (2013), that Virginia Woolf had painted her dining room at Monk's house green, where she created an atmosphere of submarine light. Woolf painted it in a lively green colour, Veronese green. Her sister, Vanessa Bell, and Duncan Grant used to pull her legs for that. Green was her favourite colour, and Monk's House reverberated with it. In the sunny afternoons, the green creepers at the windows cast their shadows on the patches of sun on the walls. It looked like being in a submarine cave (Zoob/Arber 2013: 32).

Moreover, Magda looks at airplanes writing words in the air, – to which she answers by writing words piling white stones in the desert: "The voices speak to me out of machines that fly in the sky. They speak to me in Spanish." "Forming the stones into letters twelve feet high I began to spell out messages to my saviours: CINDRLA ES MI; and the next day: VENE AL TERRA; and QUIERO UN AUTR; and again SON ISOLADO." (Coetzee 1977: 126; 132) This is certainly and openly reminiscent of Septimus Warren Smith and Mrs Dalloway watching an airplane's acrobatic writing in smoke in the sky, advertising candies:

The sound of an airplane bore ominously into the ears of the crowd. There it was coming over the trees, letting out whitesmoke from behind, which curled and twisted, actually writing something! Marking letters in the sky! Everyone looked up. [...] But what letters? A C was it? an E, then an L? [...] the airplane shot further away and again, in a fresh space of sky, began writing a K, an E, a Y perhaps?". (Woolf 1992: 22)

All this shows that somehow Woolf was at the back of Coetzee's mind while forging the character of Magda.

OLD WOMEN IN J.M. COETZEE AND VIRGINIA WOOLF

"'I love walking in London,' said Mrs Dalloway." (Woolf 1992: 6) Scholars have acknowledged how Virginia Woolf created the groundbreaking figure of a *flâneuse* in *Mrs Dalloway*. "I am hungry with love of this world" (Coetzee 1990: 18) – says Mrs Curren, protagonist of J.M. Coetzee's *Age of Iron*, while contemplating False Bay from her car. The same love for their city and its landscapes moves the two women, the same love for life. Coetzee's protagonist, aged 70, crosses and maps the city of Cape Town for readers, as Clarissa Dalloway did, aged 51, with Central London in Virginia Woolf's novel.

LOVE FOR LIFE. "For Heaven only knows why one loves it so." (Woolf 1992: 4) Life is the object of this love, this *élan vital* that characterizes Mrs Dalloway. Similarly, Mrs Curren immediately resorts to affirming her love for life, as a reaction to her condition: "To live! You are my life; I love you as I love life itself." (Coetzee 1990: 6) Mrs Curren's love for life is declared through a metonym, the love for her far away, self-exiled daughter: "Loving you, loving life, to forgive the living and take my leave without bitterness. To embrace death as my own, mine alone." (Coetzee 1990: 6)

David Attwell suggests that "while Coetzee's work is intellectually anchored in the cultural metropoles of Europe and the United States, it also belongs to a regional literature whose canons are barely known outside South Africa" (Attwell 2015: xxii). Mrs Curren becomes the suturing figure between the European tradition of flânery – although re-adapted, – and the insider's knowledge of Cape Town that we – as western readers – only acquire through her gaze. We can say that Mrs Curren flags the city of Cape Town on our map of World Literature.

As a homage to J.M. Coetzee's chiastic style in *Age of Iron*, a style that has been exhaustively delved into in the essay "Cruciform Logic ... " by Johan Jacobs (2009), and with a leap of the imagination that in David Attwell's words might be defined a "quantum leap", I would claim (borrowing one of Coetzee's favourite linguistic 'tic')[1] that Mrs Curren *is and is not* Mrs Dalloway. A woman set loose on the streets of Cape Town as her predecessor was unleashed on the streets of London.

Besides being a *flâneuse* like Mrs Dalloway, Mrs Curren has absorbed some of her traits. In spite of the obvious macroscopic differences between the two novels, their characters, their time and setting, and their authors, I would concentrate on some affinities, echoes, suggestions that connect the two literary masterpieces and their female heroines.

Old age, illness, life and death, love for life and for a city, derelicts, and above all war coalesce in Virginia Woolf's dense pages of *Mrs Dalloway*. All these same topics inundate the pages of J.M. Coetzee's *Age of Iron* and the life of Mrs Curren.

OLD AGE. In spite of Mrs Curren being older than Mrs Dalloway, and her illness being more serious, it is worth noticing how the two women measure their ageing through the gaze of men.

In her first appearance along the street Clarissa Dalloway looks like: "A charming woman, Scrope Purvis thought her [...] a touch of the bird about her, of the jay, blue-green, light, vivacious, though she was over fifty, and grown very white since her illness. There she perched, never seeing him, waiting to cross, very upright." (Woolf 1992: 4)

Similarly, once back home, Mrs Curren finds a man laying in her garden, watching her from his position: "He did not stir [...] inspecting the winter stockings, the blue coat, the skirt with whose hang there has always been something wrong, the grey hair cut by a strip of scalp, old woman's scalp, pink, babyish." (Coetzee 1990: 4)

---

1   Johan Jacobs explains Coetzee's "familiar stylistic 'tic': a predilection for doubling meaning through reflection." (Jacobs 2009: 15)

Moreover, Mrs Dalloway tries to imagine her friend Peter Walsh asking himself whether she had grown older: "It was true. Since her illness she had turned almost white." (Woolf 1992: 39) But then Peter Walsh remembers: "She has been ill, and the sound expressed languor and suffering. It was her heart, he remembered; and the sudden loudness of the final stroke tolled for death that surprised in the midst of life, Clarissa falling where she stood, in her drawing-room. No! No! he cried. She is not dead! I am not old, he cried." (Woolf 1992: 55) Mrs Dalloway "felt very young; at the same time unspeakably aged." (Woolf 1992: 8) While Mrs Curren complains and instructs:

What do I care for this body that has betrayed me? I look at my hand and see only a tool, a hook, a thing for gripping other things. And these legs, these clumsy, ugly stilts: why would I have to carry them with me everywhere? (Coetzee 1990: 12)

ILLNESS. "She was over fifty, and grown very white since her illness." After a few steps in Westminster, there she is, Mrs Dalloway, feeling silence, suspense, solemnity around her "(but that might be her heart, affected, they said, by influenza)" (Woolf 1992: 4).

Mrs Dalloway has been ill, the mark of her illness is in her white hair. Her illness remains unnamed for a while, till it shapes itself realistically into menopause accompanied by a weakness of the heart. Fictionally, however, her illness is more ungraspable, it is a sort of existential malaise.

In her essay *Illness as Metaphor* (1978), Susan Sontag claims that from the 1920s cancer replaced TB and inherited most of its metaphorical apparatus:

The fantasies inspired by TB in the last century, by cancer now, are responses to a disease thought to be intractable and capricious – that is, a disease not understood – in an era in which medicine's central premise is that all disease can be cured. Such a disease is, by definition, mysterious. (Sontag 1978: 5)

Mrs Curren inhabits the late twentieth century and her illness takes the shape of cancer in her old age, marked by "the grey hair cut by a strip of scalp, old woman's scalp" (Coetzee 1990: 4).

Moreover, Susan Sontag goes on saying that cancer immediately becomes synonymous with death: "as today in popular imagination, cancer equals death." (Sontag 1978: 7)

This was the day when I had the news from Dr Syfret. The news was not good, but it was mine, for me, mine only, for me, mine only, not to be refused. It was for me to take in my arms and fold to my chest and take home, without headshaking, without tears. "Thank you for being frank." "We will do everything we can," he said, "we will tackle this together." But already, behind the comradely front, I could see he was withdrawing. *Sauve qui peut.* His allegiance to the living, not the dying. (Coetzee 1990: 4)

Mrs Curren's illness is therefore not less mysterious than Mrs Dalloway's. Both women are vulnerable and fragile to a certain extent, but they also share a certain rigidity, straightforwardness, and uprightness: "She was like iron, like flint, rigid up the backbone" (Woolf 1992: 70), says Peter Walsh of Clarissa Dalloway, remembering the moment she refused his marriage proposal. "You are like iron too," (Coetzee 1990: 75) says Vercueil to Mrs Curren, who refuses to call back her daughter. "If I were made of iron, surely I would not break so easily," (Coetzee 1990: 75) Mrs Curren replies.

If Mrs Curren's first appearance to Mr Vercueil's eyes is characterised by her uneven skirt: "the skirt with whose hang there has always been something wrong" (Coetzee 1990: 4), the skirt that has to be mended is a gender mark, for it recurs in Woolf's novel, too. First, Mrs Dalloway is portrayed while mending her own skirt:

Clarissa, plunging her hand into the softness, gently detached the green dress and carried it to the window. She had torn it. Some one had trod on the skirt. [...] She would mend it.
Quiet descended on her, calm, content, as her needle, drawing the silk smoothly to its gentle pause, collected the green folds together and attached them, very lightly, to the belt. So on a summer's day waves collect, overbalance, and fall; collect and fall. (Woolf 1992: 41-43)

Later on Peter Walsh, who had interrupted Clarissa Dalloway in her sewing, notices how "the battered woman – for she wore a skirt – with her right hand exposed, her left hand clutching at her side, stood singing of love" (Woolf 1992: 89).

DERELICTS. As soon as Mrs Dalloway crosses Victoria Street she exclaims within herself:

For Heaven only knows why one loves it so, how one sees it so, making it up, building it round one, tumbling it, creating it every moment afresh; but the veriest frumps, the most dejected of miseries sitting on doorsteps (drink their downfall) do the same; can't be dealt with, she felt positive, by Acts of Parliament for that very reason: they love life. (Woolf 1992: 4)

This imagery, this icon, allows another leap of the imagination straight unto Mrs Curren's encounter with Vercueil, a homeless and alcoholic, taking shelter – if not too literally on her doorstep – in her own private garden:

There is an alley down the side of the garage [...] Yesterday at the end of this alley, I came upon a house of carton boxes and plastic sheeting and a man curled up inside [...] a derelict, one of the derelicts who hang around the parking lots on Mill Street, cadging money from shoppers, drinking under the overpass, eating out of refuse cans. (Coetzee 1990: 4)

Although the resonance between "dejected" and "derelict" is certainly not enough to justify a comparison between Mrs Dalloway's early twentieth century condition and Mrs Curren's reality in the Nineties, both heroines encounter a woman beggar. Woolf first provides a gendered portrait of derelicts in the figure of a female beggar at Regent's Park Tube Station. At first she is just a voice, almost inhumane: "a frail quivering sound, a voice bubbling [...] running weakly and shrilly and with an absence of all human meaning [...] the voice of no age or sex, the voice of an ancient spring sprouting from the earth." (Woolf 1992: 88) Only later she becomes "the battered woman – for she wore a skirt – with her right hand exposed, her left clutching at her side, stood singing of love." (Woolf 1992: 89) Subsequently, Peter Walsh "couldn't help giving the poor creature a coin as he stepped into his taxi." (Woolf 1992: 90) This beggar woman seems to incarnate the traditional literary figure of the old crone.

Similarly, Mrs Curren has to experience such an encounter in her own dining room, where Vercueil enters with a woman friend: "I saw that someone had followed him in. It was a woman, small, no higher than my shoulder, but old, or at least not young, with a leering, bloated face and livid skin." (Coetzee 1990: 56) Mrs Curren's only thought is to send her out of her house, and she even asks Florence to help her physically push the vagrant out. As a response, the woman produces "a rambling stream of obscenity," "in a hoarse voice" (Coetzee 1990: 59) that resembles the voice of Woolf's beggar singer. Mrs Curren's resorting to an uncharitable gestures in this case, as opposite to Peter Walsh's gesture of piety, is balanced by her own becoming a sort of homeless person, towards the end of the novel, when she is driven out of her house after a Police raid and she is compelled to sleep in a public park, side by side with Vercueil:

In Buitenkant Street, under the overpass, I sat down to rest. A steady stream of cars flowed past, heading for the city. [...] With my wild hair and pink quilt I might be a spectacle on Shoonder Street; here, amid the rabble and filth, I was just part of the urban shadowland. [...]
I wrapped myself tighter in the quilt and lay down. When I opened my eyes there was a child kneeling beside me, feeling inside the folds of the quilt. His hand crept over my body. [...]
Then something was sniffing at my face: a dog. [...] Was it Vercuil? [...] Everything grew remote: the smell of damp earth, the cold, the man beside me, my own body. [...] I lay face to face with him. (Coetzee 1990: 162)

LOST DAUGHTERS. Both Mrs Dalloway and Mrs Curren have daughters who are detached from them, almost lost, though in different ways and with more dramatic consequences for Mrs Curren. The first hint at Mrs Dalloway's daughter is between brackets: "(but one must economise, not buy things rashly for Elizabeth)." (Woolf 1992: 5) Post-war London and its almost empty shop windows impose a certain austerity, and Elizabeth, differently from her mother, seems not to appreciate luxury items. While the mother had a passion for gloves and shoes, "her own daughter, her Elizabeth, cared not a straw for neither of them" (Woolf 1992: 12).

However, the real distance between mother and daughter is due to the girl's infatuation for Miss Kilman, the Irish, catholic tutor in History, who has taken control of her life: "They were inseparable, and Elizabeth, her own daughter went to Communion; and how she dressed, how she treated people who came to lunch she did not care a bit ... ." (Woolf 1992: 12)

Quite differently, and yet similarly, Mrs Curren's daughter is painfully and inexorably absent from her life. It is to her that Mrs Curren is writing the long letter which is the novel itself:

> How I longed for you to be here, to hold me! I begin to understand the true meaning of the embrace. We embrace to be embraced. We embrace our children to be folded in the arms of the future, to pass ourselves on beyond death, to be transported.
> To whom this writing then? The answer: to you but not to you; to me; to you in me. (Coetzee 1990: 5-6)

The addressee of Mrs Curren's letter is also the object of this feeling of longing: her own daughter. Later on in the novel Mrs Curren explains to Mr Vercuil: "I have a daughter in America. She left in 1976 and hasn't come back. She is married to an American. They have two children of their own." (Coetzee 1990: 11) Distance, anyway, is not the real matter: the aggravating factor is political and ideological, for the daughter had left the country right after the Soweto uprising and had sworn never to come back "until the current rulers are swinging from the lamposts" (Atwell 2015: 148). Mrs Dalloway misses her daughter Elizabeth too, but her rage goes against Miss Killman.

In Woolf's novel, Mrs Dalloway's daughter hardly ever stays in the same room with her mother. When Peter Walsh is visiting, she just enters the room to say hello and immediately disappears. In the evening, during the party as soon as Elizabeth makes her splendid appearance her mother dramatically and unnoticed leaves the room. In Coetzee's novel, the daughter lives in another continent and Mrs Curren longs to fly to her as a butterfly or as a spirit after death.

MOTHER'S BODIES. The body can become an incarnated metaphor of femininity, a corpo-real emblem of humanity. Both Mrs Dalloway and Mrs Curren are conscious of their body to the extreme, of their life and death too:

Did it matter then, she asked herself, walking towards Bond Street, did it matter that she must inevitably cease completely; all this must go without her; did she resent it; or did it not become consoling to believe that death ended absolutely?
But often now this body she wore (she stopped to look at a Dutch picture), this body, with all its capacities, seemed nothing – nothing at all. She had the oddest sense of being herself invisible; unseen; unknown; there being no more marrying, no more having of children now. (Coetzee 1990: 9; 11)

Like Mrs Dalloway, Mrs Curren has passed the bridal and maternal age. She is conscious of her ill and decaying body:

Out of their withered bodies even the old try to squeeze one last drop. A stubborn will to give, to nourish. Shrewd was death's aim when he chose my breast for his first shaft.
What do I care for this body that has betrayed me? I look at my hand and see only a tool, a hook, a thing for gripping other things. [...] we sicken before we die so that we will be weaned from our body. The milk that nourished us grows thin and sour; turning away from the breast, we begin to be restless for a separate life. Yet this first life, this life on earth, on the body of earth – will there, can there ever be a better one? Despite all the glooms and despairs and rages, I have not let go of my love of it. (Coetzee 1990: 8; 13)

Life and death, love for life and acceptance of death are common themes in the two novels and common concerns for the two women. To Mrs Dalloway's metaphor of life as being out at sea, adrift: "She had the perpetual sense, as she watched the taxi cabs, of being out, out, far out to sea and alone" (Woolf 1992: 9), answers Mrs Curren's comparing life in South Africa to a sinking boat: "since life in this country is so much like life aboard a sinking ship, one of those old-time liners with a lugubrious, drunken captain and a surly crew and leaky lifeboats." (Coetzee 1990: 22-23) Yet, this seems an echo of Mrs Dalloway: "As we are a doomed race, chained to a sinking ship" (Woolf 1992: 85). Also, "Yet how hard it is to sever oneself from the living touch, from all the touches that unite us with the living! Like a steamer pulling away from the quay, the ribbons tightening, snapping, falling away." (Coetzee 1990: 73) And, once again, Mrs Dalloway: "all this fever of living [...] hard risen from the troubled sea." (Woolf 1992: 63)

Sea and air are two overwhelming elements in both novels: causing strong emotions of nostalgia, longing and melancholia. Mrs Curren provides an example:

In the mornings I come out of the house and wet my finger and hold it up to the wind. When the chill is from northwest, from your quarter, I stand a long time sniffing, concentrating my attention in the hope that across the thousand miles of land and sea some breath will reach me of the milkiness you still carry with you behind your ears, in the fold of your neck. (Coetzee 1990: 6)

This image of a woman sensing the wind, like a diviner, as a child would do, again quite loosely echoes Woolf's novel. Air, in the form of breeze, or solidified into mist, is not only the subject matter in the first two pages of Woolf's novel, but more literally, it makes birds and things float up and down, as a leitmotif: "Being laid out like a mist between the people she knew best, who lifted her on their branches as she had seen the trees lift the mist, but it spread ever so far, her life, herself." (Woolf 1992: 10)

In this passage the reference to the mist points back to the very opening of the novel where air was the protagonist: "How fresh, how calm, stiller than this of course, the air was in the early morning; like the flap of a wave; the kiss of a wave; chill and sharp and yet (for a girl of eighteen as she then was) solemn, feeling as she did, standing there at the open window [...] looking at the flowers, at the trees with the smoke winding off them and the rooks rising, falling." (Woolf 1992: 3)

THE BURDEN OF HISTORY. Woolf keeps on writing about Mrs Dalloway: "somehow in the streets of London, on the ebb and flow of things, here, there she survived, she being part, she was positive, of the trees at home; of the house there." (Woolf 1992: 9)

Thus, Mrs Dalloway is part of life itself, but she is also part of History. She knows only too well that post-war life in London is moulded by History: "This late age of the world's experience had bred in them all, all men and women, a well of tears. Tears and sorrows; courage and endurance, a perfectly upright and stoical bearing." (Woolf 1992: 10)

Mrs Dalloway "being part of the trees at home", but also "made into a well of tears" seems to match David Attwell's view of Coetzee's life in South Africa: "Deformation. [...] life as deformed, year after year, by

South Africa. Emblem: the deformed trees on the golf links in Simonstown." (Attwell 2015: 4) Also Mike Marais's essay "From the Standpoint of Redemption. *Age of Iron*" (2009: 95-128), insists on this same metaphor of a State that "deforms" the life of its citizens as related to *Age of Iron*.

Definitely, *Age of Iron* is a novel about mothers. Mrs Curren is a mother, and creates herself in words as connected to her beloved daughter and as ready to reach and re-join her dead mother. Florence, her black servant is also a mother of three children, envisioned in a dream as a new Amazon trailing towards the future hand in hand with her two daughters, Hope and Beauty, as an allegorical auspice for the new South Africa. David Attwell alludes to Coetzee's own mother as a possible model for Mrs Curren. He writes:

> there is Coetzee's own shrewd sense that the female narrator is a strategic way of positioning oneself on the margins of authoritative traditions. The assertively feminine position in Coetzee's writing is at times a proxy for a self-staging that has little to do with gender. Nevertheless, Vera's perseverance would have shown the way. (Attwell 2015, 142)

After trying to persuade a black boy injured by policemen and now lying in hospital, Mrs Curren – being an old woman – is highly self-conscious of her marginal position and voice: "My words fell off him like dead leaves the moment they were uttered. The words of a woman, therefore negligible; of an old woman, therefore doubly negligible; but above all of a white." (Coetzee 1990: 79)

Yet, the kind of self-trial Mrs Curren submits herself to is the same trial Coetzee imagines in order to present her with a verdict of innocence at the court of History. David Atwell writes: "Vera [Vehmeyer]'s death revived the problem of historical guilt." Then, quoting Coetzee, he adds: "It [the novel] must be about innocence. Historical innocence. How my mother, belonging to her generation in SA, was nevertheless innocent." (Attwell 2015: 144)

Mrs Curren seems to face the same dilemma, when she claims with the help of Thucydides:

I, a white. When I think of the whites, what do I see? I see a herd of sheep (not a flock: a herd) milling around on a dusty plain under the baking sun. I hear a drumming of hooves, a confusion of sound that resolves itself, when the ear grows attuned, into the same bleating call in a thousand different inflections: "I!" "I!" "I!" [...] A word of protest: I, the exception. "Were they exceptions? The truth is, given time to speak, we would all claim to be exceptions. For each of us there is a case to be made. We all deserve the benefit of the doubt. (Coetzee 1990: 79-81)

"If ever history were to become everything, we would all succumb to madness", claims Robert Pogue Harrison. Luckily we have "our religious impulses, our poetic and utopian imagination, our moral ideals, our metaphysical projections, our storytelling, our aesthetic transfigurations of the real, our passion for games, our delight in nature", he adds (Harrison 2008: ix). Our novels with their own aesthetic and ethical views provide an alternative, a correction to history, or "of rivalry with it", says Dominique Head (2009: xi).

IMAGES OF WOMEN'S GIFTS. Both Mrs Curren and Mrs Dalloway provide similar images for gifts exchanged among women, to the point of creating a sort of gender bias in the discourse on gifts. Mrs Curren imagines her long letter as a gift of words to her daughter:

Day by day I render myself into words and pack the words into the page like sweets: like sweets for my daughter, for her birthday, for the day of her birth. Words out of my body, drops of myself, for her to unpack in her own time, to take in, to suck, to absorb. As they say on the bottle: old-fashioned drops, drops fashioned by the old, fashioned and packed with love, the love we have no alternative but to feel toward those to whom we give ourselves to devour or discard. (Coetzee 1990: 9)

In the quoted passage, Mrs Curren is speaking of a gift, a gift from a mother to a daughter, made of words, in fact, a letter to be sent to destination after her death. The semantic chain "words-sweets-drops" and "to take in-to suck-to absorb" evoke the metaphor of maternal nourishing. Moreover, words in spite of being immaterial, either written or pronounced, here become corpo-real, they come from a body, they speak of that body (illness) and must be swallowed, digested, metabolized by another body.

The nerve of the style of Woolf seems to pass to the lips of Mrs Curren: this gift from mother to daughter, this act of nourishment and communion echoes the gift that Sally Seton gave to Clarissa, when they were young:

Then came the most exquisite moment of her whole life passing a stone urn with flowers in it. Sally stopped; picked a flower; kissed her on the lips. The whole world might have turned upside down! The others disappeared; there she was alone with Sally. And she felt that she had been given a present, wrapped up and told just to keep it, not to look at it – a diamond, something infinitely precious, wrapped up, which, as they walked (up and down, up and down) she uncovered, or the radiance burnt through, the revelation, the religious feeling. (Woolf 1992: 39)

The kiss here becomes a present from a woman to another woman. The idea of a present of love and words packed and unpacked is substituted by a kiss wrapped up and then uncovered. Again, the lexical shift is too fragile to allow a comparison and nevertheless Mrs Curren seems to speak as if under the spell of that ground-braking Modernist female predecessor. Finally, to "pack the words into the pages like sweets" echoes a Woolfian predilection for such a simile, as in the portrait of the nurses chatting among themselves, in *Between the Acts* (1941): "rolling words like sweets on their tongues." (Woolf 2012: 310)

STYLE. And, then, how similar is the idea of something consigned and kept almost inexorably by the two women: news about incurable illness and a gift of love! Let us compare the two pronouncements!

The news was not good, but it was mine, for me, mine only, for me, mine only, not to be refused. It was for me to take in my arms and fold to my chest and take home, without headshaking, without tears. (Coetzee 1990: 4)
And she felt that she had been given a present, wrapped up and told just to keep it, not to look at it. (Woolf 1992: 39)

If lexicon is not proof enough of a lesson learned from Modernist female speech and thought, it is interesting to notice that Mr Dalloway's interior monologue is characterized by a consistently frequent use of brackets. Mrs Curren has the same intimacy and intimation to what might be considered "asides": complicit, clarifying, almost theatrical augmented meaning for the reader.

With Woolf the parentheses are like asides, almost theatrical. Parentheses have various functions. First, they add meanings and missing pieces of information: "How fresh, how calm, stiller than this of course, the air was in the early morning; like the flap of a wave; the kiss of a wave; chill and sharp and yet (for a girl of eighteen as she than was) solemn (for a girl of eighteen as she then was)" (Woolf 1992: 3), as for instance the precise age of Clarissa, when she used to go to the seaside, at Burton.

The piece of information added in brackets is something the reader did not know and is told as an indirect confession, a piece of news broken almost secretly and in a whisper as if to the ear. When Mrs Curren describes the shelter of cardboard boxes and plastic sheets made by Vercueil, she mentions that "he produced a bag (AIR CANADA, it said) and zipped it shut" (Coetzee 1990: 5). Similarly, she describes his dog: "Why do I give this man food? For the same reason I would feed his dog (stolen, I am sure) if it came begging." (Coetzee 1990: 7)

These asides characterize the type of mental speech that the stream of consciousness produces, it is another way of talking to oneself. Yet, when Mrs Curren explains her habit of standing in front of the TV when watching the news, she adds in brackets – not to herself but to the benefit of her daughter, the addressee of her letter – "(who would choose to face a firing squad sitting down?)". (Coetzee 1990: 11) The implied reader in Mrs Dalloway, to whom the parenthesis add meanings, easily identifies with Mrs Curren's daughter, in Coetzee's novel.

THE TEXT'S SPINE. If Coetzee's language is Woolfian, the architecture of his novel is doubly so. Scholars have debated the opposing symbolism behind Mrs Dalloway and Septimus Warren Smith. They respectively represent sanity and insanity, even though the borderline between the two categories is really thin.[2] They also represent the upper classes and the middle classes,

---

2 "By implicitly stating her intention to show that the definitions of sanity and insanity in the postwar years had been skewed and that their definition ("study") need be informed and altered, Woolf was postulating a relation between sanity and insanity that might only be appreciated by recognizing that the experience of survivors of the war (whether combatants or non combatants) could lead them

the female and the male sphere and the questioning of preconceived role models. J.M. Coetzee's novel also involves a man and a woman of quite different social *milieu*, the retired professor of classics Elizabeth Curren and the vagrant Mr Vercueil, yet both of them are disabled from the very beginning.

In *Mrs Dalloway* Woolf builds up a double structure, where two stories run parallel for a while, then meet and cross over at certain moments. If the meeting of Clarissa and Septimus happens roughly after ten pages for the reader, Mrs Curren encounters Vercueil in the very first page of the novel. The balancing of a female character and a male one provides a sort of DNA spine to the novel: structuring a dialogue and an opposition, a dialectic that is similar, for instance, to Shakespeare's *Antony and Cleopatra*, where a Roman general is paired to an Oriental queen, East and West are confronted, terrestrial and naval warfare, land and water, masculinity and femininity are explored. Maybe it is not a chance that *Antony and Cleopatra* is quoted four times by Septimus Warren Smith as one of his favourite readings, one that arouses his literary inspiration and possible talent.

WAR. In *Mrs Dalloway*, tragically, war affects mothers: "the War was over, except for some one like Mrs Foxcroft [...] eating her heart out because that nice boy was killed [...]; or Lady Bexborough who opened a bazaar, they said, with the telegram in her hand, John, her favourite, killed." (Woolf 1992: 5) Although War was over, its scars are everywhere. Postwar London is characterized by almost empty shop windows. Mothers are mourning their youths. Peter Walsh watches boys in uniform, carrying guns, who "marched with their eyes ahead of them, marched, their arms stiff [...] But they did not look robust. They were weedy for the most part, boys of sixteen" (Woolf 1992: 55).

If it is undeniable that "the distance between civilian and combatant experience is explored in *Mrs Dalloway* where in postwar London the reality of a politician's wife, Clarissa Dalloway [...] is juxtaposed with that of a combat veteran, Septimus Warren Smith," (Levenback 1999: 47) in Coetzee's novel the combatant is Mr Thabane. He is a black activist and

---

to despair (what Kierkegaard called 'the sickness unto death') and, possibly, suicide." (Levenback 1999: 46)

agitator, who by inciting the young black boys to (armed) action also justifies their death.

It is significant that when Thabane (black activism) is present, Vercueil (coloured idleness?) is absent. Moreover, Vercueil almost pushes Mrs Curren towards Thabane and the township of Guguletu, for he has to push her car to make a start in the middle of a rainy night. Consequently, Mrs Curren is plunged into the middle of a war of which she knows nothing:

Shooting in Guguletu: whatever Florence knows about it, whatever you know ten thousand miles away, I do not know. In the news that reaches me there is no mention of trouble, of shooting. The land that is presented to me is a land of smiling neighbours. (Coetzee 1990: 49)

Militancy costs the black boys their death, and they are just past their childhood. Thus, Mrs Curren is confronted with death on the front, something Clarissa Dalloway is spared:

The inside of the hall was a mess of rubble and charred beams. Against the far wall, shielded from the worst of the rain, were five bodies neatly laid out. The body in the middle was that of Florence's Bheki. (Coetzee 1990: 94)

Here the mother figure, Florence, is not disconnected from the scene of her son's death in the trenches or, better, the ditches, as Mrs Flanders is, in *Jacob's Room* (1922), for instance, or as are the two mothers in *Mrs Dalloway*. For the black community is subjected to apartheid's persecutions and therefore it is compelled to witness, and live through death, day by day. This happens in the 1980s, during the years of the Emergency. Mrs Curren acknowledges this as "this... this war" (Coetzee 1990: 95), fought with bullets "made in South Africa. SABS Approved" (ibid), says Mr Thabane. It is not enough for Mrs Curren to leave the scene, she cannot avoid being haunted by those deaths. Nor is Mrs Dalloway freed from war.

SUICIDE. The suicide(s) Mrs Curren often plans, imagines, and almost enacts, asking for the complicity of Mr Vercueil, as well as the growing shame she feels towards her country can only direct her to seek freedom in thoughts of death or even in death itself.

Vercueil drove me down Breda Street and into Orange Street. Across from Government Avenue I told him to park. "I thought of driving the car all the way down the Avenue," I said. "Once I am past the chain, I don't see how anyone can stop me. But do you think there is room to get past?" [...] I closed my eyes and tried to hold on to my vision of the car, moving fast enough for the flames to fan out backward, rolling down the paved avenue past the tourists and tramps and lovers, past the museum, the art gallery, the botanical gardens, till it slowed down and came to rest before the house of shame, burning and melting. (Coetzee 1990: 113)

As happens with war, Mrs Dalloway does experience suicide only indirectly:

What business had the Bradshows to talk of death at her party? A young man had killed himself. And they talked of it at her party – the Bradshows talked of death. He had killed himself – but how? Always her body went through it first, when she was told, suddenly, of an accident; her dress flamed, her body burnt. He had thrown himself from a window. Up had flashed the ground; through him, blundering, bruising, went the rusty spikes. There he lay with a thud, thud, thud in his brain, and then a suffocation of blackness. So she saw it. But why had he done it? And the Bradshows talked of it at her party! (Woolf 1992: 201-202)

When Mrs Dalloway learns of Septimus through a narrative about his suicide, right at her party, she immediately retreats to her upper room. She absents herself from her party to the point that Peter Walsh and Sally wonder where she might be. "There he lay with a thud, thud, thud in his brain, and then a suffocation of blackness. So she saw it. But why had he done it? And the Bradshows talked of it at her party!" (Woolf 1992: 201-202) Mrs Curren, too, wonders how one could commit suicide: "But how hard it is to kill oneself! One clings so tight to life! It seems to me that something other than the will must come into play at the last instant, something foreign, something thoughtless, to sweep you over the brink. You have to become someone other than yourself. (Coetzee 1990: 119)

Immediately after receiving the bad news, Mrs Dalloway goes to the window, she parts the curtains and looks out. As mesmerized, she watches an old lady who lives opposite. Perhaps, Mrs Curren is not Mrs Dalloway set loose in the streets of another town, in another time and age. She is rather the projection of that mysterious old lady, out of the pages of Woolf's novel:

Oh but how surprising! – in the room opposite the old lady stared straight at her! She was going to bed. And the sky. [...] It will be a solemn sky, she had thought, it will be a dusky sky, turning away its cheek in beauty. But there it was – ashen pale, raced over quickly by tapering vast clouds. She was going to bed, in the room opposite. It was fascinating to watch her, moving about, that old lady, crossing the room, coming to the window. Could she see her? It was fascinating, with people still laughing and shouting in the drawing-room, to watch that old woman, quite quietly, going to bed alone. She pulled the blind now. The clock began striking. [...] There! The old lady had put out her light! [...] She felt somehow very like him – the young man who had killed himself. (Woolf 1992: 204)

That old woman who had put out her light, almost her life, might be Mrs Curren in the very last scene of Coetzee's novel:

I slept and woke up cold: my belly, my heart, my very bones cold. The door to the balcony was open, the curtains were waving in the wind.
Vercueil stood on the balcony staring out over a sea of rustling leaves. I touched his arm, his high, peaked shoulders, the bony ridge of his spine. Through chattering teeth I spoke: 'What are you looking at?'
He did not answer. I stood closer. A sea of shadows beneath us, and the screen leaves shifting, rustling, like scales over the darkness.
'Is it time?' I said.
I got back into bed, into the tunnel between the cold sheets. The curtains parted; he came in beside me. For the first time I smelled nothing. He took me in his arms held me with mighty force, so that the breath went out of me in a rush. From that *embrace* there was no warmth to be had. (Coetzee 1990: 180; emphasis added)

Once again, lexically, Coetzee echoes Woolf. While Mrs Curren narrates the impossible: her own death, her own dying folded in an embrace, Mrs Dalloway imagines Septimus's suicide as an embrace by and in death:

Death was defiance. Death was an attempt to communicate, people feeling the impossibility of reaching the centre, which, mystically, evaded them; closeness drew apart; rapture faded; one was alone. There was an *embrace* in death. (Woolf 1992: 202, emphasis added)

Threre is one more way in which the two texts resonate. The old woman appears twice in Woolf's novel, always at bed time. Therefore, it is not surprising that the vision of this iconic figure ends with the Big Ben striking the hour, as if in an ominous toll ("The Big Ben struck the half-hour." 139; "The clock began striking." 204). Although Coetzee's novel is not exactly as experimental in terms of the treatment of time as Woolf is, Coetzee's heroin alternates vigils and sleep, confusing time and rendering difficult to follow the development of both chornology and seasons. Yet, Mrs Curren often asks for the exact time, or looks it up on her alarm clock, as if there were a right time for Death to come and visit.

If "Woolf transformed the physical distance during the war into a physical proximity during the day in postwar London" (Levenback 1999: 47), as previously mentioned, Coetzee chooses the absolute physical proximity between Mrs Curren and the Other, the dizzy, alcoholic Mr Vercueil, in death. Mrs Curren not only witnesses a civil war, the war of the black young activists against the police in the townships, but she also fights a private war against her own dying body:

It seems hardly possible to believe there is a zone of killing and degradation all around me. It seems like a bad dream. Something presses, nudges inside me. I try to take no notice, but it insists. (Coetzee 1990: 119)

Writing is a way of postponing death, while also leaving an ethical testament. From the very beginning of the novel, Vercueil is identified as an Angel of death, for his arrival coincides with a bitter parody of the "Annunciation": the bad news of her terminal illness.

Their fatal union, their last embrace, might be read as a grotesque visitation of the myth of Love and Psyche. Vercuil has variously been described as an Angel, with wings, though not jet visible: "a man [...] who does not yet know how to fly" (Coetzee 1990: 197). Moreover, he only appears in Mrs Curren's house after sunset and at night:

Not an angel, certainly. An insect, rather, emerging from the baseboards when the house is in darkness to forage for crumbs. [...] I heard him [...] I wanted to whisper to him [...] but the fog in my head closed in again.
I crossed to the window. It was nearly dark. Against the garage wall the man was squatting, smoking, the point of his cigarette glowing. Perhaps he saw me, perhaps not. Together we listened.
At this moment, I thought, I know how he feels as surely as if he and I were making love. (Coetzee 1990: 14; 30)

Mrs Curren is old and physically disabled, yet intellectually and morally so lucid as to fight for civil rights to the very end. All through the novel, Mrs Curren has described herself as a butterfly, as a soul ready to take her flight from the cocoon of her decaying body. Flight and ascension towards the sky, to join her own dead mother, are frequently referenced in the novel:

Like a moth from its case emerging, fanning its wings: that is what, reading, I hope you will glimpse: my soul readying itself for further flight. A white moth, a ghost emerging from the mouth of the figure on the deathbed. [...] All part of the metamorphosis, part of shaking myself loose from the dying envelope. [...]
The moth is simply what will brush your cheek ever so lightly as you put down the last page of this letter, before it flutters off on its next journey. (Coetzee 1990: 129-130)
This was never meant to be the story of a body, but of the soul it houses. [...] The soul, neophyte, we, blind, ignorant.
We share a bed, like two wings folded. (Coetzee 1990: 186; 189)

In both novels, *Mrs Dalloway* and *Age of Iron*, death lingers in the houses of the two women protagonists, but manifests itself more clearly in the outside world. The old woman observed by Mrs Dalloway at night, in Woolf's novel, slowly stepping upstairs, slowly getting into her bed, and blowing out the candle has no agency in the plot. On the contrary, Mrs Curren has an agency in Coetzee's work till the very end, she voices her dissent and dissident views in her long letter, she shouts against policemen and armed soldiers, she takes care of black boys in her house and goes visiting them in the hospital, she admits a vagrant into her house and life. However, both Woolf's old woman and Mrs Curren are described and represented with a slowing down of the narrative pace and in a sort of close-up, in their final act of accepting repose, both affected by time (the Big Ben striking the hour; Mrs Curren's questioning the right time) in unison with their only imminent death.

When Mrs Curren started instructing Vercuil on various subjects, she spoke to him about *caritas*, the Latin translation for the Greek word "agape", a form of love that is inclusive and not selfish, universal and not particular. Her relationship to him develops from repugnance to acceptation, to a form of love: "One must love what is nearest. One must love what is to hand, as a dog loves. Mrs V." (Coetzee 1990: 190) She learns to join him, descending down into his realm, under viaducts, in the streets, sleeping on the bare ground, before finally going back to her now destroyed house and bedroom, to exhale her last breath in his arms.

Mrs Dalloway empathically imagines herself in Septimus's death as well as in the old woman's final rest as if looking into a mirror. The clock inexorably, always strikes its leaden beats when the old woman is presented (Woolf 1992: 139; 204), as well as in the moment when Septimus jumps from his window (Woolf 1992: 149).

Bibliography

Allen, Graham (2000): *Textuality*, London: Routledge.
Attridge, Dereck (2004): "Trusting the Other. *Age of Iron.*" In: *J.M. Coetzee and the Ethics of Reading*, Chicago: University of Chicago Press, pp. 91-112.
Attwell, David (2015): *J.M. Coetzee and the Life of Writing. Face to Face with Time*, New York: Viking.
Barthes, Roland (1977). *Image – Music – Text*. Trans. Stephen Heath, London: Fontana.
Coetzee, J.M. (1977): *In the Heart of the Country*, London: Penguin.
―――― (1990): *Age of Iron*, Harmondsworth: Penguin.
Concilio, Carmen (2013): "Whose War? The Influence of Virginia Woolf's *Mrs Dalloway* on Some Postcolonial Writers." In: Lucia Folena (ed.), *La guerra e le armi nella letteratura in inglese del Novecento*, Turin: Trauben, pp. 83-98.
Durrant, Sam (2004): "Speeches before Apartheid: J.M. Coetzee's Inconsolable Works of Mourning." In: *Postcolonial Narrative and the*

Work of Mourning. J.M. Coetzee, Wilson Harris, and Toni Morrison, New York: State University of New York Press, pp. 23-52.

Eco, Umberto (1995): *Six Walks in the Fictional Woods*, Harvard: Harvard UP.

Ferreccio, Giuliana/Concilio, Carmen (2009): *J.M. Coetzee. Percorsi di lettura tra storia e narrazione*, Gorée: Siena.

Golding, William (1965): "Fable." In: *The Hot Gates and Other Occasional Pieces*, London: Faber and Faber, pp. 86-101.

Harrison, Robert Pogue (2008): *Gardening. An Essay on the Human Condition*, Chicago: University of Chicago Press.

Head, Dominique (2009): *The Cambridge Introduction to J.M. Coetzee*, Cambridge: Cambridge UP.

Huggan, Graham (1996): "Evolution and Entropy in J.M. Coetzee's *Age of Iron*." In: Graham Huggan/Stephen Watson (eds.), *Critical Perspectives on J.M. Coetzee*, London: Macmillan, pp. 191-212.

Jacobs, Johan U. (2009): "J.M. Coetzee and Cruciform Logic." In: Giuliana Ferreccio/Carmen Concilio (eds.), *J.M. Coetzee percorsi di lettura tra storia e narrazione*, Siena: Gorée, pp. 13-62.

Kossew, Sue (1994): "Writing as Political Intervention." In: *Pen and Power. A Post-Colonial Reading of J.M. Coetzee and André Brink*, Amsterdam: Rodopi, pp. 179-204.

Levenback, Karen (1999): *Virginia Woolf and the Great War*, Syracuse: Syracuse UP.

Marais, Mike (2009): "From the Standpoint of Redemption. *Age of Iron.*" In: *Secretary of the Invisible. The Idea of Hospitality in the Fiction of J.M. Coetzee*, Amsterdam: Rodopi, pp. 95-128.

Riffaterre, Michel (1990): "Syllepsis." *Critical Inquiry* 6:4, pp. 625-38.

Segre, Cesare (1984): "Intertestualità e interdiscorsività." In: *Teatro e romanzo*, Turin: Einaudi, pp. 103-118.

Walcowitz, Rebecca L. (2012): "For Translation: Virginia Woolf, J.M. Coetzee and Transnational Comparison." In: *The Legacies of Modernism. Historicizing Postwar and Contemporary Fiction*, Cambridge: Cambridge UP, pp. 243-263.

Wharton, Michael/Still, Judith eds. (1990): *Intertextualities: Theories and Practice*, Manchester: Manchester University Press.

Woolf, Virginia (1992 [1925]): *Mrs Dalloway*, Harmondsworth: Penguin.

_____ (2012 [1941]): *Between the Acts*, Hertfordshire: Wordsworth Editions.

"Representing Age and Ageing in New Zealand Literature"
The Māori Case

PAOLA DELLA VALLE, UNIVERSITY OF TURIN

METHODOLOGICAL FRAMEWORK

In the last fifty years there has been a growing interest in the study of age and ageing from various perspectives, probably in response to an increasingly ageing population in contemporary Western societies. The work of social historians has also been challenged by a new perspective, promoted by cultural historians and based on a kind of 'philosophical relativism'. While the former mainly focus on the investigation of demographic research, economic data, and documents of public policy (when available), the latter privilege subjective sources such as diaries, biographies, literary and artistic works, religious and scientific texts, and prescriptive essays on old age (Johnson 1998: 12). This different methodological approach emphasises the silences of the sources and the "situatedness of historical texts within ambiguous and multiple constructions of meanings" (Johnson 1998: 1). The tension between these two different paradigms, the positivistic/empiricist and the relativistic, is still unresolved.

David Troyansky has underlined how research could benefit from transcending disciplinary divisions between social and cultural approaches to the history and representation of old age, and advocates an integrated reading of all the possible sources (Troyansky 1998: 97). Johnson, however, underlines that the construction of a 'total' history is hindered by two major problems: the lack of objective transversal social data, especially in past epochs or peripheral contexts, and the conflicting views that may arise from a subjective approach. Documentary sources from classical antiquity, the Middle Ages, early modern Europe and even more recent times such as the 19th century are in fact insufficient, as they offer only partial information about an elite and leave many social categories unrepresented. On the other hand literary, artistic and cultural representations can be contradictory or inconsistent, as they may reveal a personal bias or be a projection of the author's fears, doubts or hopes rather than conveying a larger viewpoint. Cicero (106-43 BC), for example, gives a positive picture of the elderly as repositories of moderation and wisdom, claiming they should be respected and obeyed by younger generations (Parkin 1998: 26), while satirist Juvenal (ca 55-135 AD) is unpleasantly realistic in conveying the physical and mental shortcomings of old age (Parkin 1998: 32). Even the common assumption of a golden age for elders in the past, in which "older people were in some ways more active and more valued participants in civil society" than today is not supported by evidence, at least not for elders who were "neither literate, nor wealthy nor powerful" (Johnson 1998: 6). Old age, says Johnson, would therefore be better represented if historians paid attention to a number of small specific issues and voices rather than trying to construct meta-narratives and if they focused on discontinuities rather than continuities of images, ideas and policies (Johnson 1998: 16-18).

This premise constitutes the methodological framework of the present essay on age and ageing in Aotearoa New Zealand. The tension between the two different approaches – positivistic/empiricist and relativistic – will be held. Although plenty of formal evidence, such as statistics and documents of public policy, is now available in Aotearoa New Zealand, these sources might give only a partial picture of the subject. Some categories, in this case the Māori indigenous minority, might be underrepresented or misrepresented, as their idea of age and ageing differs considerably from the dominant view. Representations of old age found in cultural documents and literary works by Māori writers are therefore quite useful to integrate the missing information provided by official documents.

THE OFFICIAL SOURCES: THE NEW ZEALAND POSITIVE AGEING STRATEGY (PAS)

New Zealand population is constantly ageing. In the early 1980s the median age was 26 years (this means that half of the people were younger than 26 and half were older). In 2014 it was 37.5 years. Comparatively, these changes align with those of other 'developed' countries, although New Zealand population is slightly younger. For example, in 2014 the median age in Japan and Germany (which have the world's oldest populations) was 46.1 years, in the United Kingdom 40.6 years, in Australia 38.3 years, in the United States 37.6 years. The number of aged 65-plus is increasing. In 2011 the first of New Zealand's baby boom generation turned 65. In 2014 650,000 people (14 percent of the population) were aged 65-plus – a 55 percent increase since 1994. That number is projected to reach 1.2 million by 2034, with people over 65 making up 22 percent of the population. There has been an even larger increase in the number of people aged 80-plus. Between 1994 and 2014 the number of people over 80 increased by 80 percent, and the trend will continue. In 2014 more than 160,000 people were aged 80-plus; this number is expected to be 368,000 by 2034, a rise of 130 percent. Over this same time period the number of people aged under 20 is expected to increase by only 3 percent ("2014 Report on the Positive Ageing Strategy": 10).

These data have been taken from the "2014 Report on the Positive Ageing Strategy", the latest update on the progress of the elaborate government plan started in 2001, the "New Zealand Positive Ageing Strategy" (PAS), and aimed at activating a practical response to the changing needs of an increasingly older society. The PAS provided not only a set of principle statements but was also a framework for policies and programmes across the government sector, that is, "a basis for action", in the words of the then Minister for Senior Citizens, Hon Lianne Dalziel ("The New Zealand Positive Ageing Strategy": 3). A total of 34 consultations were held throughout New Zealand, including four meetings specifically for Māori, to establish the goals for positive ageing according to certain priority areas, seek feedback on the principles underlying the project, identify mechanisms for regular monitoring, reporting and review of progress on the Strategy, and other practical procedures. Following the positive ageing principles, the effective policies of the Strategy will:

Empower older people to make choices that enable them to live a satisfying life and lead a healthy lifestyle;

Provide opportunities for older people to participate in and contribute to family, *whānau* [extended family] and community;

Reflect positive attitudes to older people;

Recognise the diversity of older people and ageing as a normal part of the lifecycle;

Affirm the values and strengthen the capabilities of older Māori and their whānau;

Recognise the diversity and strengthen the capabilities of older Pacific people;

Appreciate the diversity of cultural identity of older people living in New Zealand;

Recognise the different issues facing men and women;

Ensure older people, in both rural and urban areas, live with confidence in a secure environment and receive the services they need to do so; and

Enable older people to take responsibility for their personal growth and development through changing circumstances. ("The New Zealand Positive Ageing Strategy": 6-7, my emphases)

The ten aspirational goals for central and local government agencies and communities to understand and respond to the issues of ageing are:

1. Income – secure and adequate income for older people.
2. Health – equitable, timely, affordable and accessible health services for older people.
3. Housing – affordable and appropriate housing options for older people.
4. Transport – affordable and accessible transport options for older people.
5. Ageing in the Community – older people feel safe and secure and can age in the community.
6. *Cultural Diversity – a range of culturally appropriate services allows choices for older people.*
7. Rural Services – older people living in rural communities are not disadvantaged when accessing services.
8. Positive Attitudes – people of all ages have positive attitudes to ageing and older people.
9. Employment Opportunities – elimination of ageism and the promotion of flexible work options.

10. Opportunities for Personal Growth and Participation – increasing opportunities for personal growth and community participation. ("The New Zealand Positive Ageing Strategy", 20-23, my emphasis)

Although some of the principles underline respect of cultural diversity, which is also referred to in goal 6, the project has been criticised for being Western-centric, insofar as it conceives of successful ageing in terms of Western values such as productivity, activity, independence, and personal decision-making and does not fully capture a Māori perspective of ageing. This is especially evident given the rise of distinct models of well-being and Māori-defined frameworks for development that have emerged since the later part of the 20th century and the beginning of the new Millennium, such as *He Korowai Oranga* ("Māori Health Strategy") and the concept of "Economy of *Mana*" by Manuka Henare.[1]

"Māori Health Strategy", in particular, is based on the notion of *Te Whāre Tapa Whā*, according to which good health for Māori requires balance and harmony in relation to the four domains of wellbeing. They are *te taha wairua* (spiritual), *te taha hinengaro* (mental), *te taha whānau* (family) and *te taha tinana* (physical). This model is conceptualised as being equivalent to the four walls of a meeting house (*whārenui*) with each wall being of equal strength so that the house is strong and connected to the place and space around, and the ground it rests upon.

A 2010 study of a Māori doctoral student at Massey University (NZ), William John Werahiko Edwards, has proposed an alternative Māori version of PAS combining Western scientific inquiry, as found in the multidisciplinary discipline of gerontology, and *Mātauranga Māori* (Māori knowledge). Edwards's thesis is philosophically positioned at the interface between two different paradigms – Western science and indigenous knowledge – and uses the "interface approach", further developing work undertaken by Māori psychiatrist Mason Durie, an influential figure in the rise of the "Māori Health Strategy". The notion of interface works only if researchers explicitly accept the legitimacy of both inquiry paradigms, considering neither of them as superior or inferior to the other (Edwards

---

1 For *He Korowai Oranga* cp. (https://www.health.govt.nz/our-work/populations/maori-health/he-korowai-oranga). For the Economy of *Mana* cp. Paola Della Valle, "Indigenous Degrowth and Global Capitalism", pp. 218-219.

2010: 55 and 291). This approach is also consistent with Willie Ermine's notion of "ethical space", that is, "the appropriate place from which to transform knowledge because it offers a view of alternate knowledge systems in simultaneous fashion" (Edwards 2010: 53).

In his research Edwards makes two different ontological and epistemological worlds converse. While he acknowledges and uses the outcomes of gerontology (the scientific side of the interface), he also draws on two other sources of data offering Māori perspectives and values on old age: an analysis of forty-two *whakataukī* or traditional proverbs about ageing as a process, the aged and age; and a qualitative study of twenty older Māori people based on interviews. *Whakataukī* are a genre of Māori oral literature consisting in a body of highly metaphorical proverbial sayings used for the transmission of traditional knowledge. Edwards underlines how even within gerontology there has been a movement toward incorporation of literature since:

The result of such an expanded, engaged dialogue between the form of knowledge developed through literary interpretation and more familiar scientific approaches can yield unexpected and undoubtedly fruitful results. (Edwards 2010: 64; quoted from Holstein: 826)

As to the qualitative data collection, Edwards (like the previously-mentioned Johnson) believes in the importance of biographical approaches and subjective concerns, of differences and variations, in the study of old age: "the 'inside view' of life, as individuals experience it, and interpretation of their life, is crucial to understanding the human experience" (Edwards 2010: 65).

The conclusion of Edwards's research is that Māori positive ageing is characterised by a two-dimensional concept that incorporates a process dimension and an outcome dimension. The process dimension is consistent with a life-course perspective and therefore recognises that ageing is a life-long process where circumstances encountered during life may impact cumulatively and manifest in old age. Many determinants can impact this dimension such as educational achievements, employment status, the degree of material wellbeing and financial security, access to medical cure and health education, the size of one's family, and the amount of family responsibilities. More generally, these factors are also the results of historical, social and political processes.

The outcome dimension can be described in terms of complementary universal and Māori specific outcome domains. The universal outcome domains are expressed in the PAS. The Māori-specific outcome domains identified in the study are the following:

> *kaitiakitanga* (stewardship: caring for the things most valued by Māori, the environment and people);
> *whanaugatanga* (connectedness and kinship: consolidation of relationships within and beyond the family);
> *taketuku* (transmission of values and knowledge);
> *tākoha* (contribution to Māori collectives);
> *takatū* (adaptability over time, and between the Māori world and the wider world); and
> *tino rangatiratanga* (self-determination: control over life circumstances and in determining Māori positive ageing).
> The overarching outcome domain is *taupaenui* (realised potential) (Edwards 2010: 303).

Māori Positive Ageing, according to Edwards, must therefore embrace a specific cultural approach together with larger economic and health objectives, since it is concerned with "older Māori ageing in their own terms, having control of their life circumstances, enjoying a high level of social engagement and being economically secure" (Edwards 2010: 292).

Another research project, conducted by Dr Mere Kēpa and called "Bring 'Me' Beyond Vulnerability. Elderly Care of Māori, by Māori" (2006), stresses the role of the family in caring for elders, who are necessarily vulnerable. In particular, it emphasizes that care does not imply only health related matters but also cultural, political and social relationships and is grounded in *whānau* (extended family), *whanaungatanga* (connectedness) and *kanohi kitea* (presence and participation).

Finally, a feasibility study on Māori living to advanced age, commenced in 2006 and finished in 2011, also offers telling results. The research investigated 33 Māori aged 75 to 79 years living in the Bay of Plenty and Lakes District Health Board areas and was aimed at organising a future quantity and cohort research (Dyall, Kerse et al. 2011). Māori elder engagement involved participation in a series of focus groups to identify important questions that they considered should be asked in order to capture and record areas of wellbeing which are important to *kāumatua* (elders/leaders) and *kūia* (older women). The study was named *Te Puawaitanga o Nga Tapuwae Kia ora Tonu*, meaning "the blossoming of the path to maintain good health," and framed within the two models for Māori health: *Te Whāre Tapa Whā*, which has been illustrated before, and the *Pōutama* model of human development, according to which "Māori life moves through a series of stages of growth, with each stage linking to the next step creating a stairway which goes upwards with no ending, for there is no limit to growth and development of people within a lifetime or across generations" (Dyall, Kerse et al. 2006). The *Pōutama* model of human development is visible in many meeting houses. One wall depicts in some way the *Pōutama* pattern, showing the complexity of human life. Māori therefore consider that the growth and development of a person continues irrespective of their health or disability until death.

Almost all participants could identify their tribal group. Participants reported that cultural values influenced how they lived their lives. The majority of participants identified that cultural identity was important for them and this had been developed alongside their personal values, spirituality, religion, education and the upbringing provided by their parents, *whānau* and *marae*.[2] Over 50% of participants were actively involved in contributing to their grandchildren and great-grandchildren. In addition, the majority were actively involved in tribal and *marae* activities, their local community, church and wider society. The roles they played within their family and wider community were diverse and they included being mentors, guardians and elders. Two-thirds of the participants were active and were able to do recreational activities they enjoyed. The concept of retirement as 'disengagement' for them did not generally exist for almost all were still active, supporting their families and their community, or involved in paid employment. Food and access to healthy traditional Māori

---

2   A *marae* is the traditional gathering place in front of the meeting house. It also means the spiritual and cultural centre of the village, and the tribe with which a Māori identifies.

food were identified as important for over 80% of participants. They reported that they enjoyed eating this food on a regular basis.

Although the study has provided results only on 33 people, which cannot be generalised to the greater population of older Māori or be a representative sample, the quality of the information collected thanks to the involvement of the participants in the project at all stages and their constant feedback gives us an idea of the areas of importance for wellbeing in old age for Māori people.

In their monograph on life expectancy and mortality in New Zealand history, Woodward and Blakely explore the reasons why this country could boast the lowest mortality in the world for roughly 70 years, from 1870 to 1940, but only for non-Māori. If European settlers had considerably improved their living standards in the new country, this was not the case for the indigenous population. In 1881 life expectancy for Māori was 35 years less than non-Māori (18 years at birth). By 1946 the gap had closed to about 20 years: still a considerable difference (Woodward & Blakely 2014: 74). Besides the pernicious effects of the new pathogens spread by European immigrants, Māori poor ageing and early deaths were certainly a consequence of the high rate of disadvantage and material hardship suffered by Māori, due to economic marginalisation and the impoverishment of their cultural world. Today, according to the NZ Ministry of Health's data, the life expectancy of a non-Māori male and female born between 2012 and 2014 is respectively 79.5 and 83.2 years. In the Māori population it is 73 years for males and 77.1 years for females (Independent Life Expectancy in New Zealand 2013: 7). If the present trend is maintained, the gap will be closed by 2040 (Woodward & Blakely 2014: 219). These comforting statistics convey the picture of an indigenous minority that has been able to overcome colonial trauma and assimilation by militancy and resilience, and the defence of their worldview. A Māori positive ageing strategy is a further challenge they will have to face in the future.

Representations of ageing, the aged, and age however, were already present in the works of many writers of the Māori Renaissance. They allude to the role and function of elders in their society and also to the problems and hinders of positive ageing in their terms.

AGE, AGEING AND THE AGED IN NEW ZEALAND LITERATURE

In the voice of Māori writers elders are often represented as "our living *taonga* (treasures)", to use Dyall's words (Dyall, Kerse et al. 2011). This is most of all due to the fact that they are the repositories of traditional knowledge and values, and of *te reo* (Māori language). In the short story "A Game of Cards" by Witi Ihimaera (from the collection *Pounamu Pounamu*, 1972), an older Māori woman, Nanny Miro,[3] one of the young narrator's relatives, is depicted as the custodian of the *whānau*'s heritage and past. Her place, evoked in the narrator's childhood memories, is defined as a "treasure house, glistening with sports trophies and photographs, pieces of carvings and greenstone, and feather cloaks hanging from the walls" (Ihimaera 1972: 2). Nanny Miro is also the guardian of the most valuable of Māori treasures: the ancestral land, which she owns in great quantity. In rewriting the story for the 2003 new edition of *Pounamu Pounamu*, her 'political' engagement is made more explicit by Ihimaera with the addition of remarks which underline her preoccupation that the younger generations might not be up to this role:

"How are you going to do good things for your people if you can't concentrate?" she would ask. "Here I am, counting on you to get a good education so that you get the rest of our land back and you're just hopeless, he hoha koe [you are annoying]." (Ihimaera 2003: 12)

Or,

"Aue [Alas]," she would sigh. Then she'd look at me, offer words of wisdom that didn't make sense like, 'Don't let me down,' or 'If you can't beat the Pākehā one way remember that all's fair in love – or cards'. (Ihimaera 2003: 12)

Nanny Miro lives with her extended family in the Māori village of Waituhi (an omnipresent "place of the heart" in Ihimaera's fiction). Within the Māori community older people are cared for by the other members, as the

---

3 Nanny is a term for older relatives: grandmothers, grandfathers, great-grandparents, great-aunt and uncles, etc.

scene of Miro's death shows. Miro loves playing cards at home with the other *kuias* (old women) of the village, surrounded by clouds of smoke, gossiping about the village people, laughing and cheating each other. On the night she passes away all the community gathers to accompany her in the last journey while playing cards:

> The old ladies sat around the bed, playing. Everybody else decided to play cards too, to keep Nanny company. The men played poker in the kitchen and sitting room. The kids played snap in the other bedrooms. The house overflowed with card players, even onto the lawn outside Nanny's window, where she could see [...]. Everybody laughed. Nanny and Mrs Heta started squabbling as they always did pointing at each other and saying You cheat, not me! And Nanny Miro said: I saw you, Maka tiko bum [shit face], I saw you sneaking that card from under the blanket.
> She began to laugh. Quietly. Her eyes streaming with tears.
> And while she was laughing, she died. (Ihimaera 1972: 4-5)

This story represents several aspects of ageing and age among Māori. On one hand the image of the *kuias* as chain smokers evokes the notion of *manaakitanga* (hospitality, generosity), that is, the creation of a comfortable social context for members of the community or guests in general, by encouraging tobacco consumption. Sharing smokes seems to have assumed a cultural value in connection to *manaakitanga*, says Heather Gifford, but it has also become a dangerous cause of morbidity and mortality among Māori, whose rates of smoking remain more than twice that of non-Māori (Gifford 2015: 83). We can recall here Edwards' notion of "process dimension" for a Māori Positive Ageing Strategy, that is, the need to see positive ageing in a life-course perspective, which implies health education and reconsideration of the concept of *manaakitanga* in relation to tobacco smoking. Probably, in the early seventies, when the short story was written, the extent of the pernicious effects of smoking on health had not been fully realized yet. On the other hand, "A Game of Cards" evokes many Māori values which contribute to Positive Ageing: connectedness and kinship (*whanaugatanga*), caring for the things most valued by Māori (*kaitiakitanga*), and transmission of values and knowledge (*taketuku*). Also, it illustrates the importance of the extended family (*whānau*) and the presence of and participation in the community (*kanohi kitea*), two of the three factors necessary in the care of the vulnerable together with *whanaugatanga,* according to Mere Kēpa. Finally, in the story Miro recounts that she decided to leave the hospital and be treated at home, although she was seriously ill (Ihimaera 1972: 4). We can infer that she is a terminal patient who has chosen her "deathscape" (Moeke-Maxwell 2015: 170). Another Māori belief is pointed out here. As Moeke-Maxwell highlights, "Home is a place that is associated with supporting the living to live well until they die. It is widely accepted that Māori individuals want to die at home, surrounded by their whānau" (2015: 169).

The "Beginning of the Tournament", in the same collection, describes the participation of older Māori in recreational activities, deemed important in the feasibility study mentioned before. Here the account of the annual Māori hockey tournament, which draws teams from all the East coast in the North Island, becomes a way to celebrate the 'irrepressible spirit' of Māori and their values. The makeshift organisation of the event and the disregard of rules by participants are hilarious. Set in a paddock among browsing cows, an atypical match is described. The teams include kids who have never played before and grandmothers holding a walking stick in one hand and a hockey stick in the other. An older Māori man, Nanny Kepa, is a jury member of the Grand Parade, where teams compete for best attire, and is also the referee of the women's match. Cheating is admitted, as long as it does not favour the team who won the year before, according to a redistributive sense of justice. The event is in fact a way to get Māori together and revive traditions such as action songs, traditional food, and popular dances.

Two more stories in *Pounamu Pounamu* include forceful images of old age that anticipate some key points of a Māori PAS: "The Child" and "The Whale". In the former a grandmother moves to her son's house after becoming a widow. The loss of her husband has also affected her mental equilibrium. The story is narrated by the young grandchild who helps her in accomplishing everyday activities and accompanies her in long walks on the beach. Strong bonds between grandchildren and their nannies are frequent in Ihimaera's fiction, like that between Nanny Paora and his great-grandchild Pene in the novel *Whānau*. The structure of the extended family favoured close ties between generations and *whangai* (adoption) was a relatively common practice whereby the young were raised as children of their grandparents or other relatives, especially in large families (Della Valle 2010: 113). "The Child" depicts a world of warm relationships and caring for elders, which makes the inevitability of their deaths easier to be accepted. Home appears again as the favourite deathscape for Māori, and *whānau* (family) and *whanaungatanga* (connectedness) are essential for a serene end-of-life. *Whānau*, too, forcefully claims the right deathscape for the older. The novel ends with the community's collective search for Nanny Paora and Pene at night, after they have run away together. The child wanted to prevent the old man from being taken away from him to a hospital or rest home.

"The Whale", instead, opens with an older Māori in the darkness of the meeting house. He is teaching his grandchild Hera the symbolic meaning of the building in all its parts, exemplifying the transmission of values and knowledge (*taketuku*). The story, however, is the most pessimistic in the collection. While crossing his semi-deserted village the man sees images of decay and neglect everywhere. Many young people have moved to urban areas and most of those who have stayed live debauched lives, without any interest in their culture and traditions (apart from Hera). The last image of the story, "a whale, stranded in the breakwater, [...] already stripped of flesh by the falling gulls" (Ihimaera 1972: 121), is the ultimate sign of a dying animal and a seemingly dying culture. In the later novel *The Whale Rider* (1987), Ihimaera will use many images from this story. One is the figure of the despotic great-grandfather and tribal leader Koro Apirana, who is the repository of customary knowledge and feels in charge of the education of the younger generations, among whom he is seeking the future male chief of the tribe. Here the bond between elders and younger generations seems to be broken by the obstinacy of the older man to want a male successor. By not applying *takatū* (adaptability over time) in gender relations, Koro Apirana risks being an unwise guide for his community. To his surprise, he will dramatically discover that it is a girl, not a boy, his heir. Other images taken from the above-mentioned story refer to the mythical ancestor and founder of the village Paikea, who arrived ashore riding a whale, and to the stranded whales, symbolising the decay of the Māori race.

Patricia Grace also describes how *kaitiakitanga* (caring for the people and the things most valued by Māori) is carried out by an older Māori woman in the eponymous short story "Waimarie" (from the collection *Electric City,* 1987). Waimarie looks after her mentally disabled twenty-year-younger brother and is bringing up two girls, probably granddaughters, who are staying at her place because of problems with their unstable alcoholic mother. She represents the fulcrum of the *whānau* for her support to *whanaugatanga* (consolidation of relationships within the family) and *tākoha* (contribution to Māori collectives). She also participates as a *kaumātua* (elder) in traditional ceremonies and the image of her singing a *karanga* (welcome call) on the *marae* for a *tangi* (traditional funeral ceremony) closes the story. Edwards underlines how relevant is for Māori positive ageing the involvement of older people in the family, in the collectives, and in the education of younger generations. However, if the level of demand is too high and places burdens on them, it can also be harmful. So he suggests compensatory actions to be set up, such as the involvement of a larger number of older people in *marae* activities, to reduce demands on individuals, or courses to up-skill older Māori with regard to customary knowledge in order that there are more elders to take on formal roles (Edwards 2010: 298).

The participation of older people in the community life is also exemplified in *Potiki* (1986), which tells of a rural extended family, the Tamihanas, holding on to 'the old ways' and applying a form of subsistence-economy model, which allows them to be self-sufficient in times of economic crisis. The family includes old Granny Tamihana, the mentally handicapped Mary, and her physically disabled son Toko or *potiki* (the last-born), whose father is unknown. In the extended family structure the disadvantaged, the weaker, the older and the disabled are protected and cared for, and the bond between generations is stronger. Granny Tamihana looks after Mary and Toko with tender affection and is reciprocated by having the respect and love of the community. Unlike the nuclear family organised around few members overloaded with duties and roles, the extended family redistributes functions and responsibilities, valorising the potentials of each member and activating reciprocal support. As Martha Nussbaum underlines, a truly civilised society is one that guarantees the rights of the 'weaker' categories (Nussbaum 2013). In *Potiki*, as in other works by Māori writers (for example, Ihimaera's *Whānau*), it is the community that exerts surveillance on its members and looks after them, providing that social control that is often absent in large urban areas, as well as warmth and sense of belonging. The connection with one's origins and ancestors, the sense of belonging to a culturally well-defined context, and the inclusion in a family group are necessary in the care of the older and disadvantaged categories. A scene in *Potiki* clarifies different attitudes in the approach toward old age and disability. Pākehā[4] private developers, evocatively renamed Dollarman, have made a millionaire offer to the community for the land where the cemetery and the meeting house stand, which would give good access to the neighbouring site under development. The community receives Dollarman several times at the meeting house before a decision is taken. Finally, they run down the offer because they prefer to protect their sacred places, avoid pollution, and preserve their land as it is. This decision sounds incomprehensible for the developers, as it goes against their view of 'progress'. But the community claims the right to defend another notion of progress. In one of these meetings, while Granny, Mary and Toko are comfortably sitting on the mats and listening to the two parties talking, one of the developers notices the three of them, and Toko understands how he perceives them:

Right then I saw what the man saw as he turned and looked at the three of us and as my eyes met his eyes. I saw what he saw. What he saw was brokenness, a broken race. He saw in my Granny, my Mary and me, a whole people, decrepit, deranged, deformed. That was what I knew. (Grace 1995: 102)

In this sentence Grace underlines not only the gap between two notions of progress (the Western and the indigenous one), but also different approaches to the weaker categories in society. They certainly should not be there in the eyes of the Pākehā developers, but hospitalised or taken care of by special institutions, while for the Māori they are integral part of the community, with their function and role.

The literary texts that have been analysed showed many years in advance images of ageing and old age that would be later found in quantitative and qualitative studies on Māori older people. This confirms Johnson's point that research in this field should be carried out maintaining the tension between a relative and an empiricist approach, and that literature, together with other instruments, can be helpful in representing the condition and needs of older people by giving voice to the silences of the sources, especially those of categories that are less visible or socially powerful such as minorities, and by highlighting the "situatedness of

---

4 *Pākehā* is the term for a New Zealander of European origin.

historical texts within ambiguous and multiple constructions of meanings" (Johnson 1998: 1).

BIBLIOGRAPHY

Della Valle, Paola (2010): *From Silence to Voice: the Rise of Maori Literature*, Auckland: Libro International. Print.

―――― (2018): "Indigenous Degrowth and Global Capitalism." In: *Uncommon Wealths in Postcolonial Fiction*. Ed. Helga Ramsey-Kurz and Melissa Kennedy, Leiden & Boston: Brill Rodopi, pp. 207-225. Print.

Dyall Lorna/Ngaire Kerse/Karen Hayman/Sally Keeling (2011): "Pinnacle of life: Māori living to advanced age." In: *The New Zealand Medical Journey*, 25th March, 124/1330, last accessed March 16, 2018 (https://www.nzma.org.nz/journal/read-the-journal/all-issues/2010-2019/2011/vol-124-no-1331/view-dyall age). Web.

Edwards, William John Werahiko (2010): "Taupaenui: Maori Positive Ageing", A PhD thesis in Public Health, Massey University, Palmerston North, New Zealand. Unpublished.

Gifford, Heather (2015): "Is Sharing Tobacco within the Home Really Good Manaakitanga?". In: *Home Here to Stay*. Ed. Mere Kēpa, Marilyn McPherson, Linitā Manuʻatu, Wellington: Huia, pp. 83-93. Print.

Grace, Patricia (1987): *Electric City and Other Stories*, Auckland: Penguin. Print.

―――― (1995 [1986]): *Potiki*, Honolulu: University of Hawaiʻi Press. Print.

Holstein, Martha (1994): "Taking Next Steps: Gerontological Education, Research, and the Literary Imagination." In: *Gerontologist* 34/6, pp. 822-827. Print.

Ihimaera, Witi (1972): *Pounamu Pounamu*, Auckland: Heinemann. Print.

―――― (1974): *Whanau*, Auckland: Heinemann. Print.

―――― (2003 [1987]): *The Whale Rider*. (US edition), Harcourt: Orlando & New York. Print.

―――― (2003): *Pounamu Pounamu. The Anniversary Collection*, Auckland: Reed Print.

Johnson, Paul (1998): "Historical Readings of Old Age and Ageing." In: *Old Age from Antiquity to Post-Modernity*. Pail Johnson/Pat Thane (eds.), London and New York: Routledge, pp. 1-18. Print.

Kēpa, Mere (2006): "Bring 'Me' Beyond Vulnerability – Elderly Care of Māori by Māori. Kei Hinga Au E, Kei Mate Au E. Te Tiaki ā te Māori i te Hunga Kaumātua Māori". In: Paper presented at *Mātauranga TakeTake: Traditional Knowledge, Ngā Pae o te Māramatanga International Indigenous Conference*, Te Papa Museum, Wellington. 14-17 June, pp. 14-17. Unpublished.

Moeke-Maxwell, Tess (2015): "Homedeathscapes: Maori End-of-life Decision-making Processes". In: *Home Here to Stay*. Mere Kēpa/ Marilyn McPherson/Linitā Manuʻatu/Wellington (eds.): Huia, pp. 169-191. Print.

Nussbaum, Martha C. (2013): *Giustizia sociale e dignità umana. Da individui a persone*, Bologna: Il Mulino. Print.

Parkin, Tim G. (1998): "Ageing in antiquity: Status and Participation." In: *Old Age from Antiquity to Post-Modernity*. Pail Johnson/Pat Thane (eds.), London and New York: Routledge, pp. 19-42. Print.

Shahar, Shulamith (1998): "Old Age in the High and Late Middle Ages." In: *Old Age from Antiquity to Post-Modernity*. Pail Johnson/Pat Thane (eds.), London and New York: Routledge, pp. 43-63. Print.

Tangaere A.R. (1997): "Maori Human Development and Learning Theory." In: *Mai i Rangiatea: Māori wellbeing and development*. P. Te Whaiti/M. McCarthy/M. Durie (eds.), Auckland: Auckland University Press, pp. 46-59. Print.

Troyansky, David G. (1998): "Balancing social and Cultural Approaches to the History of Old Age and Ageing in Europe." In: *Old Age from Antiquity to Post-Modernity*. Pail Johnson/Pat Thane (eds.), London and New York: Routledge, pp. 96-109. Print.

Woodward, Alistair/ Blakely, Tony (2014): *The Healthy Country? A History of Life & Death in New Zealand*, Auckland: Auckland University Press. Print.

SITOGRAPHY

"Healthy Ageing Strategy", Ministry of Health, Wellington 2016, last accessed March 10, 2018 (https://www.health.govt.nz/system/files/documents/publications/healthy-ageing-strategy_june_2017.pdf). Web.

"He Korowai Oranga" (Māori Health Strategy), last accessed March 10, 2018 (https://www.health.govt.nz/our-work/populations/maori-health/he-korowai-oranga). Web.

"Independent Life Expectancy in New Zealand 2013", NZ Ministry of Health/Manatū Hauora, last accessed March 10, 2018 (http://www.health.govt.nz/publication/independent-life-expectancy-new-zealand-2013-0). Web.

Marriott, Lisa/Dalice Sim. "Indicators of Inequality for Māori and Pacific People", WORKING PAPER 09/2014, August 2014, Victoria University, Wellington (NZ), last accessed March 11, 2018 (https://www.victoria.ac.nz/sacl/centres-and-institutes/cpf/publications/pdfs/2015/WP09_2014_Indicators-of-Inequality.pdf). Web.

"The New Zealand Positive Ageing Strategy", Ministry of Social Policy, 2001, last accessed March 10, 2018 (https://www.ifa-fiv.org/wp-content/uploads/2012/11/060_NZ-Positive-Ageing-Strategy.pdf). Web.

"The 2014 Report on the Positive Ageing Strategy", Office for Senior Citizens – Te Tari Kaumātua, New Zealand Ministry of Social Development, last accessed March 10, 2018 (http://www.superseniors.msd.govt.nz/documents/msd-17470-2014-ageing-strategy-report-final.pdf). Web.

Ageing and Neurologic Disease

ENRICA FAVARO, UNIVERSITY OF TURIN

THE PROCESS OF AGEING IN THE DIFFERENT ORGANS AND APPARATUSES

Ageing is a complex and heterogeneous process defined as the gradual, time-dependent decline or loss of physiological functions; its rate and speed vary from species to species, from organ to organ within the same species, down to the tissues and cells of the same organism (Diamanti-Kandarakis et al., 2017; Carmonna JJ et al., 2016): the process of ageing is a kind of mosaic, for example kidney and lung get older faster.

During the process of ageing there is loss of some cells, and massive anatomical-functional alteration in different apparatuses (Harrison's, *Principles of Internal Medicine 19th ed.*, McGraw-Hill Medical). Here are some examples of these modifications resulting from ageing.

Skeletal Muscle System

> Decrease of muscle mass, muscle contraction and of the number of mitochondria;
> Decrease of bone mass leading to osteopenia and osteoporosis leading to high risk of fractures;
> Degeneration of intervertebral discs and high risk of hernias, joint pains, spondylosis;
> Degeneration of cartilage that leads to postural instability and to gonarthrosis with reduction of the articular line.

Central and Peripheral Nervous System

Decrease of the mass of the CNS and the vascular flow;
Decrease of the number of neurons, of gray substance, and of neurotransmitters and consequently of neuron connections;
Decrease of visual acuity and night vision; modification of the crystalline lens with risk of cataracts;
Arthrosis and reduced mobility of anvil, hammer and stirrup in the ear.

Respiratory and Cardiovascular System

Decrease of elastic capacity and muscle response in the lung;
Reduction of oxygen saturation;
Decrease of muco-ciliary clearance;
Decreased diastolic filling;
Degenerative phenomena of the arterial vessels;
Increased pressure.

Gastrointestinal System

High risk of diverticulosis and fecaloma formation due to decreased intestinal motility.

Urinary System

Decrease of kidney mass (-40%) due to loss of nephrons;
Reduction of glomerular vasculature and alteration of renin secretion;
Reduction of renal flow, glomerular filtration and tubular function;
Muscle weakening and reduced capacity in the bladder;
Increase of volume in the prostate with pollakiuria and dysuria.

Immune System

Immunosenescence that is characterized by changes in the immune system and in the apoptosis process, induced by oxidative stress (Ventura et al., 2017; Fulop et al., 2018);
Increase of inflammatory response;

Decrease of efficacy of B antibody and T response, Dendritic cells, macrophages and neutrophils;
Reduction of antibody response and Increased autoantibody response.

Endocrine System

Reduction of testosterone and of the GH / IGF-1 axis with some symptoms such as sarcopenia (reduction of strength and muscular endurance, loss of mass, tone and muscle strength);
Osteoporosis;
Reduction of appetite and food intake;
Drop in libido;
Cognitive and psychogeriatric symptoms;
Anaemia;
Increased cardiovascular risk;
Alteration in hypothalamic–pituitary unit (Diamanti-Kandarakis et al., 2017).

Molecular Alteration

Ageing is accompanied by multiple **molecular alterations** (Diamanti-Kandarakis et al., 2017). There is increase of several molecular alterations involving DNA, RNA or proteins, such as an increase in genomic instability, chromosome structural abnormalities, epigenetic alterations, DNA cross-linking and frequency of single-strand breaks, a decline in DNA methylation, loss of DNA telomeric sequences, an alteration of posttranslational changes of proteins structure (deamidation, oxidation, cross-linking, and nonenzymatic glycation) and of mitochondrial structure (Harman et al., 2001). It has recently been discovered that pathophysiological mechanisms of ageing may be also accompanied by alteration of micro RNAs functions and stem cell exhaustion (Lopez-Otin et al., 2013).

THE FRAIL ELDERLY PATIENT

The capability of an organism to keep balance and to adjust to change may promote longevity, frailty and disease (Diamanti-Kandarakis et al., 2017). There are three manners of ageing:

> Common/normal: which includes that part of the population that grows old with some disability and comorbility;
> Successful ageing: which includes those people who have a physical, cognitive and functional performance above average;
> Pathological ageing: which includes all frail patients.

Frailty is undoubtedly a negative predictor, predisposing to unfavorable clinical outcomes such as mortality, poor quality of life and disability. Being frail predicts likelihood of early death, higher disabilities, a much more frequent rehospitalization rate and more early institutionalization risks (Kelaiditi et al., 2013).

The intrinsic factors that are often associated with the development of a state of frailty are:

1) Sarcopenia: Sarcopenia is a geriatric disease caused by different factors such as: oxidative stress (ROS), changes in the endocrine system, loss of the regenerative capacity of cells. Its onset may be favored by some diseases such as heart failure, respiratory failure, immobilization syndrome.

2) Malnutrition: When malnutrition is established, the descending parable of the state of frailty is accelerated. The following may contribute to the development of malnutrition: early satiety, slow digestion, alteration of taste and smell, alvo disorders, psychic causes (depression, dementia), poverty and solitude. Weight loss in elderly subjects impacts on different organs and apparatuses (in particular on muscle, bone, immune system) and increases the risk of infections, immobility, hospitalization, mortality, anaemia, cognitive impairment.

3) Dementia: A person with dementia, 8 times out of 10, is also a frail elderly patient (cp. pharagraph **a**).

4) Life habits: Some aggravating factors of a state of frailty seem to be education level, economic problems, lack of social and family support, and smoking. On the other hand, a well balanced diet such as the Mediterranean diet, regular moderate exercise and a longer period of study and of intellectual activities seem to be good guarantee against early cognitive and physicological decay.

Modifiable lifestyle factors and a multidomain intervention – including physical activity, cognitive engagement, active social life and a healthy diet (such as the Mediterranean diet) – are a key strategy for protection against risk of developing frailty and may delay the progression and secondary appearance of adverse results related to cognitive frailty, improve or preserve the cognitive functions and may help to prevent cognitive decline (Kelaiditi et al., 2013; Ngandu et al., 2015, Phillips C et al., 2017).

NEUROLOGIC DISEASES AND AGEING

The most common neurologic diseases in older people are dementia, Alzheimer's disease, Parkinson's disease and depression (Harrison's 2017; Pinessi, et al., 2015).

a) Dementia

Dementia is a serious geriatric syndrome, an intrinsic factor of frailty and a powerful predictor of mortality and instability. This general term is used to describe a deficit in two or more functional cognitive areas diagnosed for at least 6 months.

Dementia is dramatically increasing in the general population and its evolution is progressive. Dementia is characterized by impairment of acquired cognitive capacity. It affects the memory, the intellectual and linguistic skills, and is usually accompanied by radical changes in personality and sometimes in motor skills: in particular dementia is a progressive loss of memory, concentration, thinking process, orientation, comprehension, calculation, learning ability, language, and judgment and executive functions (Rossor et al., 2007). Given prolonged life expectancy, dementia cases are increasing dramatically in the general population, in particular in persons over 85 years of age (Savva et al., 2009; Ritchie et al., 2002; Milne et al., 2008).

There are primitive forms of dementia: Alzheimer's disease (the most frequent degenerative dementia), Trisomy 21, Frontotemporal dementia (FTD), Lewy body dementia (LBD), Progressive supranuclear paralysis, Corticobasal degeneration, Parkinson's disease, Huntington disease (HD), Prion disease. Secondary forms of dementia can be reversible or associated with an organic clinical condition: vascular disease; endocrine disease (diabetes, hypo- or hyperthyroidism, hypoparathyroidism, hypocortisolism, hypercortisolism) Infectious-inflammatory CNS (Infectious pathology: HIV, cysticercosis, lue, borelliosis, Whipple disease, chronic meningitis, brain abscess); Toxic-deficiency (Nutritional causes: B12 deficiency, folate, thiamin, dehydration; Exogenous drugs or toxic substances); Lupus, rheumatoid arthritis, Antibodies antiphospholipid syndrome); Intracranial expansive processes (Brain tumors; Chronic subdural hematoma); Chronic renal and liver failure; Drugs; Different causes and different origins such as: severe anaemia, polycythemia vera, porphyria, paraneoplastic syndromes) (Pinessi et al., 2013).

Diagnosis of dementia is based on clinical examination, on neuropsychological tests, on neuroimaging and on laboratory tests (blood and liquor) (Pinessi et al., 2013). Psychiatrists, neurologists and geriatricians are involved in the management of dementia and in the assessment of the patient.

A general objective examination must always be accompanied by a neurological examination; Anamnesis should check for signs suggestive of dementia or of other diseases. It is important to investigate:

Clinical history: familiarity, trauma, signs of alcoholism, drug abuse, nutritional status (folic acid and vitamin B12 cause reversible dementia);
Other diseases or some possible confounding factors that could mimick dementia such as encephalopathies, dysthyroidism, hyper or hypothyroidism, respiratory failure, liver failure, renal failure, diabetes, arterial hypertension, obstructive sleep apnea syndrome (OSAS);
Pharmacotherapy; a possible further cause of reversible dementia is iatrogenic;
Psychiatric/neurological pathology.
Cardiovascular diseases and the risk factors of vascular cerebropathy;
Neurological examination: Focal neurological signs such as paresis, sensory alterations, aphasia (a focal deficit suggests an ictal cause); Movement and walking (parkinsonism, ataxia of the march, myoclonus).

The most frequently used test for neuropsychological diagnosis is the MMSE (Mini Mental State Examination) (Petersen et al., 2011), which is a global evaluation scale useful for monitoring dementia. It is a 30-point test to evaluate cognitive function, orientation over time and space, memory (recording and memory), attention and computational skills, language and visuospatial function. Based on the score (normal> 24-27 / 30) dementia is defined:- Mild 20-24;- Moderate 10-19;- Severe <10.

The stages of the diagnosis of dementia include: evaluation of cognitive impairment; etiology of dementia; severity of cognitive impairment; behavioral changes; social, family and environmental situation.

There is no effective treatment of degenerative dementias. Cholinesterase inhibitors and memantine may be useful in mild or moderate disease phases (Pinessi et al., 2013).

It is important to intervene at an early stage of cognitive decline to slow or prevent progression to dementia also with some approaches not strictly pharmacological (Kelaiditi et al., 2013; Ngandu et al., 2015, Phillips C et al., 2017), (cp. last paragraph).

b) Alzheimer's Disease

Alzheimer's disease is one of the most common neurologic diseases, a deterioration of memory and other cognitive domains that leads to death within 3 to 9 years after diagnosis. It is the most common form of dementia, and 50-70% of all dementias is Alzheimer's disease (Querfurth et al., 2010). It is a fact that, with the gradual increase in the population of the elderly, Alzheimer's disease has become a major sociodemographic problem in industrialized countries and developing countries. It has a prevalence of 1% in individuals 60-64 years old, but it exponentially increases with age, reaching 24-33% in subjects over 85 years of age. This number is expected to double every 20 years, in relation to the ageing of the world's population and now Alzheimer's disease is considered a priority in terms of public health.

Alzheimer's disease is a complex and heterogeneous progressive disorder of the central nervous system and is the most common neurodegenerative disease.

The disease was first described in 1906 at a conference in Tübingen, Germany by Alois Alzheimer, as a "peculiar severe disease process of the cerebral cortex." Alois Alzheimer reported the histopathologic findings of neuritic plaques and neurofibrillary tangles in the brain of a 53 year old woman with personality change and progressive dementia. More than one hundred years have passed since its first documentation, many aspects of the pathophysiology of AD have been discovered and understood, however gaps of knowledge continue to exist.

It is characterized by extensive and selective neuronal loss; Increased astrocytes; diffuse plaques in neocortex, neuritic plaques and synaptic alterations; numerous amyloid plaques; abundant neurofibrillary tangles (NFTs) in selectively vulnerable regions of the brain: deposition of amyloid plaques and neurofibrillary tangles represent the typical markers of the pathology. The preponderant pathogenic hypotheses are dysregulation of β-amyloid production and metabolism. An imbalance between production and clearance, and aggregation of peptides, may cause accumulation of β-amyloid and this excess may be the initiating factor in Alzheimer's disease. Accumulation of misfolded proteins in the ageing brain results in oxidative and inflammatory damage, which in turn leads to energy failure and synaptic dysfunction (Querfurth et al., 2010; Singh et al., 1997; Sanabria-Castro et al., 2017; Querfurth H NEJ 2010 Kang J, 1987; Goldgaber D 1987; Goedert 1966; Johson 1996; Yankner 1996; Yankner BA. 1996; Arriagada 1992; Kosik KS. 1993).

An important challenge in the field of neurodegenerative diseases is the early and timely diagnosis of the disease. For most neurodegenerative diseases, the underlying causative agent for the disease remains unknown and the diagnosis of neurodegenerative diseases related to ageing (dementias, etc.) is made on the basis of the presence of distinctive clinical features (McKhann et al., 2011). The first clinical description of Alzheimer's disease was that of 1984 by McKhann, updated in 2011, which claimed that to suspect AD it was necessary to diagnose deficit of memory associated with deficiency of at least another cognitive domain that lasted for at least six months, after excluding the causes of secondary dementia (McKhann et al., 2011). After more than thirty years, diagnosis still remains essentially clinical even if other criteria were introduced by Doubois (Doubois et al., 2007) and by the McKhann team (McKhann et al., 2011) (National Institute on Ageing and Alzheimer's Association) with some morphological and functional markers (PET and markers for β-amyloid) (Blennow et al., 2015).

In the last 15 years there has been massive research towards identifying preclinical markers of diseases such as Alzheimer. The most recent attempt includes the notion of mild cognitive impairment (MCI), initially identified by the Mayo Clinic on the basis of a cohort study of adults suffering from AD (Petersen et al., 1999). The Mayo Clinic study found that before the emergence of the clinical symptoms of AD, subclinical memory decline was observed in those subsequently developing AD (Petersen et al., 1999).

It is an age-related degenerative disease, as the principal risk factor for Alzheimer's disease is age (Querfurth et al. 2010). Other risk factors include, beside advanced age, head injury, low level of education, depression, diabetes, smoking, environmental toxicity, manual work, cardiovascular disease. The best way to prevent Alzheimer's disease is the correction of cardiovascular risk factors: it is a fact that diabetes, hypertension and heart disease increase the production of β-amyloid.

The onset modality is typically subtle, with an initial short-term memory deficit and topographical orientation in known pathways, language disorder, behavioral and cognitive disorders, gnosic, praxic and emotional defect.

Natural history of the disease begins with the onset (initial accumulation of asymptomatic β-amyloid) that may occcur 20 years before the clinical onset, which corresponds to time 0. At the clinical onset follow mild, moderate and advanced phases of the disease. The average duration of the disease is 8-10 years, with an inter-individual variability.

It affects the memory, thinking, orientation, comprehension, learning, language, and judgment. In particular: Alzheimer's disease produces progressive memory loss, difficulty in solving problems, disorientation in time and space, changes in behavior and personality, and impairments of insight, judgment, executive functions, praxis and other cognitive functions (Singh and Guthikonda, 1997).

Treatment of patients with Alzheimer is difficult, because there is currently no specific effective therapy. The drugs currently used are cholinesterase inhibitors and memantine, an NMDA receptor antagonist (Pinessi et al., 2015).

In spite of a lot of ongoing clinical trials and a lot of experimental new drugs, no cure or drug has been able to delay or halt the course of Alzheimer's disease. New findings seem to show that cognitive impairment can be prevented or delayed even in the absence of new drugs by promoting changes in behavior and by managing vascular risk factors (Ngandu et al., 2015) (cp. last paragraph).

In fact, different forms of non-pharmacological treatment for Alzheimer's disease are being studied, consisting of behavioral interventions, psychosocial support, cognitive training and physical activity. These measures may be resorted to in order to complement the pharmacological treatment and have shown positive results in the overall clinical management of the patient (Pinessi et al., 2015). Moreover recent studies indicate that cognitive interventions and maintenance of adequate levels of physical activity may even have the potential to delay the onset of Alzheimer's Dementia (F. Gomez-Pinilla et al., 2008, Curlik er al., 2013, Chang et al., 2010) (cp. last paragraph).

c) Parkinson's Disease

Two hundred years ago, James Parkinson first described the disorder that bears his name (Lang et al., 1998): in 1817 James Parkinson, an English doctor, described in his essay on "shaking palsy" the characteristic movement disorders observed in some patients (Lees et al., 2007).

Parkinson's disease is a neurodegenerative disorder due to interaction between genetic and environmental factors characterized by the coexistence of motor and non-motor symptoms and constitutes the second neurodegenerative disease after Alzheimer's disease.

It is characterized by the progressive death of selected but heterogeneous populations of neurons including dopaminergic neurons of the *pars compacta* of the *substantia nigra*. Loss of dopamine projections from the *substantia nigra* to the *putamen* causes the fundamental motor disorders of Parkinson's disease. The mechanisms responsible for cell death in Parkinson's disease are largely unknown. Increasing evidence suggests that in the neuronal death in the *pars compacta* of the *substantia nigra* may be involved apoptosis, mitochondrial dysfunction, oxidative stress, increased free radical production, the actions of excitotoxins, deficient neurotrophic support, and immune mechanisms. Symptoms occur when 70% of neurons of *substantia nigra pars compacta* have been damaged (Oertel et al., 1996).

The classic triad of major signs of Parkinson's disease is made up of tremor, rigidity, and akinesia (Gibb 1988; Hughes 1993). The condition typically develops unilaterally in the upper limbs but progresses to become bilateral and later involves postural instability and gait disorder. Later complications include response fluctuations, declining levodopa response and dyskinesia (Oertel et al., 1996).

In addition to the primitive motor deficits, PD includes dysfuntion of higher order motor control. Non-motor symptoms of PD include cognitive deficits, behavioral disorders, autonomic disturbances and sleep.

The average age of the insurgence of Parkinson's disease (PD) is approximately 60 years, but likelihood of insurgence increases with age. In actual facts, age is one of the most consistent risk factors, and with the progessively increasing age of the general population, a significant increase in Parkinson's disease will occur in the future (Lang et al., 1998).

The diagnosis of Parkinson's disease is made on the basis of clinical criteria and is based on the presence at the neurological objective examination of resting tremor, rigidity, bradykinesia and postural instability (Pinessi et al., 2013). Misdiagnosis is also an important problem, because the syndrome of parkinsonism may have a number of different causes, such as drugs, Wilson's disease, and other neurodegenerative diseases.

The therapy is exclusively symptomatic and currently there is no treatment available that can change the evolution of the disease. Drug therapy is aimed at correcting the deficit of dopaminergic transmission and there are several classes of antiparkinsonian drugs including levodopa, decarboxylase inhibitors, dopaminergic agonists, monoamine oxidase inhibitors, anticholinergics, dopaminergic agonists and NMDA receptor inhibitors. Surgical approaches and non-pharmacological approaches, such as targeted physical activity interventions, are also being attempted to complete drug therapy (Pinessi et al., 2015).

d) Depression

Depression is a condition which almost all people experience in relatively mild forms many times in their lives. Depression meriting clinical attention is long-lasting, and severe enough to interfere with normal life. In addition to a depressed mood, the patient is typically lacking in both mental and physical energy to an extreme degree, he or she has the irrational feeling of worthlessness and/or guilt and may frequently think of death and suicide.

Major depressive disorder (MDD) is a global disease burden that affects over 300 million people worldwide (Ferrari et al., 2010). It is a heterogeneous disorder with a highly variable course, different subdivisions, different treatments; its pathogenesis has not yet been fully understood. Late-life depression occurs in persons 60 years of age or older among whom it may be very common. It is often associated with coexisting medical illness, cognitive dysfunction, or both (Belmaker et al., 2008; Taylor NE).

Older people may be prone to a higher proportion of depressing events, but causes of depression in later life are different. Causes may be attributed to a variety of diseases; life factors and psychological states of mind may contribute to the worsening of depression: stressful and negative events, bereavement, illness (especially chronic pain, stroke or fracture), medical treatment side effects, dementia, memory loss, finantial problems, long lasting social and relationship problems (especially lack of social support) (Penninx et al 1996); Penninx et al., (1996) report that depressive symptoms increase with the number of illnesses patients are likely to suffer from. Some diseases seem to be more conducive to depression than others: conditions which create chronic pain, such as arthritis, were found to be more likely associated with depression than were serious but less painful conditions such as diabetes. Psychological state may also be an important factor in some cases, with various real or imagined shortcomings in capabilities, such as dementia and memory loss correlated with depressive symptoms. Lifestyle factors, such as financial problems or long-term social and relationship problems may also be exacerbating factors.

The diagnostic criteria for major depression include observation of a marked change of mood, characterized by sadness or irritability, or anhedonia, accompanied by at least several psychophysiological changes, such as disturbances in sleep, changes in appetite, or sexual desire, energy level, crying, suicidal thoughts, and slowing down of speech and action. These changes must be observed over a minimum of 2 weeks and must interfere considerably with work and family relations (Lebowitz et al., 1997, Miller et al., 2000).

Screening elderly people for depression is very important because depressed older adults are at increased risk of suicide and because depression may be a manifestation of cognitive decline or a risk factor for dementia (Belmaker et al., 2008). It is also worth considering that older depressed people run the risk of developing dementia or pseudodementia.

Beside pharmacotherapy or psychotherapy as first-line therapy, some non strictly pharmacological approaches, social and physical activities may be important to prevent the beginning or worsening of the depression process in elderly people. Depressed older adults should be encouraged to increase their social active life, engagement in pleasurable activities and social interactions, and physical activity (Belmaker et al., 2008, cp. last paragraph).

AGEING AND THE PREVENTION OF A STATE OF FRAILTY IN A MULTIDOMAIN INTERVENTION*

In the face of a multitude of drug and clinical trials failures, we now know that some neurological diseases cannot yet be cured: prevention and projects aiming to change life style may be an important way to manage some of these diseases related to ageing. In addition to improving research in the field of pathophysiology of diseases, diagnostics and research of new drugs, prevention and multidomain intervention should be extended because they may be the best way to manage some diseases related to age. Interventions aiming to change some lifestyle factors seem to be necessary to successfully fight some diseases. Older adults should be encouraged to increase their social active life, to increase engagement in pleasurable activities and social interactions, to intensify physical activity and improve nutrition. Those lifestyle factors changes may help some people even after cognitive decline and a state of frailty has already begun.

Recent studies have demonstrated that modified lifestyle factors are a key strategy for maintaining brain health during ageing and enhance brain and cognitive reserve. A multidomain intervention, including physical activity, cognitive engagement, active social life and a healthy diet (such as the Mediterranean diet), are strategic for protecting against frailty and may delay the progression and secondary appearance of adverse results related to cognition, they may improve or maintain the cognitive functions and may help to prevent cognitive decline (Kelaiditi et al., 2013; Ngandu et al., 2015, Phillips C et al., 2017).

A randomized controlled clinical trial, the Finnish Geriatric Intervention Study to Prevent Cognitive Impairment and Disability (FINGER) had the goal to assess the effect on cognitive health of improved diet, physical exercise and mental training while providing regular health advice and cardiovascular health monitoring (Ngandu et al., 2015).

Between 2009 and 2011 the FINGER clinical trial enrolled 1,260 men and women (mean age 60 years) who were randomly assigned to a control group, and to a treatment group. All of them with some risk for dementia. Members of the treatment group were then directed to follow a regimen of diet, exercise and cognitive training and received periodic clinical examination. Control group participants, on the other hand, received only basic health advice.

In comparison with the control group, the intervention group (631 participants) received a mix of nutritional guidance (healthy balance of protein, fat, carbohydrates, dietary fibers and salt and restrictions on consumption of sugar and alcohol), cognitive training (different cognitive tasks to enhance executive function (planning and organizing), memory improvement and mental speed) and physical exercise (physical training, aerobic exercise) and postural balance exercises; the subjects' cardiovascular condition was also more intensely monitored (regular checkups of metabolic and vascular health, regular measurement of weight, blood pressure, and hip and waist circumference).

The study provided good evidence that a combination of improved diet, physical exercise, mental and social stimulation, and management of cardiovascular problems can improve cognition even after age 60, maintaining cognitive functioning and preventing cognitive impairment. The multidomain lifestyle model used in the FINGER trial2 is going to be tested in different populations and in different settings across the world (US pointer, Mind-China, Singer, UK-finger study).

As the elderly population is constantly growing, projects of multidomain interventions aiming to change some modifiable risk factors such as diabetes, hypertension, obesity, physical inactivity, smoking, depression might be important in the management of diseases related to ageing and have an important role not only in the prevention of chronic diseases but are also socioeconomically relevant (Livingston et al., 2017, Toumilehto et al., 2001).

Bibliography

Arriagada PV/Growdon JH et al. (1992): "Neurofibrillary tangles but not senile plaques parallel duration and severity of Alzheimer's disease." In: *Neurology* 42, pp. 631-639.

Belmaker RH/Agam G (2008): "Major depressive disorder." In: *N Engl J Med*, Jan 3, 358/1, pp. 55-68. Review.

Blennow K/Zetterberg H (2015): "The past and the future of Alzheimer's disease CSF biomarkers-a journey toward validated biochemical tests covering the whole spectrum of molecular events." In: *Front Neurosci*, Sep 29, 9, p. 345.

Carmona JJ/Michan S (2016): "Biology of healthy aging and longevity." In: *Revista de Investigación Clínica* 68, pp. 7-16.

Chang M/Jonsson PV/Snaedal J et al. (2010): "The effect of midlife physical activity on cognitive function among older adults: AGES – Reykjavik Study." In: *The Journals of Gerontology. Series A, Biological Sciences and Medical Sciences* 65/12, pp. 1369-1374.

Curlik DM/Shors TJ (2013): "Training your brain: do mental and physical (MAP) training enhance cognition through the process of neurogenesis in the hippocampus?". In: *Neuropharmacology* 64, pp. 506-514.

Diamanti-Kandarakis E/Dattilo M/Macut D/Duntas L/Gonos ES/Goulis DG/Gantenbein CK/Kapetanou M/Koukkou E/Lambrinoudaki I/Michalaki M/Eftekhari-Nader S/Pasquali R/Peppa M/Tzanela M/Vassilatou E/Vryonidou A; COMBO ENDO TEAM (2017): "Mechanisms in endocrinology. Aging and anti-aging: a Combo-Endocrinology overview." In: *Eur J Endocrinol*, Jun 176, 6, pp. 283-308.

Dubois B/Feldman HH/Jacova C/Dekosky ST/Barberger-Gateau P/Cummings J/Delacourte A/Galasko D/Gauthier S/Jicha G/ Meguro K/ O'brien J/Pasquier F/Robert P/Rossor M/Salloway S/Stern Y/Visser PJ/Scheltens P (2007): "Research criteria for the diagnosis of Alzheimer's disease: revising the NINCDS-ADRDA criteria." In: *Lancet Neurol*, Aug 6, 8, pp. 734-46. Review.

Ferrari AJ/Charlson FJ/Norman RE et al. (2013): "The epidemiological modelling of major depressive disorder: application for the Global Burden of Disease Study 2010." In: *PLoS One* 8/7, pp. 1-11.

Fulop T/Larbi A/Dupuis G/Le Page A/Frost EH/Cohen AA/Witkowski JM/Franceschi C ([1960], 2018): "Immunosenescence and Inflamm-Aging As Two Sides of the Same Coin: Friends or Foes?". In: *Front Immunol*, Jan 10, 8, pp. 1-13.

Gibb ERG/Lees A (1988): "The relevance of the Lewy body to the pathogenesis of idiopathic Parkinson's disease." *J Neurol Neurosurg Psychiatry* 51, pp. 745-752.

Goedert M/Trojanowski JQ/Lee VMY (1998): "The neurofibrillary pathology of Alzheimer's disease." In: SB Prusiner, *The molecular and genetic basis of neurological disease*, Boston: Butterworth-Heinemann.

Goldgaber D/Lerman MI/McBridge OW et al (1987): "Characterization and chromosomal loclization of a cDNA encoding brain amyloid of Alzheimer's disease." In: *Science* 235, pp. 877-880.

Gomez-Pinilla, F (2008): "Brain foods: the effects of nutrients on brain function," Nature Reviews. In: *Neuroscience* 9/7, pp. 568-578.

Harman, D (2001): "Aging Overview." In: *Annals of the New York Academy of Science*, Apr 9, 28, pp. 1-21. Review.

Harrison's (2017): *Principles of Internal Medicine 19th*. Columbus OH: McGraw-Hill Medical.

Hogan MJ/Staff RT/Bunting BP/Deary IJ/Whalley LJ (2012): "Openness to experience and activity engagement facilitate the maintenance of verbal ability in older adults." In: *Psychology and Aging* 27/4, pp. 849-854.

Hughes AJ/Daniel SE/Blankson S/ Lees AJ (1993): "A clinicopathologic study of 100 cases of Parkinson disease." In: *Arch. Neurol* 50, pp. 140-148.

Johson GVW/Jerkins SM (1996): "Tau protein in normal and Alzheimer's disease brain." In: *Alzheimer Dis Res*, pp. 138-154.

Kang J/Lemaire HG/Unterbeck A et al. (1987): "The precursor of Alzheimer's disease amyloid A4 protein resembles a cell-surface receptor." In: *Nature* 32, pp. 733-736.

Kelaiditi E/Cesari M/Canevelli M/ van Kan GA/Ousset PJ/Gillette-Guyonnet S/Ritz P/Duveau F/Soto ME/Provencher V/Nourhashemi F/Salvà A/Robert P/Andrieu S/Rolland Y/Touchon J/Fitten JL/Vellas B; IANA/IAGG. "Cognitive frailty: rational and definition from an (I.A.N.A./I.A.G.G.) international consensus group." In: *J Nutr Health Ageing*, Sep 17, 9, pp. 726-734.

Kosik, KS (1993): "The molecular and cellular biology of tau." In: *Brain Pathol* 3, pp. 39-43.

Lang AE/Lozano AM. (1998): "Parkinson's disease." In: *N Engl J Med*, Oct 15, 339/16, pp. 1130-1153. Review.

Lebowitz BD/Pearson JL/Schneider LS/Reynolds CF 3rd/Alexopulos GS/Bruce ML/Conwell Y/Katz IR/Meyers BS/Morrison MF/Mossey J/ Niederehe G/Parmelee P (1997): "Diagnosis and treatment of depression in late life. Consensus startement update." In: *JAMA*, Oct 8, 278/14, pp. 1186-1190.

Lees, AJ (2007): "Unresolved issues relating to the shaking palsy on the celebration of James Parkinson's 250th birthday." In: *Mov Disord*, Sep 22, Suppl. 17, pp. 327-34.

Livingston A/Sommerlad V/Ortega A (2015): "2 year multidomain intervention of diet, exercise, cognitive training, and vascular risk monitoring versus control to prevent cognitive decline in at-risk elderly people (FINGER): a randomised controlled trial." In: *Lancet* 385, pp. 2255-2263.

Lopez-Otin C/Blasco MA/Partridge L/Serrano M/Kroemer G (2013): "The hallmarks of aging." In: *Cell* 153, pp. 1194-1217.

Mattila RJ, "Epidemiology" in WC Koller (1987): *Handbook of Parkinson's Disease*. New York: Arcel Deeekr, pp. 35-50.

McKhann GM/Knopman DS/Chertkow H/Hyman BT/Jack CR Jr/Kawas CH/Klunk WE/Koroshetz WJ/Manly JJ/Mayeux R/Mohs RC/Morris JC/Rossor MN/Scheltens P/Carrillo MC/Thies B/Weintraub S/Phelps CH (2011): "The diagnosis of dementia due to Alzheimer's disease: recommendations from the National Institute on Aging-Alzheimer's Association workgroups on diagnostic guidelines for Alzheimer's disease." In: *Alzheimers Dement*, May 7, 3, pp. 263-269.

Miller KE/Zylstra RG/Standrige JB (2000): "The geriatic patient: a systematic approach to maintaining health." In: *Am Family Physician*, Feb 15, 61/4, pp. 1089-1104.

Milne A/Culverwell A/Guss R/Tuppen J/Whelton R (2008): "Screening for dementia in primary care: A review of the use, efficacy and quality of measures." In: *Int Psychogeriatr* 20, pp. 911-926.

Ngandu T/Lehtisalo J/Solomon A/Levälahti E/Ahtiluoto S/Antikainen R/Bäckman L/Hänninen T/Jula A/Laatikainen T/Lindström J/Mangialasche F/Paajanen T/Pajala S/Peltonen M/Rauramaa

R/Stigsdotter-Neely A/Strandberg T/Tuomilehto J/Soininen H/Kivipelto M (2015): "A 2 year multidomain intervention of diet, exercise, cognitive training, and vascular risk monitoring versus control to prevent cognitive decline in at-risk elderly people (FINGER): a randomised controlled trial." In: *Lancet*, Jun 6, 385/9984, pp. 2255-2263.

Oertel WH/Quinn NP, "Parkinsonism", in Brandt T/ Caplan LR/Dishgans J et al. (1996): *Neurological disorders: course and treatment*, San Diego: Academc, pp. 715-722.

Penninx BW/Beekman AT/Ormel J/Kriegsman DM/Boeke AJ/van Eijk JT/Deeg DJ (1996): "Psychological status among elderly people with chronic diseases: does type of disease play a part?". In: *J Psychosom Res*, May 40, 5, pp. 521-534.

Petersen RC/Smith GE/Waring SC/Ivnik RJ/Tangalos EG/Kokmen E (1999): "Mild cognitive impairment: clinical characterization and outcome." In: *Arch Neurol*, Mar 56/3, pp. 303-8. Erratum in: *Arch Neurol* 1999 Jun 56/6: p. 760.

Petersen, RC (2011): "Mild cognitive impairment." In: *N Engl J Med* 364, pp. 2227-2234.

Phillips, C (2017): "Lifestyle Modulators of Neuroplasticity: How Physical Activity, Mental Engagement, and Diet Promote Cognitive Health during Aging." In: *Neural Plast*, Jun 12, pp. 1-23.

Pinessi, Lorenzo/ Gentile, Salvatore/Rainero, Innocenzo (2015): *Neurology Book*, Milano: Edi Ermes Edition.

Querfurth HW/LaFerla FM (2010): *N Engl J Med*, Jan 28, 362/4, pp. 329-344.

Rabassa M/Cherubini A/Zamora-Ros R et al. (2015): "Low levels of a urinary biomarker of dietary polyphenol are associated with substantial cognitive decline over a 3-year period in older adults: the Invecchiare in Chianti Study." In: *Journal of the American Geriatrics Society* 63/5, pp. 938-946.

Ritchie K/Lovestone S (2002): "The dementias." In: *Lancet* 360, pp. 1759-1766.

Rossor Martin/Growdon John (2007): *The Dementias*, Boston: Butterworth- Heinemann.

Sanabria-Castro A/Alvarado-Echeverría I/Monge-Bonilla C (2017): "Molecular Pathogenesis of Alzheimer's Disease: An Update." In: *Ann Neurosci*, May 24/1, pp. 46-54.

Savva GM/Wharton SB/Ince PG/Forster G/Matthews FE/Brayne C (2009): "Medical Research Council Cognitive Function and Ageing Study." In: *N Engl J Med*, May 28, 360/22, pp. 2302-2309.

Singh VK/Guthikonda P (1997): "Circulating cytokines in Alzheimer's disease." In: *J Psychiatr Res*, Nov-Dec 31/6: pp. 657-60.

Taylor, WD (2014): "Clinical practice. Depression in the elderly." In: *N Engl J Med*, Sep 25, 371/13: pp. 1228-1236. Review.

Tuomilehto J/Lindström J/JG Eriksson (2001): "Prevention of type 2 diabetes mellitus by changes in lifestyle among subjects with impaired glucose tolerance." In: *N Engl J Med* 344, pp. 1343-1350.

Ventura MT/Casciaro M/Gangemi S/Buquicchio R (2017): "Immunosenescence in aging: between immune cells depletion and cytokines up-regulation." In: *Clin Mol Allergy*, Dec 14, pp. 15-21.

Wilson RS/Mendes CF/De Leon/ Barnes LL et al. (2002): "Participation in cognitively stimulating activities and risk of incident Alzheimer disease." In: *JAMA* 287/6, pp. 742-748. Review.

Yankner, BA (1996): "Mechanisms of neuronal degeneration in Alzheimer's disease." In: *Neuron* 16, pp. 921-932.

Yankner, BA (1962): "New clues to Alzheimer's disease: unraveling the roles of amyloid and tau." In: *Nature Medicine* 2, pp. 850-852.

Contributors

Abbate Badin, Donatella formerly of the University of Turin, is the author of numerous scholarly essays and books in the fields of nineteenth and twentieth century English and Irish studies focusing especially on poetry, travel writing and the representations of Italy in English and Irish literatures. She has published extensively on G.M. Hopkins, Thomas Kinsella, Dickens, Sean O'Faolain, the Irish Gothic, Thomas Moore and twentieth-century women writers. On Thomas Kinsella, besides several articles and an edited collection of essays and poems, she has published a critical study (*Thomas Kinsella*, New York: Twayne 1996) and a translation of his poetry into Italian (*Una Terra senza peccato*, 1996). Her specialization in the representations of Italy in literature has led her to an in-depth study of Lady Morgan's Italy, a text which she edited for Pickering and Chatto and on which she published a book and many articles. She has been a member of the Steering Committee of EFACIS and of the editorial board of *Studi irlandesi: A Journal of Irish Studies*.

Bertinetti, Paolo Emeritus Professor at the University of Turin, has been professor of English Literature, Dean of the Faculty of modern languages and literatures, and Head of the School of modern languages and literatures of the University of Turin. Among his publications are studies on twentieth-century English Theatre, on Elizabethan and Restoration drama, on the novels of Graham Greene, on Beckett's work and on postcolonial literature. He is editor and part author of a two-volume history of English literature and author of *English Literature. A Short History*, both published by Einaudi. He has also edited the Italian translation of Beckett's complete dramatic works (1994) and of his short prose (2010); and of Graham Greene's most important novels (2000 and 2002). His translation of

Hamlet, of *The Tempest* and of *Macbeth* were published by Einaudi, respectively in 2005, in 2012 and in 2016. He is director of the journal *Il Castello di Elsinore*.

Canton, Licia is the author of the collections *The Pink House and Other Stories* (2018) and *Almond Wine and Fertility* (2008, second edition 2018) – stories for women and their men – published in Italy as *Vino alla mandorla e fertilità* (2015). She is also a literary critic and (self) translator, and founding editor-in-chief of *Accenti, the Canadian Magazine with an Italian Accent*. Her fiction, essays and creative nonfiction have been anthologized internationally, appearing in English, French, Chinese, Italian and dialect. As editor she has published ten volumes of creative and critical writing, including two on the internment of Italian Canadians during World War II. She leads workshops on healing through writing. She mentors emerging writers and editors via the Quebec Writers' Federation (QWF). A member of the Writers' Union of Canada, she has served on the board of the Quebec Writers' Federation (2007-10) and as President of the Association of Italian Canadian Writers (2010-14). She holds a Ph.D. from Université de Montréal and an M.A. from McGill University. Born in Cavarzere (Venice), she immigrated to Montreal in 1967.

Concilio, Carmen is Associate Professor of English and Postcolonial Literature at the University of Turin, Italy. Her research fields include Modernism, Postcolonial literature, photography and the visual arts, migration studies, Eco/Digital Humanities, ageing studies, Gender/Partnership studies, and urban studies. Apart from edited and co-edited works and volumes, her most recent publications include *Antroposcenari. Storie, paesaggi, ecologie* (2018); *Word and Image in Literature and the Visual Arts* (2016); *New Critical Patterns in Postcolonial Discourse* (2012). Her articles appeared on *Journal of Commonwealth Literature*, *Le Simplegadi*, *Altre Modernità*, *AION Anglistica*, *Ri-cognizioni*. She translated into Italian J.M. Coetzee, Nino Ricci and Ivan Vladislavić. She is currently President of the Italian Association for the Study of Culture and Literature in English (www.aiscli.it), and editor in the scientific board of journals and series: *Il Tolomeo*, *de-genere*, *Anglosophia* series (Mimesis).

De Angelis, Irene lectures in English Literature at the University of Turin. She is the author of *The Japanese Effect in Contemporary Irish Poetry* (Palgrave Macmillan, 2012) and she co-edited with Joseph Woods *Our Shared Japan. An Anthology of Contemporary Irish Poetry*, with an *Afterword* by Seamus Heaney (Dedalus Press, 2007). Her publications include a monograph on W.B. Yeats's *Noh* Plays (2010) and a study of Derek Mahon's international outlook in his poetry. She has written essays and book chapters on authors as varied as Rudyard Kipling, W.S. Maugham, Aldous Huxley and Alan Bennett, Seamus Heaney, Derek Mahon and Marina Carr. Her research interests include East-West Studies, Literature and the Visual Arts, the representation of ageing in Literature, Ecocriticism and Modern Manuscript Analysis.

Della Valle, Paola is a Researcher at the University of Turin. She specializes in New Zealand and Māori literature, Pacific studies, postcolonial culture, and gender theory. Her articles have appeared in the *Journal of Commonwealth Literature*, the *NZSA Bulletin of New Zealand Studies, Le Simplegadi, RiCognizioni, Il Castello di Elsinore, Textus* and *Loxias*. She has published the monographs *From Silence to Voice: The Rise of Māori Literature* (2010), *Stevenson nel Pacifico: una lettura postcoloniale* (2013) and *Priestley e il tempo, il tempo di Priestley: Uno studio sul tempo nel teatro di J.B. Priestley* (2016). She has contributed to the volumes *Experiences of Freedom in Postcolonial Literatures and Cultures* (2011), *Contemporary Sites of Chaos in the Literatures and Arts of the Postcolonial World* (2013), *L'immagine dell'Italia nelle letterature angloamericane e postcoloniali* (2014), *Antroposcenari* (2018) and *Uncommon Wealths in Postcolonial Fiction* (2018). She is a member of the International Advisory Board of the *Journal of New Zealand and Pacific Studies*.

Favaro, Enrica holds a Degree in Medical Biotechnology from the University of Turin. In 2003 she completed a PhD in the Department of Medical Sciences, in collaboration with the Department of King's College School of Medicine, London, working in the research field of coxsackievirus, endothelial cells and type 1 diabetes. Since 2003 she has been a Research Fellow at the University of Turin, in the Department of Medical Sciences, working in the field of immunology of type 1 diabetes. Moreover, since 2016 she has been the Project Manager of the interdisciplinary project "Terzo Tempo / Third Time", aimed at disseminating healthy ageing.

Folena, Lucia is Associate professor of English literature at the University of Turin. Her principal research fields are Renaissance and early modern literature, theory, cultural studies, literature and philosophy, literature and the visual arts. Her recent publications include: *"Contrées sans culture*: 'Nature' across the Anthropological Rift", *Simplegadi* XV: 17, 2017; "Playing with Shadows: Time, Absent Presence, and *The Winter's Tale"*, in *Word and Image in Literature and the Visual Arts*, ed. by C. Concilio & M. Festa (Mimesis 2016); "All that May Become a Man: *Macbeth* and the Breakdown of the Heroic Model", *Simplegadi* XIV:15, 2016; "Dark Corners & Double Bodies: Espionage as Transgression in *Measure for Measure"*, in *Plots and Plotters: Double Agents and Villains in Spy Fictions*, ed. by C. Concilio (Mimesis 2015).

Fondo, Blossom N. is Associate professor of Postcolonial studies in the department of English at the Higher Teacher Training College of the University of Maroua in Cameroon where she teaches postcolonial studies, critical theory and gender studies. She has published widely and participated in conferences on these areas. Her recent publication is a co-edited collection of essays on Toni Morrison on the occasion of her 85th anniversary entitled: *The Timeless Toni Morrison* published by Peter Lang. She is currently working on another co-edited volume of essays on the question of identity in American Literature entitled *From Essentialism to Choice: American Cultural Identities and Their Literary Representations*. Her main research interests are postcolonialism, ecocriticism, feminism and African American studies. She has been a visiting scholar at Dickinson College, New York University in the USA and Karl Franzens University of Graz, Austria.

Piciucco, Pier Paolo teaches English literature at the Department of Foreign Languages, Turin. He got a Ph.D. from the University of Bologna in 1999 for a thesis on the female figures in Indian-English literature. Since then his main fields of research have been postcolonial and postmodern studies and he has focussed his attention on the contemporary evolutions of literary forms. He has published extensively on these topics, co-edited five collections of essays, edited two works and written a monograph on the relevance of South African theatre during Apartheid. Most of his works have been published abroad by scholarly journals and publishers.

Acknowledgements

This collection of academic essays *Representation of Age and Ageing in the Anglophone Literature* has its origin in a publication based on research on the traditional literary figure of the "old crone", edited by my former PhD tutor, Elsa Linguanti (1934-2012) at the University of Pisa: *Personaggio donna. Lo sguardo dalla fine* (2001). Besides, it also owes much to the seminars held by Luisa Passerini on age and myths, at CIRSDe (www.cirsde.unito.it/). To both of them goes my gratitude for having instilled in me awareness on issues of gender and ageing in literary postcolonial studies. This publication is meant as a continuum with those early starts and all contributors to this volume have my profound indebtedness for accepting to be part of this project.

My thanks go to Marlene Goldman, University of Toronto, Canada – who always leads the way for scholars in Canadian literature – for allowing me to discuss with her my research project in the late summer of 2017, and who is author of a milestone publication in Ageing studies and Canadian literature: *Forgotten. Narratives of Age-Related Dementia and Alzheimer's Disease in Canada* (2017). The section on Canadian literature owes much to teaching and class discussions with the students of the Master in American Studies (editions 2012; 2017) to whom I taught Alice Munro's short stories. I am in debt to Canada, the country where I repeatedly pursued my research, and to Licia Canton (Montreal), who deserves a word of thanks for generously accepting the invitation to contribute the "Preface" to the volume, also given her experience speaking to seniors and women's groups via the Canadian Mental Health Association in Toronto. Roberta Meierhofer, Eva-Maria Trinkaus, Heike Hartung and Ulla Kribernegg of the University of Graz, Austria, must be thanked for encouragingly welcoming the project proposal and for allowing contact with Transcript publisher through the patient help of editor Annika Linnemann. Roberta Meierhofer also enabled the project to open up internationally, thanks to the participation of scholar Blossom Fondo, who inspired me to contribute an essay on South African literature, another of my major fields of research, and particularly on a novel I immersed myself into, when translating it into Italian (J.M. Coetzee, *Age of Iron* 1990; it. transl. *Età di ferro* 1995).

With precious tips by Simone Francescato, who first published in the "Aging Studies Series", all this has become possible. My greatest debt, as usual, is to my invaluable first readers: Valerio Fissore, Mariangela Mosca and Maria Festa. Another enthusiastic colleague, Enrica Favaro, must be thanked for broadening the scope of our project so as to include clinical analysis and to consider medical notions of well-being, which led to public readings for seniors on the topic of "Representations of Ageing in Anglophone literature" by our research group (http://www.hu4a.it/cb-profile/userprofile.html) in September 2017 and May 2018, as part of the project activities promoted by the University of Turin research marathon #HACKUNITO FOR AGEING.

Cultural Studies

Gundolf S. Freyermuth
Games | Game Design | Game Studies
An Introduction
(With Contributions by André Czauderna,
Nathalie Pozzi and Eric Zimmerman)

2015, 296 p., pb.
19,99 € (DE), 978-3-8376-2983-5
E-Book: 17,99 € (DE), ISBN 978-3-8394-2983-9

Andréa Belliger, David J. Krieger
Network Publicy Governance
On Privacy and the Informational Self

February 2018, 170 p., pb.
29,99 € (DE), 978-3-8376-4213-1
E-Book: 26,99 € (DE), ISBN 978-3-8394-4213-5

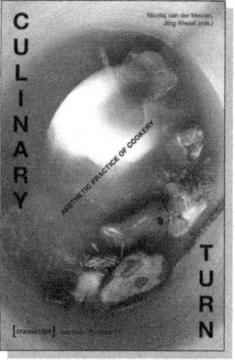

Nicolaj van der Meulen, Jörg Wiesel (eds.)
Culinary Turn
Aesthetic Practice of Cookery
(In collaboration with Anneli Käsmayr
and in editorial cooperation with Raphaela Reinmann)

2017, 328 p., pb., col. ill.
29,99 € (DE), 978-3-8376-3031-2
E-Book available as free open access publication
ISBN 978-3-8394-3031-6

**All print, e-book and open access versions of the titles in our list
are available in our online shop www.transcript-verlag.de/en!**

Cultural Studies

Martina Leeker, Imanuel Schipper, Timon Beyes (eds.)
Performing the Digital
Performativity and Performance Studies in Digital Cultures

2016, 304 p., pb.
29,99 € (DE), 978-3-8376-3355-9
E-Book available as free open access publication
ISBN 978-3-8394-3355-3

Suzi Mirgani
**Target Markets –
International Terrorism
Meets Global Capitalism in the Mall**

2016, 198 p., pb.
29,99 € (DE), 978-3-8376-3352-8
E-Book available as free open access publication
ISBN 978-3-8394-3352-2

Ramón Reichert, Annika Richterich,
Pablo Abend, Mathias Fuchs, Karin Wenz (eds.)
Digital Culture & Society (DCS)
Vol. 3, Issue 2/2017 – Mobile Digital Practices

January 2018, 272 p., pb.
29,99 € (DE), 978-3-8376-3821-9
E-Book: 29,99 € (DE), ISBN 978-3-8394-3821-3

**All print, e-book and open access versions of the titles in our list
are available in our online shop www.transcript-verlag.de/en!**